Praise for *Oral Communication in the Di
Development and Training . . .*

M000266927

It is a challenge to engage my undergraduate engineering students in oral communication, let alone increase their awareness of the importance of communication in the discipline—especially in an age of decreasing face-to-face communication. This book not only provides a number of ways to implement communication assignments, but it also explains the value of doing so. Additionally, this book goes further in addressing more subtle issues such as how to manage facework in my classroom, and how to deal with inevitable conflict students might face when doing oral communication assignments. It is an outstanding reference.

—Dr. Jon P. Rust, Professor of Textile Engineering,
Alumni Distinguished Undergraduate Professor,
North Carolina State University

Working with engineering students in a career services capacity, I see the need for students to feel confident communicating in the real world. While many colleges and universities have very strong communication programs, STEM students won't learn communication skills specific to their fields simply by taking a required general education course. These students need to be introduced to applications specific to what they'll face in a work environment and hence faculty and staff need to be skilled in integrating oral communication into their curriculum. I am confident that *Oral Communication in the Disciplines: A Resource for Teacher Development and Training* can provide the guiding philosophy for instructors who are outside of the field of communication, ultimately resulting in well-rounded students in every discipline.

—Krysta Kirsch, Employer Relations and Recruiting Manager,
Engineering Career Services, The Ohio State University

Oral Communication in the Disciplines: A Resource for Teacher Development and Training is the first of its kind to provide a clear and straightforward strategic framework to guide teachers as they incorporate oral communication activities into their course. This all-encompassing empirically and theoretically grounded book helps to ensure that communication is not just added, but thoughtfully incorporated in meaningful, context-specific ways. The practical examples and planning worksheets will guide the most inexperienced instructors and also help experienced teachers to rethink and re-evaluate their activities and assignments. The incorporation of facework and feedback helps to demystify the evaluation process. This book is a must-have for any instructor who wants to incorporate meaningful oral communication activities.

—Dr. April Kedrowicz, Assistant Professor,
Department of Clinical Sciences, College of Veterinary
Medicine, North Carolina State University

Oral Communication in the Disciplines

A Resource for Teacher Development and Training

Deanna P. Dannels, Patricia R. Palmerton, and Amy L. H. Gaffney

Parlor Press
Anderson, South Carolina
www.parlorpress.com

Parlor Press LLC, Anderson, South Carolina, USA
© 2017 by Parlor Press.
All rights reserved.
Printed in the United States of America
S A N: 2 5 4 - 8 8 7 9

Library of Congress Cataloging-in-Publication Data

Names: Dannels, Deanna P., author. | Palmerton, Patricia Ruby, author. |
  Gaffney, Amy L. H., 1982- author.
Title: Oral communication in the disciplines : a resource for teacher
  development and training / Deanna P. Dannels, Patricia R. Palmerton, and
  Amy L. H. Gaffney.
Description: Anderson, South Carolina : Parlor Press, [2016] | Includes
  bibliographical references and index.
Identifiers: LCCN 2016031994 (print) | LCCN 2016039855 (ebook) | ISBN
  9781602358522 (pbk. : alk. paper) | ISBN 9781602358539 (hardcover : alk.
  paper) | ISBN 9781602358546 (pdf) | ISBN 9781602358553 (epub) | ISBN
  9781602358560 (ibook) | ISBN 9781602358577 (Kindle)
Subjects: LCSH: Communication in education. | Teachers--Training of.
Classification: LCC LB1033.5 .D42 2016 (print) | LCC LB1033.5 (ebook) | DDC
  371.102/2--dc23
LC record available at https://lccn.loc.gov/2016031994

978-1-60235-852-2 (paperback)
978-1-60235-853-9 (hardcover)
978-1-60235-854-6 (PDF)
978-1-60235-855-3 (ePub)
978-1-60235-856-0 (iBook)
978-1-60235-857-7 (Kindle)

The cover design for this book depicts the waveform, or spectral display, of its title *Oral Communication in the Disciplines: A Resource for Teacher Development and Training* being spoken into digital audio software. The designers, Brian Gaines and April O'Brien, sought to illustrate the nature of the text's focus on oral communication while simultaneously capturing this phenomenon visually.

Printed on acid-free paper.

1 2 3 4 5
First Edition

Parlor Press, LLC is an independent publisher of scholarly and trade titles in print and multimedia formats. This book is available in paper, hardcover, and digital formats from Parlor Press on the World Wide Web at http://www.parlorpress.com or through online and brick-and-mortar bookstores. For submission information or to find out about Parlor Press publications, write to Parlor Press, 3015 Brackenberry Drive, Anderson, SC 29621, or email editor@parlorpress.com.

CONTENTS

Section IV: Evaluating Oral Communication in Your Classroom   *169*

Figures and Tables

Figures

Tables

ACKNOWLEDGMENTS

We are grateful to the many people who have contributed to this text and our scholarship throughout the years. David Blakesley's support of this project has been vital as we brought the text to fruition. We are also grateful to Jared Jameson for copyediting the manuscript. Thanks also go to the students who assisted us with sources and citations at various points in the project: Hannah Jaffe (North Carolina State University), Raven Timmons (University of Kentucky), and Aubrey Fonfara (Hamline University).

We extend our thanks to colleagues who provided reviews of the manuscript: Susan McLeod (University of California, Santa Barbara), Sean Connin (Trinity University), Jon P. Rust (North Carolina State University), Krysta Kirsch (Ohio State University), Wendy Atkins-Sayre (University of Southern Mississippi), Ann Darling (University of Utah), and April Kedrowicz (North Carolina State University). Thank you to the faculty who granted permission for us to use rubrics and assignment descriptions: Diane Clayton (Hamline University), Jon D. H. Gaffney (Eastern Kentucky University), and George Vane (Hamline University).

Deanna Dannels would like to acknowledge several people who have influenced the project in important ways. Co-authors Patricia Palmerton and Amy Housley Gaffney have been collaborative and engaged partners; their commitment to the project and the process of writing made the time working together fulfilling and productive. Deanna is also grateful for Ann Darling who provided her with the initial opportunity (twenty years ago) to learn in the trenches about what it means to do communication across the curriculum. Working with the engineers during that time changed the path of her work and forever sculpted the way she thinks about and tinkers with teaching and learning. She would also like to acknowledge Chris Anson, who has been a partner in communication across the curriculum for many years; her faculty development commitments and practices cannot be unraveled from what she has learned from her collaborations with Chris. Finally, she would like to thank Karl Lehmann and Emma Grace Lehmann; this project took attention and time and they were there, throughout, always with loving smiles and hugs.

Patricia Palmerton would like to acknowledge the pioneers of Speaking Across the Curriculum, Robert O. Weiss of DePauw University, and Charles Roberts of East Tennessee State University who provided support and insight to her in the early stages of her work on communication across disciplines. She is also grateful for the help and support of Hamline University faculty, in particular Alice Moorhead, for her pedagogical insights, and James Francisco Bonilla and Colleen Bell for many long discussions about diversity in the classroom. Finally, she is indebted to her good friend and mentor, Robert L. Scott, for his insights into rhetoric as epistemic, which has influenced her thinking about the implications of communication pedagogy.

Amy Housley Gaffney would like to thank Deanna Dannels and Chris Anson for providing strong role models of what cross-curricular work should entail. She extends thanks to the students and faculty who have been open to exploring new ways to understand competent communication in teaching, learning, and research. She also thanks Jon D. H. Gaffney (Eastern Kentucky University) for continued discussions about curriculum, pedagogy, and life in general.

Finally, the administrators, faculty, and students we have worked with over the years from many disciplines have made this project possible. In your struggles and triumphs, you have brought to life the work in this book; propelling us to continuously share our passion for communication across the disciplines. You deserve our utmost thanks.

Oral Communication in the Disciplines

Section I: Oral Communication—Why and How?

In our experience, faculty members have mixed feelings when it comes to teaching students about oral communication. On the one hand, you might believe it is a good idea to provide your students with experience in discipline-specific communication activities. Yet, you might also think the teaching of speech would feel like an add-on to the content-focused work you do in your courses and, hence, is less central to your mission. You might truly want to help students learn to be better communicators, but you might also have limited ideas about how to do so. In this introductory section, we discuss these issues, provide a rationale for including oral communication instruction in your classes, and attempt to address some of the more common concerns that faculty members like you express when integrating oral communication activities and practices into the classroom.

1 WHY INCLUDE ORAL COMMUNICATION IN YOUR COURSE?

What we've got here is a failure to communicate.
— Frank R. Pierson

Good communication is as stimulating as black coffee, and just as hard to sleep after.
— Ann Morrow Lindbergh

Speak not but what may benefit others or yourself; avoid trifling conversation.
— Benjamin Franklin

You can have brilliant ideas, but if you can't get them across, your ideas won't get you anywhere.
— Lee Iacocca

The most important things are the hardest to say, because words diminish them.
— Stephen King

Be sincere; be brief; be seated.
— Franklin Delano Roosevelt

From American presidents to CEOs, inventors to aviators, and authors to film directors—the importance of communication can be seen in cliché after cliché, heard in motivational speech upon motivational speech, and read in one inspirational book after another. Its importance is not debatable; its presence in our lives, a given. Yet, doing it well requires conscientiousness and effort. Doing it poorly can have devastating consequences. And as with many things, teaching it well is a completely different beast than actually mastering it yourself. Furthermore, teaching it well when it is not your primary area of study, course content, or research may seem like a challenging task. This book is meant to help you in this endeavor— to teach communication within your discipline in a way that serves your own instructional goals. By incorporating communication in your courses, you have the potential to help your students learn what it means to interact as a member of your discipline, to prepare your students for future success in the workplace, to engage your students in the course material in more thoughtful ways, and to encourage civic participation and responsibility. Helping students learn to communicate well is helping them learn to be confident, thoughtful, and proactive agents of change. Helping students use communication to learn course material is helping them learn to be independent, invested critical learners. Helping you learn to help your students communicate is what this book is about.

Why Oral Communication? Why Now?

The quotations at the beginning of this book illustrate the widespread recognition of the importance of communication. There is evidence, as well, in a number of different arenas (beyond popular quotations) to support the centrality of communication. In the business world, for example, what is clear is that businesses and industries are consistently recognizing communication competence as critical and necessary for college graduates. Key points include

- The National Associations of Colleges and Employees'(NACE) 2015 Job Outlook Report describes results of a survey of employers on the qualities that make up an ideal candidate for a job. Communication skills (the ability of students to write and speak clearly) ranked high, with nearly 80 percent of respondents identifying team work skills, 73.4 percent identifying written communication skills, and 67 percent identifying verbal communication skills as attributes sought on a candidate's resume (National Association of Colleges and Employers, 2014).
- CollegeGrad.com conducts a survey on employers' desired qualities for new college graduates every two years. In the past two surveys, the second identified "most important" quality was a student's interviewing skills—ranking above GPA, internship experience, and computer skills (retrieved from http://www.collegegrad.com/press/whatemployerswant.shtml).
- Silicon Valley employers surveyed reported wanting new employees to have better communication skills—including the ability to use vocabulary appropriately and the ability to professionally use language (Stevens, 2005).
- In two qualitative studies completed by the Microsoft Corporation on struggles new employees faced with socialization in the Microsoft workplace, new employees identified communication as a key struggle—articulating the need to learn to work in large teams and to learn how to ask good questions of colleagues and managers (Begel & Simon, 2008).

- Greenberg Quinlan Rosner Research, on behalf of the California Foundation for Commerce and Education and funded by the Gates and Hewlett Foundations, conducted a survey and focus groups among California business leaders to get their opinions on public education. One emerging theme was a desire for graduates to have skills such as communication, personal responsibility, and a better work ethic—skills well suited for the workplace. In fact, 55 percent of the respondents rated "communication skills" as the highest priority for educational focus (Tulchin & Muehlenkamp, 2007).

- Robert Half Technology commissioned a recent poll that illustrated that chief information officers believe the skills necessary for new employees have changed in the past five years—with more of an emphasis on project management, oral communication, writing, and getting along with others—in addition to the traditionally high-rated technical skills (Tucci, 2007, May 16).

As illustrated above, the importance of developing communication skills for the professional arena is undisputed.

Additionally, there is increasing evidence that communication skills are critical for citizen engagement as well. Susan Bickford, in her book *Listening, Conflict, and Citizenship: The Dissonance of Democracy*, suggests that democracy, by definition, necessitates communication: "It is precisely the presence of conflict and differences that makes communicative interaction necessary. This communicative interaction—speaking and listening together—does not do away with the conflicts that arise from uncertainty, inequality and identity. Rather, it enables political actors to decide democratically how to act in the face of conflict." (Bickford, 1996, p. 2). Likewise, in his book *The Magic of Dialogue: Transforming Conflict into Collaboration*, Daniel Yankelovich (1999) suggests there are three key skills necessary for authentic citizen engagement: empathic listening, treating others as equal partners in dialogue, and examining unearthed assumptions without judgment. Such works point to the necessity of communication competencies in civic settings, and hence, the importance of teaching those competencies in classrooms where they are relevant.

Not only is it clear that communication is important, but in the past decade, there has been quite a bit of press suggesting that it is a skill that is lacking. Popular press articles lament students' inability to speak clearly as proficient members of society. Take for example, the following:

- In a newspaper article in *The Boston Globe* (Zernike, 1999) titled "Talk is, Like, You know, Cheapened," the issue of "mallspeak" (like, you know, goes . . .) is brought up as a critical problem for American democracy and education.

- The problem of inarticulateness was serious enough to be addressed in the legislative session—one senator even mockingly imagined whether Abraham Lincoln could have rallied the nation's determination if the Gettysburg address began, 'Four score, and like, seven years ago, you know, our forefathers, uh, brought forth, you know . . . .'"
- In the poem, "Totally Like Whatever," Taylor Mali asks, "Have we just gotten to the point that we're the most aggressively inarticulate generation to come along since, you know...a long time ago?" He encourages this generation, in the poem, to "speak with conviction and authority." (http://www.taylormali.com/poems-online/totally-like-whatever-you-know/).
- The *LA Times* article "College, Like, Focus on Speech" (Mehren, 1999) describes the proliferation of the youth "mall-speak" or "teen-bonics," reflecting students' inability to craft arguments, make clear points, and to deal with crucial issues without fighting over them or avoiding them. This article also describes oral communication as an important competency for all students to have: "The premise is that writing skills and a degree from a prestigious institution are no longer enough. In order to face the world beyond college, students must speak effectively, be able to organize cogent arguments and be ready to function in an increasingly team-oriented workplace. It's verbal competence-cum-confidence: understanding that mall-speak is fine when you're with your buddies, but beginning a meeting with 'I was, like, y'know, whatever' just won't cut it."
- *The Chronicle of Higher Education* article "Taking Aim at Student Incoherence" describes the problem of inarticulateness as a serious and substantive one—moving beyond the delivery issue of "mall-speak"—reflecting problems with students' thinking. The article illustrates how attention to communication can address not only the issue of inarticulate and vernacular speech, but also students' competencies in organization, critical thinking, argumentation, and learning of course material (retrieved from http://chronicle.com/colloquy/99/speech/background.htm).

Clearly, the development of articulate communication is a critical concern. Integrating oral communication activities in the classroom can help alleviate this concern. Additionally, integrating oral communication activities into the classroom can also be beneficial to students' learning. In higher education, there are a number of different initiatives that have recognized the importance of student oral participation to the learning endeavor. The rise of active learning as a viable, necessary, and important alternative to lecturing has been documented widely (e.g., Barnes, 1980; Helman & Horswill, 2002; Johnson & Johnson, 1974; Silvan, Wong Leung, Woon, & Kember, 2000; Slaven, 1995; Springer, Stanne, Donovan, 1999; Yoder & Hochevar, 2005). In fact, in many disciplines, there is clear research that active learning improves students' performances on exams and other performance-based measures. In addition to increased content performance, active learning research has shown other benefits in terms of development of critical thinking skills, independent learning abilities, motivation for lifelong learning, and problem-solving skills. Other educational endeavors (e.g., cooperative learning, inquiry-guided instruction, service learning, etc.) have supported and built upon this basic premise—that getting students involved as active participants in the classroom (as opposed to passive recipients of content delivered through a lecture) is productive, valuable, and beneficial.

Research on the "writing to learn" initiative has also documented that the active writing process enhances learning of course content (e.g., Herrington, 1981; Odell, 1980). Scholars in composition have studied this relationship between writing and learning for several decades, and such a history is well documented (Bazerman, Little, Bethel, Chavkin, Fouquette, Garufis, 2005). In articulating the unique characteristics of written communication that make it a valuable mode of learning, Janet Emig (1977) argued that "verbal language represents the most available medium for composing; in fact, the significance of sheer availability in its selection as a mode for learning can probably not be overstressed" (p. 122). Although Emig argued that writing, by its nature, was more useful than talking for the development of learning, research on the effects of oral communication—or the verbalization of material—on learning has shown, among other things, the following:

- Vocalized stimuli are recalled more often than non-vocalized stimuli (Carmean & Weir, 1967; De Vesta & Rickards, 1971; Weir & Helgoe, 1968).
- Adults are more likely to locate errors in the course of a computation if they verbalize the ways the errors could have occurred (Marks, 1951).
- Vocalization during problem solving tasks produces better performance than not vocalizing (Davis, 1968; Gagne & Smith, 1962).
- Students who studied verbal material in order to teach it to another student learned more than students instructed only to learn it (Bargh & Schul, 1980)
- Students who give and receive explanations learn more than those who don't (Webb, 1982; Webb, 2009).
- Learning is increased when students are engaged in oral interaction with those who have a greater degree of knowledge and also communi-

cate within the zone of knowledge held by the learner (Hatano, 1993; O'Donnell, 2006; Vygotsky, 1978).

- Students who ask questions but are not answered suffer; in fact, this occurrence is a strong predictor of poor performance (Webb, 1982, 2009). This result suggests a relational dimension to the oral communication experience within the learning context: Students who ask, but do not receive a response, may be prone to quit asking.
- Students restructure their knowledge when engaged in small-group discussions, affecting their learning positively. This restructuring was not observed as happening as effectively in individual learning. (O'Donnell, 2006; Schmidt, DeVolder, DeGrave, Moust, Patel, 1989; Webb, 2009).
- Small-group discussion appears to activate prior knowledge, mobilizing existing knowledge and restructuring this knowledge by creating new relations between concepts in ways that make sense to the persons who produce the relations (Schmidt, et al., 1989)
- Small-group discussion appears to be one way that learners can learn things that they do not relate to, or that are incompatible with existing beliefs, because it helps the learner become aware of his or her own perspective and the potential limitations of that perspective (Schmidt, et al., 1989; see also Hogan, Nastasi, & Pressley, 2000; Schwartz, 1995).
- When students provide explanations and elaborate upon those explanations, there is increased learning (O'Donnell, 2006; Webb, Franke, De, Chan, Freund, Shein, & Melkonian, 2009).
- In a meta-analysis of forty-two empirical research studies on discussion in the classroom, classroom discussion was shown to be "highly effective at promoting students' literal and inferential comprehension" (Murphy, et al., 2009).

As illustrated by the above points, students who have the opportunity to speak about their learning or hear how others have construed a problem or approached a solution benefit by seeing that there are multiple ways to approach an issue or problem, expanding the possibilities for exploring an issue in new ways. To realize that there are multiple paths to a solution or to come to understand the strengths and limitations of various paths is a gift that many students never receive. Discussions about life experiences—as related to course content—whether offered by students who have experienced discrimination or by students who have had a change of perspective, expand horizons in ways otherwise not possible. Speakers who struggle with apprehension and get the courage to make a claim and argue for it during a class discussion gain valuable experience that can move beyond the classroom.

Oral communication assignments and activities have the potential of changing students: their learning, their outlook on life, their approach to interaction. Students' engagement with communication activities can have significant effects on their learning, their ultimate success in the professional world, their interactions as citizens, and their interpersonal relationships. Therefore, we suggest it is important for you to consider additional ways in which you can use communication in your course. We advocate, though, that you do this in a way that will help you meet your teaching goals. For some, you might design high stakes, formal, graded assignments that focus on fostering professional communication competencies. For others, professional communication competencies might not be as relevant, so your focus might be on lower stakes, ungraded assignments in which students use communication competencies to learn course material. It is important to note that ungraded communication activities may only be low stakes in terms of grades, but they are in fact quite high stakes in the sense that we ask students to disclose their thoughts and opinions. Class discussion and small-group discussions, for example, are highly self-disclosive activities. We are asking students to disclose their thinking while it may still be quite unformed. We are asking students to make public their opinions and attitudes when those opinions and attitudes may not be shared. We are asking them to let others in on their degree of expertise, their ability to do close reading, their ability to analyze, etc. The stakes for how an individual is seen by others, and how that person sees him or herself are pretty high.

COMMUNICATION COMPETENCE

As you begin to think about what kinds of assignments and activities you want to design for your course, it is important to consider the question: "What counts as a competent communicator in my course or discipline?" Communication competence has been defined in a number of different ways within the communication discipline. Although there are numerous models of communication competence, many share similar assumptions, four of which are important here. First, communication competence is measured in some degree by the achievement of a communicator's goals. Second, competence must not only focus on individual achievement of goals, but also is dependent on whether the communicator is interacting in ways that are effective and appropriate to the social relationship (Spitzberg, 1988). That means maintaining an awareness of an appreciation for the goals and objectives of the other parties to the communication event: The other member of a dyad, the other members of a group, the audience for a public presentation. Third, communication competence is also dependent on the constraints of the social context in which the communication is occurring. Finally, although we often judge competence solely by looking at the actual behavior displayed, as noted earlier, many scholars suggest competence is not only about the skills of communication, but also about the motivation a communicator has toward particular communication events and the knowledge a communicator has about how to act within that situation (Spitzberg & Cupach, 1984).

The dynamics of competence show through in common experiences. First, consider a typical interaction you might have when buying a car. Your goal might be to get a used car for a less-than-bluebook price. One measure of communication competence is whether you actually purchase the car for your price. Yet, a more full measure of communication competence would also consider the extent to which you used strategies that were effective and appropriate to the relational and situational context. You might get the car for the price you wanted but not use strategies that were necessarily appropriate for the situation. If you communicate in a way that leaves a bad impression, for example, you might not be able to return to this dealership and expect good service on your car. Or, you might eventually get the car for the price you want but it might take you a number of different strategies to be effective with a particular salesperson. In this case, you would not be considered as competent as someone who was able to use more appropriate and effective interactions. Part of being successful in this situation is having the knowledge about what it means to negotiate for a used car and the motivation to engage in the interaction fully. The most competent buyer, then, is the one who not only achieves his or her goals, but who does so with the knowledge and skills appropriate to the relationship and situation.

In a different example, imagine a doctor interacting with a patient. It is paramount that the patient understands the conditions requiring a particular treatment or medication, and the importance of taking the medication as prescribed. The communicative competence of the doctor might be measured in terms of the level of understanding of the patient—but we also know that simply understanding does not necessarily mean compliance. The doctor must take into consideration the concerns and issues (the objectives, if you will) of the patient. Can the patient afford the medication? Are there mitigating factors that will make it difficult or impossible for the patient to enact the treatment plan? In this case, as with our used car example, part of being successful is having the knowledge about what it means to clearly articulate the problems and the ways to address those problems, and also to listen carefully to the needs and concerns of the other party in this interaction, having the motivation to engage fully in the interaction. The most competent communicator, then, is the one who not only achieves his or her goals, but who does so with the knowledge and skills appropriate to the relationship and situation.

Moving back to the classroom, helping your students become competent might not only involve the behavioral aspects, but also the knowledge and motivation aspects relevant to the situation and relationship. As you design graded formal communication assignments or ungraded, more informal, communication activities, it is important to consider the important skills, motivation, and knowledge involved in being successful within the communication activity—to consider how you want students to communicate well in these situations that you design.

Communication as a Situated Activity

Clearly, being successful as a competent communicator can vary across contexts, disciplines, and courses—and it should. Much as writing-in-the-disciplines scholarship argues against a one-size-fits-all approach to writing, we believe communication is a situated, disciplinary activity. We do not advocate for generic communication instruction being dropped in your courses and curricula. Your students need to learn to communicate within your discipline (Dannels, 2001) and within the norms, values, and expectations that your discipline holds. For example, what kinds of questions are valued and expected in the humanities? What form should those questions take? How do these question forms differ from those asked in physics? In sociology? In composition? Should questions lead to answers that are quantitative? Should questions be focused on discerning evidence, or upon expanding vision? Are narrative answers appropriate? How appropriate are anecdotes or testimonials? How new—or old—should evidence be that is provided in answers to questions in order to be deemed legitimate? How do the rules of evidence differ in history from graphic arts, economics, anthropology, or mathematics? Is discussion tightly organized in your discipline? Or, is there an expectation that creativity flows from wide-ranging tangential forays? Are agendas crucial to success? Or, are agendas seen as something that unnecessarily curtail creativity? What evidence is appropriate to sound credible as a speaker in political science? Engineering? Religious studies? Art? Should evidence have been gathered using the scientific method in order to be acceptable? Furthermore, what about organizational structures? Argumentative forms? Professional standards? Additionally, how are expectations for oral communication similar to and/or different from expectations for written communication in your discipline? Are there other forms of communication competence that are valued in addition to writing and speaking? How do all expectations for varied modalities and competencies intertwine? Although these variations in communication competence often go unaddressed, they do exist, and students have to manage them. In this book, we advocate for teaching students how to understand those variations so that they can work within them. Many faculty members tend to assume that students will somehow discern what the variations are. The astute students will. However, many students will never understand that there are criteria being applied that are not just arbitrarily chosen by their professor but are part of a larger cultural system. In a parallel example, students may learn how to write a lab report in an introductory chemistry course and, in doing so, may implicitly learn to differentiate that writing from more creative pursuits. The cultural norms surrounding writing in the sciences are well documented, but such norms are not always clearly conveyed to students.

What does this mean for us as teachers? We need to think proactively about what these rules are for our students—whether in small-group discussions, interactions to facilitate close readings of texts, presentations to illustrate professionalism, or teamwork aimed at advocacy of a particular political agenda—and help students learn to think proactively about them as well. We cannot possibly map all of the elements in any given situation that point to the specific behaviors that will inevitably be competent in that situation (see Pearson & Daniels, 1988). Rather, we need to work with students to help them learn how to discern the characteristics of all situations—academic, professional, interpersonal, civic—that they encounter. We need to help them understand communication within the disciplines, rather than communication as a generic skill that works in the same way in every situation. We also need to help them figure out how to learn what the rules are. Instead of charting a map of competence, we must look at how such maps are constructed and teach students how to discern the nature of that construction. We cannot separate what we are teaching—and what we are asking of our students—from the contexts within which they are functioning. Communicative competence implies knowledge of cultural, social, and interpersonal rules that will facilitate the negotiation of meaning among the participants. Part of our task it to help students gain this knowledge so that they can enact behaviors that are appropriate and successful in their various communication situations.

2 A STRATEGIC FRAMEWORK FOR COMMUNICATION IN THE DISCIPLINES

The question now is simply—Where do you start?

First, we acknowledge the constraints under which you are able to work with students. In many cases, you have very limited time to devote to anything other than your course subject. In many cases you do not have the opportunity for an extended mentoring relationship with students because they take one class with you and move on. How can you help students learn to be confident, thoughtful, proactive agents of change in nine or fifteen weeks while at the same time covering the material you need to cover; keeping up with the dramas of the classroom; grading homework, quizzes, and tests; managing attendance; considering excuses; responding to student emails; and perhaps every once in a while actually reading new material for the course in your "free" time? It is possible if you take a focused, discipline-based approach to oral communication. Your best chance at engaging in oral communication in your courses and your best chance to maximize your impact with students is to do so with your feet firmly planted in your own disciplinary traditions, norms, and contexts and using those to help guide your choices about how oral communication fits in. This book will provide you with a framework—a trellis, if you will—to act as a support for exploring how oral communication can contribute to your own disciplinary and course-based content, activities, and goals.

Before we introduce the framework of this book, we want to recognize that many of you have come to this initiative as a result of outside forces. It could be that your campus has an established communication-across-the-curriculum program that has invited you to participate. Perhaps your campus has a writing across the curriculum program that has incorporated more attention to speaking and they are looking for people who might be interested. It could even be that you are feeling pressure from the administration to participate in more teaching and learning enhancement activities. Or, if you are an administrator, you could be feeling pressure from the alumni, industry, or accreditation agencies to produce outcome-based evidence of student learning and communication competence. It could also be that your campus or department is not involved with these initiatives, but you have become curious and intrigued by the possibility of doing something new in order to revitalize your departmental participation. Whichever of these "sparks" (or perhaps there are others, too) has brought you to this book, our goal is to provide you with a framework and practical supplements to that framework to help you consider, seriously and efficiently, a focus on oral communication in your classrooms and curricula. The premise of this book is that focused attention to goal-based, discipline-specific oral communication activities can benefit teaching and learning in significant ways, facilitating engaged and interactive learners and teachers, proficient and coherent soon-to-be professionals, and participatory citizens within and outside of your classroom.

While there are many reasons to consider oral communication as a viable contribution to your classroom, the task of incorporating oral communication in your courses could be a daunting one, especially if you are already teaching a packed curriculum, dealing with larger and larger classes, or managing other instructional initiatives. The framework we present is not intended to simplify this task, but rather to provide you with a number of options to explore using that which you already know—your discipline. One of the key assumptions of this book is that oral communication is a situated activity that, when taught across the curriculum, is best implemented with a discipline-specific, goal-based foundation. We do not start with the five oral communication assignments that every student should participate in or the oral communication skills that should be present in each course, nor could we even establish what assignments or skills should be included in every class. Instead, we suggest several decision points and elements to consider while developing your own approach to teaching oral communication in your own discipline.

As you move forward, we encourage you to be strategic in locating where oral communication best fits within your instructional emphases. To help you explore these issues, we propose a framework that focuses on five decision-making points about oral communication: Consider institutional context, articulate oral communication instructional objectives and outcomes, design oral communication assignments and activities, support students' learning, and evaluate learning. These decision points follow a traditional instructional design model that moves from institutional context to goals to design to implementation, and then finally, to assessment. Figure 2.1 provides an illustration of these decision points.

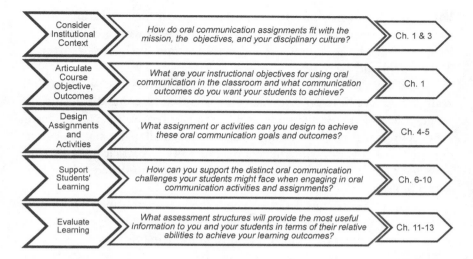

Figure 2.1. Strategic Framework for Oral Communication in the Disciplines

We tailor this model to oral communication in the disciplines by high-lighting the situated nature of these decisions. For each decision, you should consider the particular norms and values of your course and discipline so that you can construct a learning environment that is useful and authentic to the students involved. We will introduce each of the five decision-making points in brief here, and then will expand on them in later chapters by providing teaching resources for each of the constructs.

Decision Point I: Considering Institutional Context

Guiding Question: How do oral communication assignments fit with the institutional mission, the department objectives, and your disciplinary culture?

Before you think through your work within your specific courses, it is important for you to consider the contextual issues that might surround your particular course and discipline. How you integrate oral communication activities and assignments into your course occurs within the context of your institution's goals as well as your discipline's expectations. Consider the institutional mission, and the ways in which that mission fits with the local region and community. What historical issues influence this mission? How do these relate to the role of your discipline within the larger institution? What other initiatives (such as writing across the curriculum) are present and how are they implemented on your campus? How does your particular department contribute to larger initiatives, a broader sense of your discipline, and/or institution? If you are in a department that is one of many within your larger discipline, what historical or current departmental issues are relevant to your department's activities? How does the class fit within the larger curriculum? What is the communicative culture of your discipline, department, and curriculum?

There are also considerations related to logistical issues: What are the realities you face in terms of elements such as time, space and students' demographic? What are your students likely to face relative to expectations in other courses that they are taking—for example, if all major courses require extensive group work, will students be able to fully participate if they are expected to be fully functioning group members in four different long-term group projects?

Finally, there are considerations about the impact of using new kinds of pedagogy in your own teaching and upon how your teaching is evaluated. To what extent have you had some experience working in other communication-related initiatives? How prepared do you feel for turning over some control in the classroom to student discussion? How ready do you feel to assess oral communication efforts of students? What kind of institutional support is available to you to help you develop your pedagogical approaches? What kinds of criteria are used to evaluate you as a teacher, and do they take into consideration investment in new pedagogies?

Once you have a better understanding of these institutional considerations, it is important to consider the cultural, disciplinary issues that will impact the teaching and learning of communication. Some of those could emerge from particular historical traditions in your discipline, others might emerge from standards of practice that have become entrenched in the way in which the faculty and students in your discipline go about approaching communication. Yet others possibly emerge from the pragmatics of your students, faculty, and institutional structure. These situated, disciplinary issues are important to understand because the teaching and learning of communication within your courses will be driven, in many ways, by the context in which it is occurring. Chapter 3 addresses this decision point in more detail.

DECISION POINT II: ARTICULATING OBJECTIVES AND OUTCOMES

Guiding Question: What are your instructional objectives for incorporating oral communication in the classroom and what communication outcomes do you want your students to achieve?

As you think about incorporating oral communication in your course, consider the reasons it might be beneficial for your classes. What purpose could oral communication serve in the larger context of the course? The answer to this question will help you in defining broad instructional objectives for incorporating oral communication in your classroom. For some, you might want to use oral communication in a supporting role—to push students to engage in the reading more thoroughly or to help students talk through their opinions and ideas about course content. For others, you might want to help students master certain professional communication skills they can later use in the workplace. Yet, others might be most concerned about using communication to encourage students to participate as active citizens of their local and national communities. Instructional objectives are typically written in the goal-statement form, beginning with "My goals for using communication in this course include . . . " or "The purpose of this communication activity or assignment is . . ." Sample instructional objectives are:

- to become familiar with critical thinking approaches necessary for understanding course content, issues, or problems
- to increase group cohesiveness
- to increase student responsibility for learning in the class
- to become proficient at asking questions in the context of your discipline
- to develop facilitation and discussion skills
- to increase awareness and skills for dealing with group conflict
- to be able to use vocabulary needed for professional contexts outside of the classroom
- to learn how to do close reading of texts
- to gain insight into a particular author's work
- to develop the ability to address a hostile audience.

Instructional objectives or goals are not exactly the same as specific communication outcomes, although they are clearly related. Not all of our objectives or goals as teachers are measurable, yet it is important to articulate that we have them. We may, for example, have an objective that students will become more ethically sensitive, or have empathy for alternative points of view. It would be difficult to measure these kinds of objectives, yet they still provide direction. Student-learning outcomes, on the other hand, are measurable, and as such they can be evaluated should we choose to do so. Therefore, beyond your broad-scale instructional objectives or goals, it is important to identify the specific communication outcomes you want your students to achieve by taking your course. It is possible your institution will refer to these outcomes as "learning objectives" as there are varied definitions for objectives and outcomes dependent on the context. For this context, though, outcomes identify the desired capabilities you want your students to have when they leave the course, as opposed to goals that are broad statements of purpose, and at times what we simply hope will happen for students.

One often-used framework for articulating objectives and outcomes is Bloom's taxonomy. While there have been revisions to this taxonomy (Anderson & Krathwohl, 2000), and there has been some controversy about its use, we believe it is useful to consider the three major classifications of student learning outlined by Bloom and colleagues (1956): cognitive, affective, and psychomotor. The cognitive domain deals with what you want students to know—the "recall or recognition of knowledge and the development of intellectual abilities and skills" (Bloom, 1956, p. 7). The affective domain deals with values, attitudes, and interest. Finally, the behavioral domain (or *psychomotor learning*, the term used by Bloom) is focused on motor skills, and commonly is related to speech, handwriting, and technical proficiencies (Krathwohl, Bloom, & Masia, 1964).

When you are writing course-based outcomes and when you are designing assignments, it might be helpful for you to think about which domains you want to focus on. In Chapter 4, for example, when we discuss outcomes for informal activities, you will often be focused on the cognitive domain and affective domain (what you want students to know and value after engaging in communication), whereas when you design more formal assignments (Chapter 5) that typically have a grade or greater credit value attached to them, you are often adding a psychomotor domain (what you want students to be able to do, communicatively, as demonstrated in the assignment).

There are a number of different formulas for writing student-learning outcomes. For example, the A.B.C.D. framework refers to writing outcomes that identify: the audience/target of the outcome, the expected behavior, the conditions under which this behavior will be expected, and the degree/standard by which acceptable performance will be judged (Heinich, Molenda, & Russell, 1989). Another highly adaptable structure is the S.M.A.R.T. framework for writing student-learning outcomes that are specific, measurable, attainable, realistic, and time-sensitive (Doran, 1981). To the extent that these frameworks help, use them. However, we suggest that as you adapt and use these frameworks, you do so in ways consistent with your context.

A couple of examples might illustrate how objectives/goals and outcomes could work together in a course. First, in a mechanical engineering design course, instructional objectives and outcomes could be as follows:

> "One objective of this course is to engage you in communication events that simulate professional contexts in the engineering design industry."

For the same course, the learning outcome could be:

> "By the end of this course, students will be able to translate techni-
> cal material into understandable language for a lay audience during
> a design prototype presentation."

In a composition course, you might have this instructional goal:

> "This course will provide you with experience in expressing written
> ideas in an oral communication setting."

A student learning outcome supporting this objective could be:

> "By the end of this course, students will be able to translate written
> work into oral talking points for a public presentation."

In a modern dance course, you might have the following as an instructional objective/goal:

> "The goal for the course is to help students develop multimodal
> ways of thinking and talking about dance."

The student learning outcomes for this course might be:

> "By the end of this course, students will be able to articulate, in suc-
> cinct performance review presentations, the rationale behind a series
> of movements within multiple eras of dance."

You might notice that these objectives and outcomes blend communication and content in varied ways. Content-oriented goals/objectives are the
meat of your course—and they essentially articulate what you want your
students to learn in terms of course material. For some of you, there will
be distinct content-oriented goals and communication-oriented goals. For
others, your content and communication goals will blend. For example,
in a software engineering course, the following outcome blends content
and communication:

> "By the end of this course, students will be able to accurately and
> succinctly diagnose unreported bugs in new software applications in
> impromptu managerial role plays."

In an anatomy and physiology course, you might have separate content
and communication outcomes:

> "By the end of this course, students will be able to identify differ-
> ent parts of the skeletal, muscular, lymphatic, and respiratory sys-
> tems" and

"By the end of this course, students will be able to accurately synthesize information about the human body when analyzing health and disease cases."

How you articulate your content/communication outcomes is up to you. What is important is that you begin to articulate these objectives and outcomes so you can get a sense of how communication fits within the larger context of the course. Although we will spend additional time on teachable, measurable, and observable outcomes when we move to evaluation, it is critical that you begin writing those outcomes now, at the beginning of the process. They will stand as a map to help guide your decisions about assignment design and evaluation. Table 2.1 provides you with questions to help you think about the relevant objectives and outcomes for your course.

Table 2.1. Planning Questions: Relevant Objectives and Outcomes

What are your key content-focused objectives and/or outcomes for the course?
What current assignments help you achieve your content-oriented objectives and/or outcomes for the course?
What are your key communication-focused objectives for the course?
What particular communication outcomes do you want your students to achieve by the end of this course? To what extent are they cognitive, affective, or behavioral?
What current assignments (if any) help you focus on your communication objectives and outcomes?

Guiding Question: What assignment or activities can you design to achieve your oral communication goals and outcomes?

As you might have noticed, the process of identifying measurable student-learning outcomes leads you to consider the assignments within which those outcomes can be realized. The third decision point focuses on designing assignments and activities to achieve your objectives and outcomes. When thinking about the nature of the assignments, you will need to make decisions about the stakes, structure, and format of each assignment. Specifically, some of these assignments will be very formal, high-stakes events. Others might be very informal activities with little, if any, credit attached. You might structure some of these assignments as collaborative (e.g., team-based), or you might structure them in combination with other assignments (e.g., writing). Additionally, you will need to decide what type of oral communication activity you will have your students engage in during and outside of class. Some might look like traditional public presentations, and others might be more focused on teamwork or small-group communication competencies. The structure and nature of the communication assignment or activity should directly flow from your communication objectives and expected outcomes. If one of your objectives is to help students understand their readings more critically, then you can consider a wide variety of oral communication activities or assignments that could achieve that objective. Your decision, though, should be to go with whichever option is best aligned with the outcome you expect students to demonstrate. It might not make sense, for example, to have students give a formal thirty-minute presentation to achieve the objective of understanding readings more critically. A more aligned activity might be to have students rotate, with each student providing a two-minute critical review presentation in which they articulate the argument of the reading and one criticism of it to start the day's discussion. An alternative might be for each student to pose two questions for clarification and one or two questions for evaluation in a two-minute informal presentation to the class. The point is, you get to decide how to construct oral communication activities and assignments, but those decisions should align with your goals.

Some of the questions you will need to consider in this decision point include

- What type of communication assignments or activities will best meet your objectives? (e.g., presentation, small group or team-based, one-on-one, etc.)?
- Where on the spectrum between formal (high stakes) and informal (low stakes) will the assignments or activities fall?
- What particular constraints do you want to place on the assignment or activity in order to focus students on your communication goals?
- What guidelines do you want to give students about the assignment or activity in order to focus them on your communication objectives?
- Are there ways to scaffold assignments and activities so that they work together to meet overall course goals (see Chapter 5 for a discussion on scaffolding)?

These questions will get you started. Chapters 4 and 5 of this book provide information on designing both formal communication assignments (often used to foster professional communication competencies) as well as informal communication activities. These chapters also provide information about how to scaffold these activities and assignment to best meet your desired goals.

DECISION POINT IV: SUPPORTING STUDENT LEARNING

Guiding Question: How can you support the distinct oral communication challenges your students might face when engaging in oral communication activities and assignments?

Like any new skill or process, oral communication does not come naturally. Although some would argue that talking is a skill that many have naturally, and therefore need no help with, we suggest that when using oral communication to achieve particular goals, there are issues that need to be addressed in terms of student support. Regardless of your assignment decisions, oral communication opens the door for a number of challenges students (and you) could face. Specifically, when asking students to participate in oral communication assignments, there is a possibility that you will need to deal with issues of apprehension, participation, difficult interactions (conflict), and diversity. This fourth decision point is about figuring out how to deal with these issues and provide students with the support they need to work through the potential challenges and be successful. As faculty, your primary job is to teach content, and we realize you probably do not have the time to fully explore these challenges. Yet, there is a wealth of information about these challenges that you could use to preempt them or diffuse them when they arise. We suggest that you seriously consider attending to these challenges because it is these that usually become critical factors in whether or not you accomplish your objectives.

Some of the questions you will need to consider within this decision point include

- To what extent do your assignments and activities open the door for communication apprehension? What fears might students have about engaging in these assignments and activities?
- What challenges do students face when participating in class activities or group discussions? Are students likely to be quiet, and even resistant to speaking up in class? Or are students eager to participate in communication activities such as discussions?
- What are student experiences with group communication activities? For example, how will you manage students who have had bad experiences with group or teamwork and who are discouraged at the prospect of being involved in yet another group project?
- What conflicts or difficult interactions do you anticipate could emerge when students work on and perform their communication activities and assignments?

- What issues of diversity (e.g., gender, ethnic, cultural) might cause challenges to students as they work on and perform their communication activities and assignments?

Section III of this book (Chapters 6 through 10) discusses each of these challenges and provides suggestions of activities and assignments to help support students who face these challenges.

DECISION POINT V: EVALUATING LEARNING

Guiding Question: What assessment structures will provide the most useful information to you and your students in terms of their relative abilities to achieve your learning outcomes?

Nine times out of ten, the first question faculty members have when thinking about using oral communication in their course revolves around assessment. We recognize that assessment takes time, and assessment of oral communication might feel daunting, given your expertise is on the content of your course. Yet, assessment is tied directly to your goals, assignment design, and student support. This final decision point asks you to consider various assessment mechanisms that could help you understand the ways in which students are fulfilling your goals and the ways in which they need to improve. Additionally, we believe it is important—specifically when assessing oral communication—to consider the relational nature of assessment, and to pay attention to the ways in which you can respond to students in order to increase the potential for learning. Students often feel that when they speak, whether in front of a large group or in a small team-based setting, whether formal or informal, that they are putting themselves out there. Therefore, there is the potential that students will become defensive when given feedback. For this reason, we address issues related to this personal and embodied nature of oral communication feedback and response.

Some of the questions you will need to answer within this decision point include

- What mechanisms will you use to assess students' oral communication assignments and activities? How formal or informal will the assessments be?
- How will you provide feedback to students?
- What face issues (i.e., ego management) could emerge when providing feedback to students on their communication performances and how can you mitigate those issues?

- What various response structures might provide students with useful feedback on their communication performances (e.g., technological, face-to-face, etc.)?
- How can you construct a rubric that reflects your communication goals and disciplinary culture?
- What kinds of rubrics will be most useful to you and your students for assessment purposes?

Section IV deals with these assessment issues and provides guidance in making decisions about response and evaluation, creating rubrics, and managing ego-related issues (facework).

WHERE TO START?

You might have already noticed that although we discuss each of these decision points separately, they are intricately intertwined. For example, the ways in which you assess oral communication activities need to be directly tied to your objectives and outcomes (e.g., you don't want to hold students accountable for something that is not necessarily part of your objectives or outcomes). Writing good student-learning outcomes automatically gets you thinking about the kinds of assignments that will achieve those outcomes. And the ways in which you support students will differ depending on the challenge brought up by the differing assignments (e.g., there might not be apprehension issues if you are using low-stakes pair-and-share assignments). Finally, all of these decision points live within the broader culture of your discipline and your institution. The key here is to start with your objectives and to stay tethered to them as you move through each of your decisions. We present these decision points linearly and individually in order for you to have a clear and useful framework to follow. However, to use an analogy borrowed from one of our experiences with textiles faculty and students, these decision points are meant to be "wovens." Each of these decision points depends on the others, and although you might choose to focus your energy on only one, we encourage you to consider the full range of these decisions so that you can take advantage of the ways in which they are integrated.

3 Considering Institutional Contexts and Challenges

If you are like many of the faculty we work with, you are probably thinking "Why me? Why should I teach communication? Why not let the communication department deal with it?" This is a good question. We do not presume all faculty members are professional communicators, or that faculty in other disciplines should have the theoretical background to teach communication in the same way as do communication faculty. This book does presume, though, that you have the disciplinary background and expertise to understand the communication life of your discipline. You are the expert on how communication is enacted in your own context. If an audience member watching your students says something like "emotion doesn't work here" or "the visual speaks for itself," it is likely that you can make sense of those comments in ways that are different from how we might make sense of it given our background in communication (presuming those comments are typical of your disciplinary culture). You can probably tell students pretty quickly what they should definitely not do when they give a presentation to industry sponsors (for example) or what they should do if they want experts in the field to find them credible. You probably understand the nuances of productive and cohesive teamwork in your discipline. You know the particulars about your disciplinary tradition that might influence the extent to which women participate, or the extent to which minorities become active members of communicative events. You have very good localized understandings of the types of communication events that typify your discipline, the evidence that is considered valid in your discipline, the competencies or skills that are important for your students to master, and the performative roles students will need to enact to be successful.

So, how can communication specialists help you? Communication specialists working in cross-curricular programs can provide you with the vocabulary from communication theory and research to help you name, understand, and teach so that you can achieve your instructional goals. From their own expertise, communication specialists can help you by asking you the questions that are important to ask in order to help you best tailor your choices to your own instructional emphases. Based on research, communication specialists can help you understand the particular issues students might face when trying to learn communication in your discipline. For these reasons, if you have access to initiatives on your campus focused on oral communication across the curriculum, we strongly encourage you take advantage of them. Even if you do not, if you have writing-across-the curriculum specialists, they can assist you in thinking about using this book as you think through multiple modalities of communication assignments and activities. This book should ideally supplement your work with these specialists. If you do not have access to these resources, we hope this book will provide the vocabulary, ask the questions, and give some insight into the teaching and learning issues relevant to oral communication in the disciplines.

We recognize that there might be some other challenges and concerns you have with incorporating oral communication in your courses. We discussed some of those institutional constraints in Chapter 1, in fact. We, however, want to address the more individual challenges (the "yeah but's . . .") here, because we acknowledge the valid constraints many faculty are under and the important concerns that emerge from these constraints. Our goal is not to deny that these constraints and challenges exist, but rather to provide insight on how to best handle these constraints using the strategic framework we present in this book.

Time, Time, Time . . . in Class

"Ok, so I have thirty-five students. Even if I simply have them do short presentations—say 4–5 minutes each—that will take 2–3 class periods away from my lecture material. Also, what if they don't do a very good job with the content? Then I have to go back and review the stuff they were supposed to address. If I put them in teams to save time, well—then there's the whole team issue. So, maybe I'll just scrap the whole idea. Plus, I have a lot to get through and can't waste class time."

Statements like this are typical—many of us feel the pressures of trying to find class time to cover all the material we want. The coverage issue is an extremely valid and important concern when considering incorporating oral communication activities in your courses. We all have material that is important to provide for our students in whatever content area we are teaching. In fact, many of us spend hours and hours of time trying to figure out how to get everything in—ultimately having to make painful decisions about what readings to cut, what lectures to combine, and what to assign for out-of-class work because the in-class time is full. Time in class is particularly an issue in courses where students' knowledge of the content is essential before they move on to other courses. Additionally, some courses are flagged for gathering assessment data in order to address accreditation issues, and therefore covering the material is essential. In other courses, students are completing a final project that necessitates a significant amount of class time. So why would you bring in something that will take precious time away from lecturing on course material?

One of the primary reasons coverage is an issue for many faculty members is that they have a narrow view of what it means to incorporate communication in their courses. The first thing that comes to mind are formal, business-like presentations—students in suits using PowerPoint, perhaps in research teams, giving 30+ minute presentations with a question-and-answer round afterwards—a situation that most definitely takes up a large amount of class time. For some of you, these high-stakes presentations are important and you can create the class time to allow them. But when these kinds of communication events are not relevant to your goals or your discipline, there are other options. The strategic framework starts with your goals—not with a presumed set of communication activities. You decide how to best use communication within the confines of your content area. The decision, however, begins with your goals. If high-stakes business presentations do not help you achieve your goals, then you should choose something else. If you are teaching a course in which the content is packed, consider using communication to help your students learn about the course material. Perhaps two-minute reading summaries or pair-and-share critical questions about the content will help students engage with the material is new ways. If you are interested in professionalizing your students, consider a variety of communication assignments that might help you do that. For a faculty member in business management, that might be a "performance review." For someone in soil science, that genre might be a "customer response." Or, if your goals revolve around having students critically analyze material, you could use discussions to encourage students to synthesize ideas, put information in a coherent form, listen to others, and critique ideas of others in constructive ways. These kinds of activities can help students more fully integrate course content, far beyond what they would be able to do by just listening to a lecture. The point is that you get to decide how to weave communication within and around your content so that it supports the material, instead of detracting from it.

It is worth remembering that using communication in the classroom can be about both developing students' abilities to communicate orally and developing students' abilities to understand course content. Part of the answer to the in-class time crunch is that in order to be successful, the oral activity should clearly help students learn the course material. In Chapter 3 we will discuss this particular goal in more detail. For now though, consider oral communication as integrative, rather than additional. Oral communication assignments and activities should not simply be add-ons, created to meet an abstract requirement. Course content must be fully integrated into the requirements for the activity.

TIME, TIME, TIME . . . OUT OF CLASS . . .

> This sounds like a great idea if I didn't already have three syllabi to prepare, an evaluation report to write, a faculty retreat to go to, and—oh yeah—that is only before the semester starts. Then there's the undergraduate committee, the scholarship committee, the publications committee—I actually think I've also agreed to be on a committee on committees! And then—keeping up with email questions from students, excuses about missing homework—sick grandparents, dying pets, technology problems . . . ah! Like I said—great idea. I just don't have any extra time during my day to think about this or make this happen. I already work long hours after I leave the office—there's just not enough time.

Sound familiar? One of the primary challenges faculty face when considering the possibility of adding communication activities to their course(s) is time. Regardless of the type of institution you are in, there are likely to be a number of requests, requirements, and commitments eating up your daily time slots. Not that these are necessarily negative activities—in fact, many of them are extremely important and are simply part of what we, as faculty, signed up for. But oftentimes the daily activities that we engage in leave very little time for us to focus our attention on initiatives such as communication across the curriculum. And if we are asked (or required) to engage in such initiatives, we find the time—but do so at times regretfully, at times unwillingly, and at times even spitefully.

If we could add more hours to the day or relieve you of some of your duties so that you could focus on communication across the curriculum, we would (and we would probably become rich in the process!). Time is an issue—an important one. Many of you have particular professional, personal, or administrative commitments that make such an initiative challenging. We understand that these constraints might be overwhelming. Our goal with this framework is to make your time spent on your course more efficient. The strategic framework does not necessitate you to completely revamp your course. It is flexible and rests on you making choices that fit within your disciplinary context and help you achieve your instructional emphases. Your choices might, in fact, support the teaching tasks you are already spending time on in your course preparation. If this is the case, you might be able to jump right in—try a small activity tomorrow in class or next week in lab that makes sense given what you are already doing. Just doing something small might lead to significant changes in student engagement. In other cases, the strategic framework might spark new thinking about your courses, students, and goals. This thinking could lead you to making some changes on larger assignments. This integration does take time, but we believe it is time well spent if you are able to better achieve your goals.

ME? BUT . . . I'M NOT PERFECT

"Easy for you to say. You teach communication. You are probably pretty good at this communication thing. If I'm grading my students on their communication abilities, don't I have to be perfect? How can I help my students when I don't think I am an expert in communication? Won't they start judging me? Communication specialists are much better prepared to deal with these kinds of things. I'm not the expert!"

Very few faculty members are professional communicators. In fact, many faculty members did not receive any training in communication, and if they did, it was probably informal and provided by a close mentor or colleague. Your training focused primarily on your content area—which is exactly where it was supposed to be focused. So it is definitely a valid concern when you think about opening your students up to a new experience in which you have had little, if any, formal training. When one of the authors considered asking her students to engage in a web-based portfolio assignment, she felt similar angst. She is not a web designer. How could she grade them if she was not an expert? Shouldn't they expect their teacher to be an expert in this? Similarly with communication, you might be concerned about your own level of expertise with particular communication skills or competencies. Even if you do not worry about your own communication abilities, perhaps you worry about providing sufficient feedback on communication—given you want your focus to be on the content.

Similar to many athletic, musical, and technical skills, communication (both written and oral) is an ongoing activity that should be considered developmental. If every music teacher had to be of Beethoven's stature, we would be short of music teachers. If every basketball coach was required to be as consistent as Michael Jordan, we would have a limited pool of people from which to choose a team. As a teacher of your content area, you do not have to be an expert communicator in order to engage in this process. You have to be willing and open to learn. Your primary responsibility is to teach and master your content area. That is why you are in the position you are in at your institution. You are a member of a discipline that has judged you competent to handle those particular content areas. The good news is that it is this content competence that opens the possibility for you to focus on communication in your courses. The strategic framework of this book allows you to take advantage of your disciplinary goals and competence and to use that competence to better understand and implement oral communication activities. As previously stated, as a member of your discipline, you are steeped in communication norms, activities, and values every day. The framework in this book asks you to bring those to the table—and with support (if possible), you will build more and more expertise. For example, using the framework of this book, a pre-med teacher can focus on the goal of teaching students how much self-disclosure might make a patient-physician interaction fruitful for both parties. A communication expert can give this faculty member the language of "self-disclosure," or illuminate the different kinds of self-disclosure, but the teacher steeped in the experiences and values of the pre-med context can best illustrate how self-disclosure is enacted for successful communication. So, why you? Because you have the disciplinary expertise to make oral communication meaningful and useful to your students.

SEND THEM TO A COMMUNICATION CLASS

"Why do I have to do this? Why can't I just send my students to communication? They have a public speaking course . . . this really isn't my job. What are they doing over there anyway? If they were doing their job, I wouldn't have to deal with students who did not know how to communicate."

In many universities there are communication courses that fulfill general education requirements. Similar to freshman composition courses, which often introduce students to writing competencies, processes, and genres; general education oral communication courses are important courses for students to take—as they typically introduce students to the vocabulary of oral communication. Sometimes these courses focus squarely on public speaking. At other times, they provide a hybrid view of public speaking, small-group, interpersonal, and organizational communication. Other courses are more focused on business communication. Yet, what these courses do not do is help students understand the particular, situated communication expectations for your discipline. They might teach students how to construct a logical persuasive argument, but they do not and cannot teach them the kinds of evidence that professionals in your discipline value. They cannot teach students the types of communication events that are important to your discipline because there are too many disciplines and content areas with varied communication events—there simply would not be time. You know your discipline. You are the expert in what it means to communicate competently and coherently for your audiences, in your professional situations, and in your classroom. If all you want for your students is to have them gain a basic vocabulary about communication, or increase their confidence in generic communication situations, a communication class will suffice. In fact, it might be very important for your students to gain this exposure. We, however, hope that we have made the argument that you have the potential to help your students in much more situated and profound ways by infusing communication within your course. This book is committed to help you make communication work—within your course and your discipline—so that you see it as an opportunity to achieve your teaching and learning goals.

Not My Class

"Uh, this is fine for other people. But mine is a large class. And my students do not really have the motivation to be engaged with the material. Half the time they don't even show up. The other half they spend on Facebook. And those who are there really just want a grade and want to get out of my class. I could never make this work. And if I tried, it would be a nightmare to grade."

We all have particular demographic, contextual, or institution-specific issues that could make this initiative challenging. Some of you are teaching large classes in which any thought of formal communication activities is impossible. Some have particular populations (e.g., freshmen, second-year students, less academically-inclined students) for whom anything outside of the course content is a real challenge. Others have particular physical constraints that preclude any interactive, communication activities (we've had our share of rooms with the desks bolted down!). Perhaps others have teaching content that is not as suitable for oral communication activities or assignments.

The framework provided in this book was designed to be adaptable for individual courses, students, and disciplines. We do not assume that communication activities will fit every course, student, or faculty. We are not advocating for a global, generalized communication instruction. In fact, our focus is entirely opposite. The strategic framework is fiercely committed to the goals of your course, curriculum, and discipline. We don't start by offering blanket, generic communication assignments, competencies, or genres. We start with your instructional objectives/outcomes, and encourage you to consider the various assignments or activities that fit with those emphases. For large classes, you might consider the instructional emphasis of learning course material—perhaps focusing on helping students better understand course readings or historical sources. For freshmen courses in which students are just getting exposed to the content in your discipline, you might choose to help students think about the most valued communication competencies within professional arenas in various disciplines. The point here is that the strategic framework is broad, and while it might not work in its entirety in your class, we hope you can glean something from it that will support your students' experiences within and outside of your discipline.

JUST ANOTHER INITIATIVE

"Let's see, a couple of years ago I tried the whole inquiry-guided learning thing. Then I got really excited about service learning. Hmmmm, then my department head made us do portfolio-based assessment. These were all fun, but I didn't have time to really continue with any of them. Now this? I'm already doing some communication work in my class. My students all participate in critiques and sometimes I help them learn how to avoid 'ums' and 'uhs'—so why take on more? I don't want to try any more new initiatives."

It seems like there are constantly new initiatives and teaching foci for us to explore. If we were to attend every workshop that we came across in our email inboxes with a focus on new teaching and learning initiatives, we could probably keep our calendars full five days a week. And although many of you might not have engaged in a formal initiative focused on communication across the curriculum, you might have focused some attention on communication in your current assignments and classroom activities. Some of you have probably helped students learn to participate better in discussions. Others might have asked students to problem-solve in teams or in groups and helped with the process. You might have even assigned an end-of-semester presentation. For some, these efforts may not have been particularly successful. Many of you may have questioned whether the time was worth it—were your assignments really helping students achieve what you hoped? Were they really learning the content they needed to learn? Were the assignments seen by students as integral to their disciplinary learning, or just as another "hoop" to jump through? Some of you may have tried oral verbal assignments, only to have them fail miserably. So why spend more time if you are already doing this? Why engage in this particular initiative given the high risk of failure and the multiple other pedagogical options? In the next section, we tell you why, but first we ask you to look specifically at some of the challenges you may face institutionally as well as individually, when considering integrating oral communication activities into classes. Table 3.1 provides questions for examining these aspects in the context of your institution.

Table 3.1. Planning Questions: Considering the Institutional Context

What is the mission of your institution?
What role does your discipline/department play in achieving the institution's mission?
How do the goals of the course you are teaching fit within the institutional mission and the larger curricular objectives of the institution?
What logistical issues are of concern? For example, classroom design, class size, equipment availability, etc.
What concerns do you have about the impact of taking on this pedagogical approach in your classes at an individual level?
What kinds of support do you need in order to undertake this pedagogical approach? How can you find that support?

BENEFITS OF COMMUNICATION IN THE DISCIPLINES

As we have already mentioned, we suggest that you spend time and attention to oral communication (and specifically to the framework in this book) as it will allow you to better achieve a number of your instructional objectives and outcomes. As disciplinary cultures and contexts change, adapt, and transform over time, so too, will your use of this book. We do not agree with the argument that communication is like riding a bike—once you learn, you don't forget. Communicating well, within a particular disciplinary context, is complicated by values, norms, social relationships, and power structures. The framework in this book provides applicable, flexible constructs that are meant to dive deeper in order to move beyond the surface issues related to communication. In this way, even those of you who are already doing something with communication in your courses might benefit from a new perspective committed to those disciplinary "deep waters" that are often the ones that make or break a communication event.

Yet, the question still remains—why this initiative, as opposed to the numerous others that arrive in your email inbox, especially if you have any of the concerns outlined above—all valid concerns that pose real challenges to faculty interested in incorporating communication in their courses. So, why do it? In this section we will outline benefits of this initiative for students, faculty, and programs.

Benefits for Students

As indicated earlier, there are a number of different reasons for you to incorporate communication in your courses—professional calls from industry, accreditation processes within particular disciplines, and public reportage on communication inabilities of students. Yet beneath all of these is the primary focus of communication across the curriculum—the students. Presumably, within each of these calls, lamentations, or desires is the assumption that communicating better will help students. So, the question is—how can this initiative help students?

We know from the business surveys that students who are able to communicate clearly and coherently will be ahead of the game when it comes to getting what many of them want—a job. We also know that those skills will benefit them once they enter the workplace in that they will help them cope with the realities of workplace communication events. Additionally, if your focus is on using communication to enhance learning, these skills will engage students in the processes of critical thinking, discussion, analytical questioning, and problem-solving that will not only serve them in academic situations, but in other situations in which they are called upon to learn new material or processes. Finally, communication instruction can prepare students for contexts outside of the workplace and classroom. It might make them more prepared and willing and motivated to speak up at a PTA meeting or at a town hall debate in their local community. Or, it might make them better prepared to make a clear argument about a local issue to friends or neighbors who ask for their opinion.

We will admit, some students will perceive communication work as busy work or as unnecessary to the "real" work of the discipline. Our experience, though, is that these students are either facing very typical learning challenges related to communication (that will be discussed in Section III) or that the communication activities are dropped in without a goal-based, discipline-specific focus. Therefore, when students claim that the communication feels like it is not related to their "real" work, they could be right because the activities might not have been designed in a way that intertwines with the content. With a clear goal-based rationale, careful, strategic design of discipline-based communication assignments and activities, and appropriate support and feedback to enhance learning, many of these students realize that communication is inextricable from their disciplinary lives and actually appreciate their experience in richer ways than they did prior to having it.

Benefits for Faculty

Not only are there benefits for students when they engage in communication within their discipline, but there are also benefits for the faculty. First and foremost, and we've said this again and again, the communication activities and constructs you choose to focus on should help you achieve your course goals and outcomes. If particular activities or assignments do not help you do this, don't use them. Perhaps one of your course goals is to have students become more competent in responding to the public with accurate yet simple information about your discipline. A renewed focus on communication could and should help you achieve this. In terms of teaching, perhaps one of your goals is to become a more interactive teacher. Increased focus on communication could provide you an opportunity to do this. Again, focusing on oral communication will not meet all goals, but it certainly can help you achieve many of them. Another way of looking at this is that communication can help you address some of the challenges you want to fix in your classrooms. At a recent faculty workshop, for example, one of the authors was working with dance faculty who could not see how communication could fit into their course goals. When the author asked what problems students had with the course that the instructors would like to see changed, one faculty member immediately said: "They don't understand how their movements tell the story." Bingo. Now, the question is: How can you use communication to help students understand the narrative behind movement? At that point, the faculty member thought of a number of possibilities.

In addition to being better able to achieve your course goals or solve course problems, we have found that many faculty members experience a renewed excitement and engagement with teaching when incorporating oral communication assignments and activities. A number of early surveys done on faculty involvement with communication across the curriculum showed that faculty liked the process of using communication in their courses and found the experience rewarding as a teacher (e.g., Cronin & Glenn, 1991; Cronin, Glenn, & Palmerton, 2000; Roberts, 1983). As you think about refining your course(s) to increase attention towards oral communication, you might experience new insights about your discipline, content area, and teaching in the process.

Also, as you better understand the genres, arguments, competencies and performative cultures that define your discipline, you might find benefits for your own communication abilities within disciplinary and professional contexts. Perhaps you will be able to navigate those communication activities and events you are called upon to participate in with an increased knowledge about what is considered persuasive, valued, and pertinent to the audiences you interact with because you have taken the time to help your students understand and learn the same.

Finally, and pragmatically, a focus on oral communication activities could provide you with tangible products to help you evidence successful teaching and improved learning. If assessment or accreditation is a concern in your department or institution, it could be important for you to gather information that illustrates teaching development and achievement of particular learning outcomes. If you are expected to engage in research and have an interest in instructional research or the scholarship of teaching and learning, a focus on oral communication activities provides you with the opportunities to engage in research about communication in your courses or programs. Essentially, there is a possibility that some of the pressures you face as a faculty member or program director could be reduced by creating opportunities to gather information about students' oral communication processes and abilities.

Benefits for Departments and Programs

If your department is considering a more sustained focus on communication across the curriculum, or if you are working administratively within a cross-curricular program, there are several benefits to including oral communication as one of the initiatives you implement. First, if you are in a department or program with an already established focus or educational initiative (e.g., writing, technology, service-learning), broadening to embrace oral communication will provide your constituents with more options. Perhaps faculty members you work with are having a difficult time embracing the concept of technology in the classroom, but it seems easier to consider oral communication activities given their disciplinary culture. A focus on oral communication provides them an option that they wouldn't have had with a narrowly defined program. This option could translate to increased participation, more likelihood of sustainability, and a more diverse participant pool.

Second, providing a breadth of options could allow support for other initiatives. Perhaps, for example, faculty who fear the technology initiative but are less fearful of oral communication activities will be able to better comprehend and embrace technology as it is woven within informal speaking assignments. For those in writing across the curriculum programs (in which there is already a national movement towards including oral communication) oral communication can be used in support of writing instruction. Students in psychology, for example, could give one-minute oral presentations describing an outline of their research project (perhaps in poster session format, informally) to help them talk through the logic of the project and get feedback on it. There are a number of different ways oral communication can support writing, and/or other educational initiatives, depending on the focus on your program or department.

Finally, and again, pragmatically—there has been increased focus nationally and internationally on communication across the curriculum, and participating in this movement could provide you with an opportunity to engage in an initiative that is gaining strength, popularity, and attention in educational conversations. The national and international interest in this initiative is growing and is opening doors to opportunities that could lead to productive and interesting teaching and learning collaborations and good public relations for your department or program.

MANAGING CHALLENGES

Before we move into the section with examples of different kinds of communication assignment designs, we want to return to where we started in this chapter—recognizing that you might face challenges when considering incorporating communication in your courses and curricula. Take some time to consider what those challenges might be in light of the discussion in this chapter. Table 3.2 provides planning questions to help you think about institutional challenges you may face.

As you answer these questions, we hope you begin to gain a broad sense of the communicative life of your discipline. As you continue on to the next chapters, we ask you to focus in on your own objectives and to consider various communication activities and assignments that could help you meet those objectives. Our goal is to help you align your own goals with the broader context of your discipline, your students, and your own teaching style.

Table 3.2. Planning Questions: Managing Institutional Challenges

What distinctive challenges do you face that could influence the success of using communication in your course(s)?
What distinctive challenges do your students face when preparing for and engaging in oral communication assignments?
What distinctive challenges does your department or unit face that might influence whether or not efforts to integrate oral communication activities into your unit's classes will be successful?
How would you describe the communication culture of your discipline, and in what ways would using communication activities be viewed positively/negatively?
How would you describe the communication culture of your students, and in what ways might that influence their participation in oral communication activities in your class?

SECTION II: DESIGNING ASSIGNMENTS

In this section we provide examples of the kinds of assignments that you might create in order to achieve your course objectives. The examples we discuss should by no means limit you. In our experience, faculty members are amazingly creative, and once they start looking at ways in which oral communication assignments can help them achieve what they want to achieve—whether it is better integration of content knowledge or development of professional oral communication competence—the variety of approaches developed is exciting.

4 DESIGNING INFORMAL COMMUNICATION ACTIVITIES

As we articulated in the first chapter, research shows that professional communication competence is a worthwhile pursuit in the classroom, given the multiple contexts outside of the classroom in which communication competence could make a difference in students' lives. Similarly, we need to recognize that students can use communication within the classroom in ways that are not necessarily limited to professional competence, but more focused on enhancing their learning experience. In our experience, when faculty members think about using oral communication in the classroom, most automatically think about the formal presentation. Yet, when you think about the important learning and critical thinking processes that occur in your classroom, you may think of classroom discussions, group lab work, and small learning groups. These also involve oral communication—just a different kind of communication than the formal presentation. These kinds of communication activities—sometimes referred to as *communication-to-learn* activities or *informal communication* activities—presume a different way of thinking about oral communication in the classroom. We prefer referring to these activities as *informal* activities, because we believe that whether formal or informal, the communication activities in the classroom are all *communication-to-learn* activities.

Informal communication activities have many benefits. For example, small learning groups of three or four people can facilitate talk because it is a safer place to try out ideas before coming to the larger group. Discussion, and experience with discussion, can desensitize individuals to public talk to some extent and decrease the threat of formal presentations. This kind of interaction enables change because it is part of an on-going transaction—thought evolves while interacting. The exposure to a diversity of skills and thinking decreases myths about what others think. It helps create a realistic comparison base because students hear and are exposed to others' work and thought. There is the potential for students to realize the equifinality of learning: the

43

same end can be reached in a variety of ways. Exposure to other ways of approaching ideas helps students explore multiple approaches to learning, and expands options for them. Preparing students for these kinds of activities helps students learn what is expected of them.

Although you might assume students will have the communication abilities to engage in discussions, group work, or in-class activities, many do not. Therefore, many students are unable to reap the learning benefits of the communication activity and you are left lamenting over students' lack of engagement with course content and discussions. Some of these problems will happen regardless of what you do. Yet many of these problems can be dealt with proactively. This chapter will provide you with information on designing communication activities that maximize the learning that can happen in your classroom and engage your students in skills that are important in situations outside your classroom. For example, engaging in critical analysis of problems is a crucial skill for citizen engagement, whether acting as an advocate, a facilitator, or voter. The process students go through to gather information about course requirements for a major involves skills of questioning, inquiry, research, and analysis—much of which relies on their abilities to communicate. Informal communication assignments address skills such as these. While they do not necessarily focus on helping students achieve polish as professional communicators, they help students learn to think critically, engage in course material, and learn content in deeper ways.

It is clear, though, that just talking won't aid in learning. The character of the talk matters. Webb (1982), in a series of studies on cooperative learning, has convincingly established that the character of the interaction makes a difference in individual learning. Interaction patterns differ by demographic group (e.g., male/female, age, life experience) and students' abilities to learn are influenced by ethnicity and socio-cultural background—that is, students learn better when interaction patterns are consistent with the way communication functions in their home culture (Byrd & Sims, 1987; Jordan, Au, & Joesting, 1983; More, 1987; Philips, 1983; Rhodes, 1988; Vogt, Jordan, & Tharp, 1987). These kinds of activities also involve a certain degree of risk for students. While they may appear to be low risk because they may not be graded, what a student says in class does not necessarily just stay in class. A student struggling with a text or question may be subject to teasing, ridicule, disdain, or just plain impatience expressed by the peers in subtle or not-so-subtle ways. Publicly stating an opinion brings with it the possibility of responses from others that may be difficult to manage.

So what does this mean for us? If we accept that talk by students helps them learn and that the character of the talk in the classroom will make a difference in the quality of the learning, then we are obligated to help students learn how they can use communication to engage in course material within the instructional setting. Experience with talk can contribute to the development of communicative competence, but experience alone is not enough. Students enter our classrooms with a wide variety of experiences in communicating in classroom learning activities. What counts as competent communication in one academic setting, may not be considered competent in another. Disciplines differ in terms of the types of questions they value, the norms of student interaction, the forms or reasoning, and the preferred methods for providing explanations. When students come to your class, they come with varied experiences related to these kinds of activities. Therefore, students need to be provided with examples of how to use communication in the effort of learning. In this chapter, you will find information about various informal communication activities that are intended to facilitate specific learning objectives, how to design these kinds of communication activities, and how to hold students accountable. This chapter is intended to begin the process of designing these kinds of assignments. Chapter 7 provides further information on ways to help prepare students for participation in activities such as these (specifically those that necessitate discussion). Chapter 8 looks more specifically at how to support activities that necessitate group and teamwork.

Regardless of the type of activity you are using, there are important issues related to participation in all communication activities. Student participation in informal communication activities is often seen by instructors as a low-risk process. Yet, for many students, engaging in oral communication of any form is not low risk. A student who chooses to participate in class is essentially publicly committing him or herself to a position of some sort. In doing so, participation becomes a self-disclosing activity. Face issues are always present, more relevant for some students than for others (see Chapter 13 for an extensive discussion on facework). As instructors, we are often not aware of the ramifications of a student's choice to participate. Evaluation by classmates occurs both inside and outside of class—whether we require it or not—and we often do not see the latter. Consider the assessments of faculty members made on the basis of their participation in a faculty meeting, and you will have a sense of the potentially risky nature of class discussion. Furthermore, research on participation in classrooms indicates that faculty or instructor behavior affects the extent to which students participate, as well as the quality of their participation (Webb, 2009; Webb et al., 2009). Therefore, the way in which you, as the instructor, engage in informal communication activities could influence the eventual learning outcomes of the activities themselves.

It is also important to realize that some students will experience a high degree of anxiety with any oral communication expectation—even those that are not formal public presentations. There are things one can do to help deal with high levels of communication apprehension. For example, studies have shown that multiple experiences with public speaking can help decrease public-speaking anxiety for some people. Preparation generally makes a difference in the degree of anxiety that students feel, and structuring activities that integrate a preparatory mechanism such as freewriting prior to discussion may help. Experiences with different kinds of oral communication situations can also be helpful; for example, communicating in a small group in order to prepare for a more formal presentation. Courses that focus on some aspect of oral communication that feels less threatening can help decrease anxiety in those situations perceived as more threatening. One of the best ways of dealing with communication apprehension is to experience situations where one can begin to try out and develop coping mechanisms that help. Informal communication activities can begin to do this (see Chapter 6 for a discussion of communication apprehension and for suggestions on helping students who experience a high degree of apprehension).

Finally, it is important to think about how students' past experiences might influence the communication activities you do in your class. Students may have learned "appropriate" behavior in another class, another discipline, or another group that would alienate individuals in your class. For example, what is assertive in one setting may be interpreted as grandstanding in another; qualifying one's remarks may be expected in one setting but may be interpreted as waffling in another. Gender, ethnic, racial, and cultural elements also enter into the mix. English proficiency, differences in cultural values, responses to status, the perception of status differences—all influence interaction in a group (Lee, 2009; O'Donnell, 2006; Webb, 2009). Since the dynamics of any group have a bearing upon the skills exhibited by the participants, performance of skills depends upon the pattern of interaction developing in the group as well as upon individual ability (chapters 7 and 8 provide a more extensive discussion of issues related to participation, whether in large class discussions or in teams; Chapter 10 provides information about diversity in communication activities). Part of communicative competence is developing the ability to adapt, be flexible, and be aware of multiple contextual issues, but students do not always come with those abilities, and so we believe it is important to address them up front. Therefore, even in these early stages of developing assignments, it is important to consider these issues in more detail.

There are several steps to consider when designing informal communication activities. It is important to note that not all informal activities should look the same. Some you will do quickly, in class, with very little follow-up (other than the activity itself). Others might require students to engage in some preparation outside of class. Yet others could necessitate more detailed instructions and practice in the kinds of critical thinking skills that will facilitate learning. The way in which you design the activity will determine the kinds of information you will need to provide for students. Table 4.1 provides some planning questions to help you identify what is important in as you think about informal activities.

Table 4.1. Planning Questions: Informal Communication Activities *-structure*

What learning goals are most important to your course content?
What forms of inquiry are important for your students to be able to master?
What structures of communication activities would fit best given your course constraints?
What kinds of follow-up strategies could hold students accountable for these informal activities?
What challenges do you expect your students to have with informal communication activities?
How can you proactively address these challenges in designing the activity?

The seven steps in designing informal communication activities include

- Delineating learning outcomes and forms of inquiry
- Identifying the structure of the task you want students to complete
- Articulating the particular areas of content you want students to focus on
- Designing prompts/tasks that have multiple possible responses and audiences
- Designating guidelines for interaction and potential relational issues
- Setting clear expectations for outcomes of the exercise and, if appropriate, instructions for reporting the results of the process/product
- Holding students accountable for their communication choices and behaviors in these activities.

The first step in designing informal communication activities involves thinking about what you want students to learn and what forms of inquiry you want them to engage in or practice during the activity. This decision involves a process similar to articulating course-based outcomes and objectives but is focused at the level of this exercise or assignment. Put this activity in the context of your entire course: What particular student-learning outcomes do you want to achieve for different parts of your course? How does this activity or exercise help you achieve those outcomes at this point in your course? As mentioned in Chapter 1, many of you have probably been exposed to the taxonomy of questioning developed by Benjamin Bloom (often used when articulating students learning outcomes, as well). While Bloom's taxonomy is widely cited and is often used as a guide for developing levels of outcomes for assessment purposes, it might be helpful to use Bloom's three domains—cognitive, affective and behavioral—to guide designing communication outcomes.

Given that your goals for these communication activities will be more focused on how well students learn course content, it is likely you will be writing outcomes that focus more on cognitive and affective outcomes. You will focus on the form of the communication itself primarily as a means to achieve these ends. One way to think about the learning outcomes for activities is to consider the forms of inquiry that you want your students to engage in for this activity. Do you want them to evaluate? Interrogate? Compare? Contrast? Regardless of the final format of the exercise of assignment(s) you create, the kinds of inquiry you are expecting of your students needs to be made explicit, both to yourself and to your students. For example, if you want your students to "compare and contrast," what does that mean?

As you think about generating outcomes for informal communication activities, it is also important to consider the kinds of questions you think are important for students to ask as they participate in those activities. Students often believe that what is most important is imparting their knowledge. They need to be encouraged to ask questions—and you will need to prepare them to be able to accomplish what you are asking them to do, in part by identifying the multiple ways to approach problems, texts, and issues. There are many different kinds of questions, and it is often enlightening to students to realize these different forms. Students often get stuck at the level of asking factual/knowledge questions, never considering that there are different forms of questions that can illuminate a text or an issue. It is helpful to discuss with students the different ways of asking questions and the types of insights that might be associated with different question forms. There are many different taxonomies of question types, ranging from highly abstract categorizations to fairly mundane descriptions. We have listed typical categories here in Table 4.2, although the categories are not all mutually exclusive. Of particular note are convergent and divergent questions. There are those who assert that convergent thinking and divergent thinking utilize different brain functions (divergent thinking utilizes the right brain, developing imaginative and creative abilities; convergent thinking utilizes the left brain, thus developing the deductive, rational, and analytic abilities (Guilford, 1967; Robinson, 2011; Runco, 1991).

Table 4.2. Types of Content-Focused Questions

Form of Question	Examples
Factual/Knowledge: To get information, open discussion, or test for knowledge	Questions that ask "who, what, why, where, and how"
Explanatory: To elicit reasoning, create an opening for further information, or to clarify a purpose or goal	"What other factors contributed to this problem?" "Why did the author use this analogy?
Leading: To introduce a new idea or focus attention on an idea introduced by someone else	"Now consider XYZ. How would these additional factors have changed your solution?"
Analytic: To focus on relationships among concepts or to break issues into smaller parts for further examination	"How does A relate to B?" "If X is true, what do we do with the fact that . . .?"
Hypothetical or Application: To focus on a potentially unpopular position, or to try out how a concept or solution would work to solve a problem or address an issue	"What would happen if…?" "Let's say we decided to….?" "Now let's change the scenario and see what happens if…."
Justification and Evaluation: To challenge old ideas, develop new ideas, or focus on reasoning and evidence	"I'd like to hear your reasons." "What observations did you make that led you to your conclusions?" "Does this solution meet our criteria?"

Table 4.3. Questions to Expand Ways of Thinking

Form of Question	Examples
Disjunctive: To clarify alternatives or show problems with oversimplification	"Of the two most likely possibilities, which is preferable?" "If A is not the answer, then what must the answer be?"
Convergent: To develop accuracy, think deductively, develop consensus, move toward action, or direct attention to specific elements	"Based on our information, what conclusions can we draw?" "Where are the points of overlap?" "Where do we agree?"
Divergent: To develop open-minded thinking, discover new ways of approaching an issue, show connection, focus attention on many elements	"How else might we approach this?" "If you were to research this topic, how would you proceed?"

The second step is to clearly identify the structure of the task. Given what you are trying to accomplish at this point in your course, as well as the character of students in your course, does it make sense to use a more or less structured exercise? Will you have students do small-group discussions in order to try to gain insight into a text? How structured do these small-group discussions need to be? What kind of preparation will students need in order to be ready to ask the kinds of questions that will lead to insight, and be able to talk intelligently in response (for example, reading the text, preparing discussion questions, freewriting, journal-writing, outlining essential arguments)? Will this be an in-class debate? Micro presentations? Poster presentation? Discussion? Role play? Pair-and-share (see example at the end of this chapter)? Will the task be completed fully in class or will there need to be preparation work or follow up work outside of class? How much class time will you devote to the activity and how much out-of-class time (if any) will students need to devote to the preparation and/or follow-up?

The third step is to identify the content with which they will work. Is it a particular text? A chapter in the book? Their own opinions? Web-based research they will do during the activity? Experiential events? Clearly specifying the content they need to have read, found, experienced, generated, or otherwise prepared will make the process more efficient and will help students prepare.

Fourth, you will need to design prompts that lead to multiple responses and that have varied audiences. A prompt that has one right answer will likely not lead to discussion, and students will likely find the process to be one of busy work. The best communication tasks/prompts have a breadth of possible answers and responses (see Chapter 7, Class Discussion, for more information on question-asking). Ideally, prompts should encourage students to look for answers, but also lead students to even more questions. For example, if you are having students engage in a mock psychological client role-play, use multiple psychological problems in the plays and perhaps each "client" brings to the role-play a different psychological profile. There needs to be room for true inquiry, with openness for discovery. If there is a "right" answer, then inquiry might be "how did you get there?" Such an approach will help explicate the methods of your discipline, surfacing how inquiry works.

Fifth, designate guidelines for interaction and consider relational issues that might emerge. How much time will you give students? Will they leave class or stay in the classroom? Will you ask one person to be a recorder? Is the material controversial? Is it likely that participants may become angry, concerned, fearful of potentially offending others in the class, or be reminded of difficulties in their own life? How will you address these possibilities (see Section III for discussions of approaches to these kinds of difficult situations)?

Sixth, articulate clear expectations for the outcomes of the exercise. Students need to know what they are aiming for; provide that direction by giving instructions for reporting products and processes. Depending on how you structure your exercise, not every student has to talk every time. Nor do students have to turn something in. For example, the outcome of an exercise may be one student from a small group reporting back to the class for a large class discussion on the section of the text assigned to that group. Yet another outcome might be for students to identify possible paper topics as a result of the discussion.

Finally, when designing informal communication activities, you need to consider how you will hold students accountable for the process. Will you do a post-exercise debriefing? Will you help students identify and articulate the content they have learned? How will you do so? What kinds of feedback will you provide, and based on what criteria? Will there be peer feedback? Will your feedback be connected to a grade? Will students self-reflect on their own oral communication choices and behaviors? How will you facilitate that self-reflection? Will you use rubrics? If so, what kind of rubric and what elements need to be included? The important issue to know at this point is that holding students accountable should not translate into heavy grading for these kinds of informal communication activities. Rather, you are helping them discern how their communication behaviors relate to their learning. You can easily use part of your participation grade for these kinds of activities. For example, you could have 10 percent of your course grade focused on participation, in which students get points for either attendance or for turning in some form of product from multiple communication activities (e.g., an index card reporting group processes, a one-minute paper indicating learning reflections, etc.). The key here is accountability for learning, not evaluation of the communication itself. Identify efficient processes for giving feedback that focus entirely on the learning. If you design a rubric, keep it simple, short and focused on the learning goals and processes you want for your students. Table 4.4 illustrates some examples of how to hold students accountable without creating excessive grading.

Table 4.4. Holding Students Accountable for Informal Communication Activities

Accountability Schema	Example Related Activities
Full credit if completed	*Sociology*: Group problem-solution discussion; group presentation of an example sociological problem *Astronomy*: Full class working to sort pictures into moon phases; role-play of timeline of astronomical understanding *Plant Pathology*: Sharing of a specimen with brief explanation; engagement with lab partner
Rated 1–3 on criteria such as clear interpretation, evidence-based argument	*English*: short analysis of a poem followed by a reflection; in-class debate about some aspect of a text (e.g., the true motivation of a character) *Art*: Oral presentation of a piece of art with interpretation; in-class discussion comparing different periods or different pieces of art *History*: Discussion comparing two accounts of the same event
Rated 0 or 1 on whether a particular aspect is present	*Engineering*: Individual demonstration of lab protocol; progress presentations of a design project *Psychology*: Group discussion of relevance of characteristics to a diagnosis; group presentation of a possible interpretation of a case study *Nursing*: Role plays of specific patient interactions

TEMPLATE FOR INFORMAL COMMUNICATION AND ACTIVITY DESIGN

In this section, we provide several informal communication activities and an activity-design template (Figure 4.1) to use as you think about using informal communication activities in your classroom. This template can be thought of as a way to think through designing these kinds of informal communication activities and to structure the oral instructions that you give in class. Or, for more complex activities, you can use this template to design a written prompt (in a handout, PowerPoint, or on chalkboard) and then create a handout that deals with the additional complexities.

We have situated the following examples in particular disciplines so you can get a flavor of how they might be used for different content areas. Any of these examples, though, can be adapted to your own content and discipline. Not only can you adapt the content, though, but you can also adapt the timing and structure of the activity. For example, if you want to extend an activity beyond a single class period, you can break it up into discrete tasks. Or, if you want to shorten an activity based on time constraints, you can choose to adapt the prompt for your context. The point is that you get to decide how to implement these activities based on your goals, desired learning outcomes, and contextual constraints. We provide examples in six general categories: micro presentations, in-class debates, pair/group work, discussion, dialogue/role plays, and visual/poster presentations. We also provide examples of discussion-based exercises (an analysis of Romeo & Juliet, and the Gallery Walk) as they might be presented to students in order to illustrate how an assignment created by utilizing the template might be presented to students when implementing the assignment in class.

Activity Title
Course Name/Number

Class Date(s):
[Provide the in-class day(s) of the activity and/or preparation dates as
appropriate to give students an idea of the
complexity of the activity.]

During this activity, you will...
[This initial statement should tell students the learning outcomes
you have for the activity as well as the forms of inquiry they will need
to engage in during the activity.]

Your task in this activity is to...
[Provide students with an idea about the structure of the activity
or task. You will also indicate if there are varied audiences/roles/
or cases you want students to address (in different groups or pairs).
Additionally, you should provide students with any particular guidelines for interaction that are important to the activity (e.g., time on
task, selection of groups or teams, etc.).].

To complete this activity you will need to focus on...
[Outline the key areas of content the activity will focus on and where
students are expected to get that content, as well as any preparation
they will need to do out of class with that content.].

At the end of this activity...
[Provide students with instructions for reporting out (e.g., designated group speaker, rotating speakers) and any products that need to
accompany the reporting out (e.g., written summary, visual, etc.)].

You will be accountable for...
[In this section, you will tell students the ways in which you will
hold them accountable for the learning in this activity, if any].

Instructional Logistics:

As you plan, be sure to note any particular logistical considerations
(e.g., what students need to have completed ahead of time, the amount
of time the activity or assignment will take). This template can be used
to help you consider the oral instructions you will give to students, the
PowerPoint prompt you will put up, or the handout you will design
(depending on the complexity of the activity).

Figure 4.1. Template for Informal Communication Activities

Analysis of Romeo & Juliet
English
Rotating Discussion Leaders

During this activity, you will work with a partner to do a close analysis of the text Romeo and Juliet in an attempt to understand the story from Shakespeare's perspective. In order to do this, you will need to explain and justify decisions about plot, characters, and intent using the text as evidence. You must read the play before class.

Choose one of the following prompts and discuss it with your partner. Discuss the question in the prompt for 10 minutes, using evidence from the text. We will then come back together as a large group. I will ask one person to volunteer to be a discussion leader for the first prompt. After discussing that prompt, the discussion leader will give the discussion "baton" (rolled up newspaper) to another person who will pick the next prompt on the list.

1. Assume you and several friends have been listening to the opening scene of Romeo and Juliet. You have been laughing during the early minutes, and that has disturbed your friends who contend this is a tragedy. Go over this early section and explain just why the early speeches and action are funny.
2. Another friend is simply confused about what is happening up through the Prince's speech. "There are too many characters to get anything straight," she contends. Untangle the confusion for your friend. To help her, explain how the scene begins to characterize Benvolio and Tybalt and introduces potential themes to be developed in future action.
3. Your friends have been awaiting the appearance of Romeo, but when he first comes on stage, they react negatively and their attitudes don't change as they hear him in scenes 2 and 4. Are they reacting as Shakespeare would want them to? Just how is Shakespeare presenting Romeo in these scenes? What's your evidence for your response? We see Juliet only briefly in Scene 3, but from what others say about her and how she reacts, what should be our first impression of her?
4. Benvolio, Mercutio, and the Nurse are important secondary characters. We meet Benvolio in Scenes 1,2, and 4; Mercutio in Scene 4, and the Nurse in Scene 3. How to their speeches characterize them? Note especially Mercutio's Queen Mab speech and the Nurse's anecdote about young Juliet. In what ways are Mercutio and the Nurse alike?.

There will be material from this discussion on the next exam.

Figure 4.2. Sample Informal Communication Activity (Rotating Discussion). Adapted from an exercise created by created by Professor George Vane, Hamline University.

Analysis of Romeo & Juliet English
Informal Communication Activity (Less Structured)

During this activity, you will work with a group of 4 or 5 people to do a close analysis of *Romeo and Juliet* in an attempt to understand the story from Shakespeare's perspective. In order to do this, you will need to explain and justify decisions about plot, characters, and intent using the text as evidence. You must read the play before class.

Each group will focus on one of the questions posed below. Before you start talking, take 5 minutes to free write. At the end of 5 minutes, discuss the question with the other members of your group, keeping track of the points the group members make, and how the text supports those points. What additional questions emerge from your discussion? Keep track of these too.

1. Assume you and several friends have been listening to the opening scene of Romeo and Juliet. You have been laughing during the early minutes, and that has disturbed your friends who contend this is a tragedy. Go over this early section and explain just why the early speeches and action are funny.
2. Another friend is simply confused about what is happening up through the Prince's speech. "There are too many characters to get anything straight," she contends. Untangle the confusion for your friend. To help her, explain how the scene begins to characterize Benvolio and Tybalt and introduces potential themes to be developed in future action.
3. Your friends have been awaiting the appearance of Romeo, but when he first comes on stage, they react negatively and their attitudes don't change as they hear him in scenes 2 and 4. Are they reacting as Shakespeare would want them to? Just how is Shakespeare presenting Romeo in these scenes? What's your evidence for your response? We see Juliet only briefly in Scene 3, but from what others say about her and how she reacts, what should be our first impression of her?
4. Benvolio, Mercutio, and the Nurse are important secondary characters. We meet Benvolio in Scenes 1,2, and 4; Mercutio in Scene 4, and the Nurse in Scene 3. How to their speeches characterize them? Note especially Mercutio's Queen Mab speech and the Nurse's anecdote about young Juliet. In what ways are Mercutio and the Nurse alike?.

After 15 minutes all groups will report back to the class as a whole, in order to highlight the points you discovered, and to identify additional questions that came up for the group. These reports will help guide the large class discussion.

Consider the questions that emerge from each group. What further perspectives or questions do you have? How might these provide you with a thesis for a paper analyzing this play?

Figure 4.3. Sample Informal Communication Activity (Less Structured). Exercise created by Professor George Vane, Hamline University.

Gallery Walk
Geoscience
Class Activity Dates: Monthly
(September 15, October 12, and November 10)

There are five stations set up around the room (see poster board with "STATION #" on it). During this activity, you will get into groups of 5 and place yourself at a "Home Station." You will notice that each station has at it large posters with questions on them taped to the wall (there are 5 posters at each station, each with the same question on them; but each station has different questions). You will start at your home station and, as a team, discuss answers to the questions and writes those answers on the poster provided. After 5 minutes, I will say "rotate." At that point, fold your poster so that the next team cannot see your answers and move (clockwise) to the next station. You will continue rotating until you reach "Home Station" (having gone through all stations). During the activity, I will circulate around the classroom and clarify any questions you have or address any misconceptions that you have about the content. You will be allowed to refer to course materials during the Gallery Walk, but be warned that the time at each station is so short that it will be best if you review materials on the topic of the day prior to the Gallery Walk.

At the end of the activity, your group (having returned to "Home Station") will need to-as a group—synthesize the answers to the questions and make an oral presentation (3-4 minutes long). Prepare one visual to use during your micro presentation and hand in that visual at the end of class.

Station #1: What are the effects of weather on the following systems a) transportation b) agricultural c) forestry d) banking systems.

Station #2: Outline typical temperature and wind direction patterns before and after the passage of a cold front.

Station #3: Given the passage of warm front, how would you dress your five year old for school? An elderly person for a doctor's visit? How would you explain these decisions to the elderly person or five-year old?

Station #4: Consider these cities: City A, at 8000 ft. elevation, is located on the windward side of an island at 2° S near the middle of a large ocean. City B, at 44°N, is located on a 500 ft. plateau on the lee (downwind) side of a 14,000 ft. mountain range and is over 1000 miles from the nearest water body. Explain the climate of these cities relative to latitude, altitude, continentality, mountains.

Station #5: How is weather discussed in your three favorite songs (any genre)? List specific lyrics.

Station #6: Prepare a list of criteria for reducing the risk of heat related illness for inner city elderly. Prioritize the list and justify your rating.

Figure 4.4. Sample Informal Communication Activity Template (Gallery Walk). Adapted from: http://serc.carleton.edu/introgeo/gallerywalk/examples.html

Tables 4.5 through 4.10 provide examples of informal communication activities, potential student learning outcomes relevant to the activities, and sample prompts from various disciplines. We begin with the less structured approaches that are typically found in various forms of informal communication activities, in both large and small groups. It is important to note that the prompts are short examples and might or might not be sufficient for the particular communication activity, depending on the way in which you have designed the task. You will still need to think about additional guidelines for the activity and ways to hold students accountable. As they stand, though, the sample activities are meant to provide you with ideas that will stimulate your thinking. Following the examples in Tables 4.5–4.10, we provide the extended samples of a discussion-based communication activities that illustrate how to flesh out a basic idea into a more complex activity.

Table 4.5. Sample Discussion-Based Informal Communication Activities

	Learning Outcome/ Form of Inquiry	Example Activity
Large-Class Discussion	Consider multiple perspectives or alternatives; extend benefits of a small-group or individual task	Discuss, as a class, different views on an issue (e.g., in astronomy, the origin of the universe). Explore evidence for different perspectives and have students examine what aspects of their background affect their views (e.g., religious views; skeptical nature).
Small-Group Discussions	Consider responses to texts; clarify personal views	Have individuals free write responses to a scenario related to previous material or readings. Students then discuss reactions in a group, then share the group's insights to facilitate large class discussion.
Connections	Connect course material with non-classroom events.	Ask students to bring in one example from contemporary culture that connects with the readings for the day (e.g., newspaper article, YouTube video, blog). Use these examples to start discussion about the topic.
Benefit/ Drawback Discussion	Explore topics from multiple perspectives	In preparation for discussing multiple perspectives on an issue or event, have students begin by identifying their own position and the rationale for that view. As a class, discuss the multiple perspectives, focused on generating discussion rather than arriving at a "correct" answer.

Table 4.6. Sample Micro Presentation Informal Communication Activities

	Learning Outcome/ Form of Inquiry	Example Activity
Article Evaluation	Critically analyze texts	Using an issue from a local or national newspaper, have students evaluate the article in relation to a class topic (e.g., content, persuasiveness, evidence used). Random students will present 3–4 minutes to start class.
Defending your Ground	Use reason in argumentation	Have students take a position on an assertion relevant to a class topic. Give students time to jot down notes in defense of their position to present (2–3 minutes) to a specific audience (e.g., potential employers)
Myth or Reality?	Critically evaluate sources	Provide pairs of students with website links to a variety of sources that have varied levels of credibility (spoof websites work as well). Each pair should prepare a two-minute oral review and analysis of the website to be used in an upcoming student newsletter podcast.
Cost/Benefit Analysis	Articulate complexities of solving problems	Have students research one example solution proposed to a problem relevant to your disciple. Each student should prepare a two-minute presentation in which the student argues the relative benefits and costs of this particular solution.

Table 4.7. Sample In-Class Debate Activities

	Learning Outcome/ Form of Inquiry	Example Activity
Justifying Actions	Synthesize research in persuasive manner	Tell students that they have been asked to provide justification for an action/decision relevant to the course content (e.g., in soil science, the use of pesticides at schools and parks). Divide students into "pro" and "con" teams. Each team should synthesize relevant research to support the assigned side.
Summit on the Issues	Generate evidence-driven claims and counter-arguments	Assign students (individually or as pairs) a particular group who may be affected by an issue (e.g., in a course on world health issues, assign countries; in a course on education, assign parents, teachers, or administrators, etc.). Students then prepare research on a particular issue (e.g., health problems; standards-based funding for schools) and each group presents their arguments and is given the opportunity to present counterarguments to other groups.
Sensitizing Arguments	Generate arguments without personal attacks	In teams, have students provide arguments for or against a prompt that has very real implications for various groups of people (e.g., in Kinesiology, better physical education curricula could solve obesity epidemics). Have students support claims with evidence while also being sensitive to how various groups might hear arguments (e.g., how obese people may hear arguments about obesity).

Table 4.8. Sample Dialogue and Role Plays

	Learning Outcome/ Form of Inquiry	Example Activity
Beyond Being Right	Gain empathy for different views	Have students create a hypothetical dialogue between 2–3 people who disagree about a topic and have a stake in being "right" (e.g., in a case about vaccination: a doctor, a mom, and a child). Dialogues should move past stances to the complexities of the problem. Students should come prepared to speak the dialogue.
Role Reversals	Understand various audience needs	Ask students to prepare a role play where 2–3 people would have a stake in an issue. Students will role play the discussion and switch between different perspectives.
Voting in the "Greatest"	Understand contributions of various scholars	Groups of students should prepare a role play of a reality TV show in which the host is interviewing key scholars in your discipline—each of whom wants to be named "The Greatest." The host and scholars should focus on eliciting reasons for why each should get the viewers' votes.
Interrogation Interview	Position with evidence	Have students prepare to participate in an interview with the local public radio station on a current issue relevant to course content. Students should do research in preparation to be either interviewer or interviewee.

Table 4.9. Sample Pair/Group Work

	Learning Outcome/ Form of Inquiry	Example Activity
Translating Theories	Difficult material into understand-able language	Each group will be given a theory or relevant construct. The group's task is to generate an explanation of the theory that could be understood by a third grade class while being sure to do justice to the theory.
Group Decision Responses	Collaborate about a controversial issue	Each pair will pick a prompt from a bowl that includes a statement about what should (not) happen or the value placed upon an action (e.g., math standards are disastrously low in primary education). Students should take individual time to respond, then talk with the partner to come to an agreed upon response.
Gallery Walk	Brainstorm various answers to com-mon questions	Assign each team to one station around the room as a starting point (e.g., 6 sta-tions in the room). At each station, there is a question relevant to a current class topic (e.g., what can be done to reduce the risk of heat related illness for inner city elderly). Teams should brainstorm answers to the question and write them on the poster provided. After five min-utes, teams will rotate to the next station. When teams return to their home sta-tion, their task as a team is to generate a coherent synthesis of the responses on the paper.

Table 4.10. Sample Visual Activities

	Learning Outcome/ Form of Inquiry	Example Activity
Seeing the Problem	Principles into understandable visuals	Advanced Algebra: Individuals or groups should construct a visual that explains the basics of some course principle(s) to be presented to middle schoolers. Students should also prepare a 5-minute presentation explaining the visual.
Visual Results	Observations in new, compelling ways	Provide students with a set of data and/or relevant basic charts (e.g., bar charts). Have students represent the same data in a more compelling visual manner that relates to the content of the data.
Team Development	Cohesiveness in project teams	When students form groups for a project, have them discuss their team's mission and identity. Have each team generate a visual logo for the team that represents who they want to be and how they want to be perceived throughout the project.
Theory Quarters	Theoretical principles with different modalities	Tell students they have been asked by the Department of Treasury to design a quarter (twenty-five cents) that represents a major era or school of thought studied. Have students design the quarter to illustrates key beliefs and assumptions. Students can share their designs with the class; alternatively, have students try to identify other students' eras and provide rationale for their guess.

CONCLUSION

Research shows that the active involvement of students facilitates learning. Oral communication activities additionally require that students process their learning in ways that makes it available for others. While in this chapter, we have focused on activities that primarily intend to facilitate learning of course content as distinct from learning specific communication skills; activities that are intended to help develop communication skills will also enhance learning of course content. The next chapter discusses approaches when your priority is also the development of more formal communication competencies.

5 Designing Formal Communication Assignments

O ne of the reasons faculty often choose to incorporate communication in their classrooms is that they want to help students develop competencies that will benefit them in the workplace, or other contexts they might encounter outside of the classroom (e.g., as a public citizen). Designing assignments that meet such goals requires a different way of thinking about oral communication than we discussed in Chapter 4. In informal communication activities, communication works as a means of learning content, but when your goals and outcomes involve increasing students' communication competence (explicitly), assignments tend to be more structured and formal. While success in informal communication activities is driven by the extent to which students interrogate material or engage in content, more formal communication assignments have an added layer of expectations focusing on the extent to which students' communication performance is effective and appropriate given the context.

Yet, as we mentioned earlier in the book, what counts as effective and appropriate—as competence—varies across contexts, workplaces, and disciplines (as we have already mentioned). For example, in architecture, an effective communicator might need to be visually logical in their presentation of the actual design in order to achieve the goal of having the audience understand the design. In contrast, an effective communicator in engineering might need to be visually efficient in their presentation of the design. In public health, an appropriate strategy to help an audience make a decision about a particular campaign might be to incorporate detailed descriptions of particular issues, whereas in computer science, getting an audience to make a decision about a particular proposal might require a big-picture framework without the details. In a local township, competence could be judged by a citizen's ability to synthesize diverse voices, using experiential examples to create emotional appeals about a new housing development. In a large city school board, competence could mean providing statistical evidence for a new school reassignment plan. In these examples, competence is locally negotiated and defined within the relational and situational context of the communication event. As mentioned in Chapter 1, developing that competence requires knowledge of that context and motivation to interact within it. If you are interested in incorporating oral communication in order to explicitly build students' competence, the first step is defining what that communication looks and sounds like. This chapter will help you do that. We hope to provide you with a number of different resources in this chapter that will help you design more formal assignments that will accomplish your goals in terms of desired communication competence. Before we move to teaching resources, however, we want to provide you with some foundational definitions of one key term we will use in this chapter—*oral communication genres*.

WHAT ARE ORAL COMMUNICATION GENRES?

In academia, there are a number of disciplines that use communication events to help students understand the future workplace or civic expectations and norms. These communication events typically have recognizable structures, features, and purposes. These recognizable types of communication events are called "genres." A political rally speech is a type of communication event that has identifiable and patterned features. Yet the genre is not simply defined by the structure or form. It is also defined by its rhetorical actions: "A rhetorically sound definition of genre must be centered not on the substance or the form of discourse but on the action it is used to accomplish" (Miller, 1984, p. 151). Political rally speeches, eulogies, or any other recognizable communication structure are all designed and performed to accomplish certain ends important to the context in which they occur. Therefore, when your students participate in these genres, they are learning to understand the actions and interactions of social contexts and how they can engage with those contexts effectively.

Communication genres vary across disciplines, situations and subject areas—request for funding proposals, design review presentations, the performance evaluation, business meetings, design juries, political acceptance speeches, client diagnosis interviews, telephone information response messages, introductions, small talk, cocktail discussions, and town hall presentations to name a few. Some are more formal than others, and some have more at stake than others. Some are more interpersonal in nature, such as one-on-one sessions. The commonality between them is that they are all recognizable oral genres—perhaps not all are recognizable by everyone, but recognizable by those who use them regularly. For example, in disciplines such as architecture and industrial design, the genre of the "jury" or "critique" simulates a professional client presentation that architects might face with a future customer. It has a particular structure, form, and purpose. Yet, as indicated in the earlier section, it also has historical, cultural, and disciplinary understandings about what the event looks and sounds like, how it is used within the disciplines, and why it is important to those who are learning to be new designers. For many designers, just the mention of the word "critique" will bring to the fore emotions, memories, stories, and strong opinions about their own experiences engaging in the critique or about their experiences teaching the critique. Other pre-professional oral genres hold within them historical and contextual knowledge that is critical to understand.

Oral genres that focus on preparing students for contexts outside of academia (e.g., professional workplaces or civic engagements) can be, therefore, extremely complex (Devitt, 2004; Engstrom, 1990; Russell, 1997). Students' success requires an understanding of the social, cultural, and rhetorical elements of the context. Students need to learn what is acceptable in terms of speaking, and they need to be willing to take the opportunity—should they be so bold—to explore the boundaries of acceptability as they test out what it means to be a member of a particular disciplinary, workplace, or civic context. These oral genres typically have rules and norms that are not necessarily explicit, until broken. Learning these oral genres, then, involves learning the structural and expected behaviors as well as the present and future cultural and social expectations that influence those behaviors. The picture becomes more textured and complex when you delve into complex oral genres such as the "performance appraisal," the "request for funding proposal," or the "design review presentation," each of which has multiple intended and implied audiences, complex structures, and multilayered purposes and functions. Therefore, the teaching and learning becomes much more textured and complex as well. Students in medical school, for example, learn what it means to be in the medical field when they see interns participate in the "presentation of symptoms" oral genre. Yet they also learn about the expected relational interactions, about the cultural norms of the field, and about the necessary hierarchies to attend to in this setting. In another example, students in business management learn what it means to be a supervisor when they experience or watch others experience the "performance appraisal" genre. Yet they also learn about the expected climate of the supervisory relationship and the social conventions of being in that role. In both these cases, students—while learning to speak in these particular genres—are learning about the social and relational rules of particular contexts.

STEPS IN DESIGNING FORMAL ORAL COMMUNICATION ASSIGNMENTS

As you think about designing formal oral communication assignments, it is important to understand that you get to decide which genres help with developing the competencies that are important to your course, discipline, future professional contexts, or civic spaces. In some cases, a genre you choose to use for professional development may be used by someone else to help students learn to advocate in civic settings. For example, the "public hearing" might be a genre that achieves civic goals in engineering whereas it is more focused on professionalization in sociology. You get to choose.

To summarize, the checklist for designing formal communication assignments includes the following.

- Identifying assignment rationale
- Writing student learning outcomes (cognitive, affective, behavioral)
- Articulating features of the genre
- Describing the communicator's purpose
- Defining pertinent audiences for the assignment
- Delineating the necessary skills, processing, and scaffolding
- Describing standards for success

As you move through these steps for designing formal oral communication assignments, you will be creating an assignment description that will be extremely helpful for students as they prepare for the assignment. Therefore, use these steps to help you design the assignment, but also use them to frame your articulation of the assignment to students.

Rationale

The first step in designing formal communication assignments is to consider the rationale for the assignment: How does this assignment fit within the larger context of the course? Is it a "warm-up" assignment for a more significant one that will occur at a later date? Is it the pinnacle assignment for a project? Is it more of a formative assignment to help students gain in-progress feedback? Having a clear sense of the larger puzzle will allow you to articulate to your students the role of this particular assignment in the course.

Student Learning Outcomes

Second, just as you wrote course-based objectives and outcomes, you will need to write specific outcomes for the particular assignment. As illustrated in Chapter 1, there are three types of student-learning outcomes to consider: cognitive, affective, and behavioral. Below are some possible student learning outcomes for formal communication assignments.

After completing the oral communication assignment, students should be able to:

- Respond to a critic in a way that illustrates listening and understanding of the feedback given (behavioral)

- Analyze patients' presenting problem in order to generate possible solutions (cognitive)
- Engage in collegial interactions with simulated professionals who are providing feedback on your work (behavioral)
- Appreciate distinct contributions of team members to the product development process (affective)
- Demonstrate the quality of a research project by presenting the project's justification, methods, and results, employing professional conventions that characterize use of PowerPoint in presentations (behavioral)
- Empathize with citizens' concerns about local political issues (affective)
- Succinctly summarize technical design specifications in a way that is understandable to a lay audience (behavioral)
- Understand clients' needs for and parameters for design projects (cognitive)

Again, the important point here is not to dictate what type of outcomes you write, but to design your assignment outcomes based on your overall course goals, student learning outcomes, and content.

Genre Features

The third step in designing formal communication assignments is to consider the assignment itself and the features of the genre. It is often helpful to think about these features in terms of those characteristics of the oral event specifically tied to the civic, academic, or workplace contexts in which it typically lives. Although we mentioned earlier that genres are time-bound and dynamic, what makes them recognizable is some identifiable form, defining features, or rules. Some oral genres are identifiable by a typical organizational structure. In other oral genres, the genre itself can be defined by the visual support or the models involved in the presentation. Let's take the example of the "client interview" in social work or psychology. Some of the defining features of the "client interview" include a question-answer structure where the social worker or psychologist uses background or historical questions to get a broad understanding of the case. Within the larger context, this oral genre is the initiation rite—the space in which the client and psychologist/social worker are assessing the relationship between them. This genre, then, looks different than many of the later therapy sessions because of its unique place and purpose. It is important to distinguish the defining features of these different genres so that students can understand the particular place of these features in the overall social context. When thinking about the oral genres you are asking your students to follow, ask yourself: What are the defining features of this oral genre, and how does it fit within the larger picture of the classroom and professionalization goals? What is the general structure or format of the genre? Are there distinguishing features that make it recognizable?

Purpose

Fourth, it is important to identify the communicator's purpose. What is the communicator supposed to do in the oral assignment? It might be helpful to think about the communicator's purpose in terms of both content and relational elements. For example, in a performance appraisal, the communicator's purpose is to articulate a balanced and fair assessment of an employee. Relationally, though, the communicator's purpose might focus around fostering collaborative interaction or motivation. In the example of the "client interview," the communicator's purpose could be focused on gathering information (or listening to information). Relationally, the communicator's purpose could be to build trust. Your decision-making point, therefore, is in thinking about what the communicator is supposed to do in this assignment—relationally and with the content.

Audience

Fifth, identify the participants and audiences of the oral genres that are important to your discipline. Typically, classrooms involve teachers, students, and sometimes graduate teaching assistants. In these cases, the teachers and assistants often simulate professional audiences. Yet, in some classrooms there are other participants who directly influence the oral events that happen there. Some courses involve outside industry representatives to participate in student projects. Others involve service-learning partners. Yet others involve tutors, translators, and technology support staff. As you consider oral genres in your classroom, you will need to define the participants in these oral genres. Let's expand the example of the "client interview" in psychology or social work. In this genre, the participants typically include the psychologist, psychiatrist, or social worker and the client. In some cases, there is an admitting nurse or aide who gathers basic information for the file. The initial client interview typically presumes the interactants do not have a prior relationship—they are presumed to be meeting for the first time. Alternatively, more presentation-type genres typically include a speaker or team of speakers and the audience of classmates. The audiences for this speaker may change as well, depending on this speaker's identity, goals, and genre. Some audiences will incorporate other participants in the activity system—industry representatives, guest faculty, etc. Some oral genres you might incorporate in your classroom only involve one speaker and one "audience" member—a performance appraisal or a client interview, for example. In these cases, you might involve participants from the local community or you might have students act as participants in industry.

Process and Skills

Sixth, it is important to delineate the skills and processes students will need to be successful in this assignment so that you can consider ways of scaffolding instruction to allow students to practice these skills. For some assignments, for example, students will need to know how to do a database search for academic journals. For other assignments, students will need skills in PowerPoint or other presentation software. Yet for others, students might need interviewing skills to complete research. Identifying these discrete skills and processes helps the students gain an understanding of the assignment, and can also help you build in some communication-to-learn activities that could create scaffolding for the formal assignment. One way to do this is to identify the following:

- The knowledge students need to be successful in the formal assignment
- The skills or competencies that are important for the students to master in the formal assignment
- The learning processes that are important for the students to master in the formal assignment

Following this, you can design informal activities that address discrete aspects of the knowledge, skills, or processes. We also suggest you schedule activities strategically, so that they either build a particular skill through levels of complexity or address distinct skills multiple times, essentially scaffolding your assignments. Informal communication activities can work well to build to more formal communication assignments.

Table 5.1 shows examples of how you could scaffold informal communication such as those described in Chapter 4 in order to support formal communication assignments. Note that decisions about frequency of activity, type of activity, and focus of activity are entirely up to you. You get to decide if this is a skill or competency that needs additional work or if one activity will give students enough experience to do well.

Standards for Success

Finally, you need to articulate standards for success. This articulation involves decisions not only on what counts as a successful performance, but also on the kinds of evaluative tools you will use, the ways in which you will respond to students, and the particular evaluative criteria that are important for the assignment. Although section IV will provide additional information on assessment, evaluation, and response, at this point it is worthwhile to consider the key standards for success that you believe are important to the assignment.

Table 5.1. Scaffolding Informal Communication Activities

Objectives	Informal Activity Scaffolds	Resulting Formal Assignments
Summarize information; synthesize and analyze arguments	1: Summarize the argument of a reading (one-minute micro presentation)	Position presentation on controversial event or topic
	2: Debate two opposing views (in-class debate)	
	3: Identify strengths and weaknesses in particular scholar's stances on an issue (dialogue)	
Deliberate diverse perspectives and opinions of an issue; use reasoning and evidence to persuade	1: Problem-solution presentation about weekly topics (micro presentation)	Formal presentation of solution to large-scale problem
	2: In-class debate on components of larger topic	
	3: Evidence Poster (in-class poster presentation)	
Succinctly report progress; translate technical information	1: Weekly progress presentations (in-class micro presentations with one visual)	Poster presentation for external audiences
	2: Gallery walk display of past projects (in-class)	
	3: "Translation Tuesdays" consisting of in-class micro presentations based on translating technical material to common language	

After making decisions about the assignment itself, there are several instructional logistics to take into consideration: How much class time will the assignment take? How will you deal with team versus individual contributions? What materials will you need to give to students to prepare them for the assignment? What particular characteristics of the course and students might influence students' performance in the assignment? What particular issues might arise with students when preparing for and participating in oral communication assignments? Section III will provide some recommendations for you to consider when supporting students in this process.

Template for Formal Communication Assignments

To demonstrate the considerations that go into successfully crafting a formal communication assignment, we present a template for detailing such assignments (see Figure 5.1). The template items parallel those found in Figure 4.1 for informal activities. Following that template, we describe several oral communication genres and activities that have the overall goal of building students' communication competencies for professional, civic, or other contexts. Within each activity, we provide the instructional goal, student-learning outcomes, genre features, genre audience, and genre purpose, all described in a way that can be used with students. We also note some of the instructional logistics relevant to accomplishing competence in the oral genre. We have four caveats before giving these examples. First, these examples are not exhaustive. There are a number of different oral genres in a variety of disciplines and civic contexts. We have chosen to provide examples based on our own work with these disciplines that best illustrate the student learning outcomes. We hope they will spark your thinking about the oral genres that are pertinent to your own discipline. Second, the specifics of each assignment are not set in stone. You might re-write the student learning outcomes to better fit your course or you might articulate different classroom structures that better meet your classroom demographics. These are malleable templates for you to adjust to your own needs or courses. Third, you will notice that there is no discussion of evaluation of these genres. Section IV will discuss evaluation and assessment specifically and we will return to the examples throughout the book to illustrate different evaluative issues and recommendations. Fourth, even though we may suggest discipline(s) in which assignments fit, it is highly possible and probable that the structure of the genre (if not the genre itself) could fit within other disciplines. In the next section, we present a number of oral genres, and for each one we provide the details that you, in turn, would want to provide to students when assigning such projects. Several assignments are fully detailed and we have included multiple other examples in the tables that follow.

Assignment Title
Course Name/Number

Due: [Provide the in-class due date and/or presentation dates as appropriate to give students an idea of how large-scale this project is.]

In completing this assignment, you will...
[This initial statement should tell students the objectives you have for the assignment and what specific outcomes they should achieve by completing this assignment. You can also provide the rationale for the assignment in conjunction with the objectives and outcomes.]

Your task in this assignment is to...
[Provide students with the communicator purpose.]

To complete this assignment you will...
[Outline the key components of the assignment and provide genre features for the assignment. This section will also clue students into audiences/participants.

In preparation for this assignment, you should...
[Tell students the skills/processes required to complete the assignment. These skills/processes may be tied to scaffolding.]

Your work will be evaluated...
[Provide standards for success, such as the rubric you will use to evaluate their work.]

Instructional Logistics
As you plan, be sure to note any particular logistical considerations (e.g., what students need to have completed ahead of time, the amount of time the activity or assignment will take). This template can be used to help you consider the oral instructions you will give to students, the PowerPoint prompt you will put up, or the handout you will design (depending on the complexity of the activity).

Figure 5.1. Template for Formal Communication Assignments

Table 5.2. Presentation-Focused Communication Assignments

Assignment Name	Learning Outcome(s)	Example Assignment
Request for Funding	Persuasively advocate for a cause/idea to a non-technical audience while illustrating competence and credibility.	This formal presentation (10–15 minutes) will be geared toward an audience who has the potential of providing resources for a particular project, cause or idea. Presentation should include a clear argument about the value of the project and clear evidence to support its development.
White Boarding	Orally and visually solve project development problems	When students are in project-based groups and need to make a decision, one student is charged with "white boarding." The student takes control of the meeting by moving to the white board and sketching out the visual representation of the problem and some potential solutions. The team then moves through a problem solving process in order to generate ideas about how to solve the problem.

Table 5.3. Interview or One-to-One Focused Communication Assignments

Assignment Name	Learning Outcome(s)	Example Assignment
Elevator Pitch	Students will provide a focused yet engaging synopsis of professional interests or their understanding of a topic	An elevator pitch is a short interaction (2–3 minutes) intended to mimic a conversation occurring between strangers in a time-bound setting (e.g., an elevator at a conference). Within the allotted time, students provide a clear, succinct, and interesting response that either presents their professional interests or highlights their grasp of material.
Cocktail Talk	Students will be able to both ask concrete and specific questions about professional interests and succinctly respond to questions asked of them	The "cocktail party" is a simulated social gathering where students walk around and talk with each other and invited guests as they would at a professional cocktail party. During this assignment, students should wander through the cocktail party and practice asking and answering questions—in order to begin forming professional networks.
Citizen Questioning	Students will provide a logical rationale for a professional decision in language understandable to the public	Students role play an interaction between a professional in their discipline and a public citizen. The public citizen is given a question that is typical of the profession and the professional should answer it without technical jargon. The goal of the professional is to clearly answer the question for the public citizen in a way that builds trust between the professional and the public.

Table 5.4. Debate-Focused Communication Assignments

Assignment Name	Learning Outcome(s)	Example Assignments
Policy Statement	Students will present a succinct argument with appropriate evidence about a "hot button" issue during a formal debate	Students prepare a two-minute argument about a hot button issue for their discipline. The argument is much like a politician's stance on an issue as presented in a debate. The summary should be appropriate for a broad audience.
Closing Arguments	Students will synthesize evidence and present a narrative in a compelling and persuasive manner	Students engage in "mock" closing arguments about a controversial issue in the discipline. Students are to give a mock 4–5 minute closing argument about the case. You could have several students doing mock closings for the same issue or you could vary the issues to have a number of different ones.

Progress Presentation
Mechanical Engineering

Due: Weekly by one group member (speakers will rotate)

In completing this assignment, you will gain experience summarizing your design process and develop communication skills relevant to engineering. Specifically, by the end of the progress presentation, you should be able to succinctly summarize your design progress for an interested, moderately invested audience of peers and supervisors. These progress presentations will provide you with feedback on your project to help your design process while also honing your communication skills, which are vital to engineering.

Your task in this assignment is to synthesize your group's design progress in a succinct and efficient manner for an audience moderately familiar with the design (e.g., supervisor; other design team members) and to build a productive working relationship with a design team and supervisors.

To complete this assignment you will, on your designated week, provide a two-minute progress presentation that includes one visual to another design team, faculty, or your project sponsor. In this presentation, you will address:

- What your group has accomplished in the past week
- Your group's goals for the upcoming week
- Any challenges the group is facing

These informal presentations will take place at the start of lab time, with all groups' designated speakers presenting to small audiences simultaneously.

In preparation for this assignment, you should reflect with your group on the progress you have made to ensure a comprehensive, accurate, and succinct summary. You will utilize the summarization skills developed throughout this semester.

Your work will be evaluated on the extent to which you succinctly and accurately summarize your group's progress while incorporating a visual. A complete rubric is attached.

Instructional Logistics

One way of handling these presentations is to allow approximately 10 minutes for the simultaneous presentations. It will help students if you can determine and stick to a consistent time (e.g., the first 10 minutes of Tuesday labs) so students can be prepared. Students also benefit from examples of successful progress reports.

Figure 5.2. Formal Communication Assignment Example, Progress Presentation

Artist Introduction
Music/Art

Due: End of semester

In completing this assignment, you will synthesize key information to spark audience interest in an artist. Specifically, you will combine research and presentation skills to provide an informative and interesting oral introduction to an artist.

Your task in this assignment is to mimic the introduction you might hear at a concert spotlighting this artist or musical work. You should create an engaging narrative that connects the audience and the artist.

To complete this assignment you will research your chosen artist or artistic selection to find pertinent and compelling information. You will prepare a brief oral presentation (2-3 minutes) in a moderately formal tone, utilizing introductory language (e.g., "welcome, it is my pleasure to..."), and employing audience- centered information about the artist and/or work. Prepare your remarks considering the audience (your classmates) and their previous connection to your artist.

In preparation for this assignment you should utilize multiple sources of information to research your artist, research the piece of work that is being introduced, and tailor the presentation of information to your audience.

Your work will be evaluated on both content (the research you complete) and the delivery of your information. A complete rubric will be provided.

Instructional Logistics
You can choose to assign students the artists or allow them to select appropriate artists. Presentations may take as little as one class period or may be spread out over multiple class meetings; presentations could also be in conjunction with other components of a related project.

Figure 5.3. Formal Communication Assignment Example, Introduction Presentation

Pin-up
Architecture; Landscape Architecture

Due: Weeks 3 and 8

In completing this assignment you will learn more about your design, design process, and project through speaking. By the end of the pin-up presentations, you should be able to clearly explain the visual components of a design by creating a coherent and logical oral narrative of design choices.

Your task in this assignment is to explain two different visual pin ups of drawings and to do so with limited time.

To complete this assignment, you will revisit one set of drawings you completed for this project and provide two different organizations of the material. You will present to a small group of your peers and faculty (playing the role of clients), talking the audience through both visual set ups. Following your presentation, the audience will provide feedback on which visual/oral logic is easiest to follow.

In preparation for this assignment, you should select drawings and determine two appropriate organizations of the material. You should prepare notes to remind yourself of the key points of each organization. You should think about how a potential client would understand and follow the visual flow of a design concept.

Your work will be evaluated on the extent to which you provide a clear, coherent explanation of your process that incorporates your visuals as well as your response to audience questions and feedback; a precise rubric will be provided before the first pin-up.

Instructional Logistics:
Depending on class size and length of class meetings, this activity could take one or two class periods. We recommend providing students with a list of pin up dates. Be sure you can meet in a room that allows for items to be attached to the walls. This assignment is best done during the earlier stages

Figure 5.4. Formal Communication Assignment Example, Pin Up

CONCLUSION

Although we have provided you with a number of ways to design formal communication assignments so that they are clear, explicit, and strategically focused on your goals and outcomes, we recognize that students' success with those assignments is related to a number of factors. When you incorporate oral communication assignments and activities in your course—whether they are focused on learning course content or gaining more formalized experience with communication competencies—there are several other issues that might emerge that beg for some support. Issues revolving around anxiety, diversity, conflict, discussion, and teamwork could emerge, and the way in which you manage them could influence the ultimate success of the communication assignment. In the next section of the book, we provide you with suggestions on how to best support students when these issues emerge.

Section III: Support for Student Learning of Oral Communication

While it sounds like a great idea to integrate student oral communication into a variety of different classes, doing so is a complex process. In this section, we address several issues you may confront as you take on this task. First, in Chapter 6, we discuss the common occurrence of nerves and jitters often referred to as "stage fright," which we explore as communication apprehension—the more technical term. In Chapter 7, we go into more detail about factors that affect class discussion and the oral participation of students in classes. Again, we provide background information, and then highlight ways to help students prepare for successful participation in discussion. Chapter 8 is focused more specifically on communication in small-group settings and teamwork. Chapter 9 addresses difficult interactions and dealing with conflict when it arises. Chapter 10 addresses issues of diversity as they affect classroom interaction. When asking students to talk in class, we necessarily encounter many differences due to communication styles and patterns related to different kinds of socialization. Ethnicity, race, gender, disability—all have implications for the ways in which communication will function in your classroom.

6 MANAGING COMMUNICATION APPREHENSION

W hen you start to incorporate oral communication in your course, you might notice a few things about some of your students: Some students get flushed when they get up to present their projects

- When doing informal communication activities, there are a group of students who never volunteer to be the group reporter
- One of your students emails you and asked if he could do a paper instead of the oral presentation you originally assigned
- Several students who are typically gregarious in class end up speaking very softly during presentations
- Some of the students, when participating in a class discussion, speak very short sentences and look like they are terrified.

What might be happening in these cases? It is possible, in each of these scenarios, that your students are experiencing communication apprehension. Often, in an effort to help students deal with this fear or anxiety, faculty or tutors will tell students that the fear of public speaking ranks above other fears, including death. While this tidbit is intended to make students feel less alone in their anxiety, there are better ways to help students manage their fears about speaking in front of others. Regardless of your discipline, if you ask students to speak in front of others—even small groups of peers or in informal communication activities—you are going to encounter students whose fears may be debilitating. When you want students to learn to communicate, how do you handle this situation? While simply excusing those students from the assignment may seem the easiest way out, doing so will not address the underlying situation, nor will it help students with apprehension meet the learning goals of the course. In this chapter, we will address what we know about communication apprehension and ways to deal with students' apprehension.

What You Need to Know about Communication Apprehension

Communication apprehension is fear or anxiety associated with real or anticipated communication with others (McCroskey, 1977). Communication apprehension can be manifested as a form of either fear or anxiety (or some combination of the two) and can be in relation to communication that is actually happening or in relation to anticipated communication (e.g., an upcoming speech in class). Communication apprehension can take on two primary forms: trait apprehension and state apprehension (including audience, context, and situational). Table 6.1 provides general definitions of these two kinds of communication apprehension. Regardless of the kind of communication apprehension, all are influenced by both previous experiences and genetic predispositions.

Table 6.1. Types of Communication Apprehension

Communication Apprehension Type	Examples
Trait: a general state of apprehension about communication that is an enduring aspect of personality	Appears in any communication situation, such as: Classroom discussion Out-of-class communication Public presentations
State: temporary experience of apprehension tied to a particular aspect of the communication event (audience, context, situation).	Appears only in specific communication situations, such as: • High-pressure situations • Large group discussions • When speaking to a full class
Audience: experience of a state of apprehension tied to particular audience members or demographics	Appears only in specific communication situations, such as: • Speaking with the teacher • Speaking in front of large, unfamiliar audiences • Interacting with unfamiliar peers in discussion • Speaking with audiences who are dissimilar
Context: experience of a state of apprehension tied to particular aspects of context of communication	Appears only in specific communication situations, such as: • Speaking in the classroom • Communicating in public situations • Speaking in professional spaces
Situational: experience of a state of apprehension tied to particular aspects of a situation in which communication happens	Appears only in specific communication situations, such as: • Novel experiences • Formal situations • Situations that are unfamiliar • Spaces where communicator feels in the "spotlight"

Trait-like communication apprehension is apprehension that is highly resistant to change and is typically similar across time. This type of communication apprehension is not easily altered but can be improved with work. State-based communication apprehension (context, situation, and audience) can be relatively enduring as well. For example, a student who has apprehension about the generalized situation of a job interview will likely experience that apprehension in all job interviews; a student who has apprehension about talking with a teacher is likely to have that apprehension when dealing with most teachers.

Causes of Communication Apprehension

Research has suggested that there are a variety of situational features that could induce apprehension. Addressing those situational features, then, becomes an important way you can help your students. These causes include novelty, unfamiliarity, formality, subordinate status, dissimilarity, conspicuousness, and degree of attention. Although these situational influences do not always induce apprehension, we know that they are likely to play a role in the ways in which many students experience apprehension. Seven common causes are

- Novelty. New situations produce uncertainty about how to behave and what to expect. Think about the first day of class versus the end of a semester. Many students may be hesitant to speak up or are otherwise apprehensive on the first day of a class because they do not know what to expect. For example, is it OK to ask questions? Can I speak up without being called on?
- Unfamiliarity. Just as with new situations, situations that are otherwise unfamiliar are likely to increase apprehension. At the same time, as the level of familiarity increases, the level of apprehension decreases.
- Formality. The more formal a situation is, the more constraints on "acceptable" behavior likely exist. For example, a student may feel comfortable responding to a question in class because the situation is relatively informal. However, that same student may be highly apprehensive when he has to give a presentation in front of the class.
- Subordinate status. Apprehension is often increased when a person is the subordinate within a communication event, such as an employee who is speaking with a supervisor, or a student speaking with an instructor.
- Dissimilarity. Often (but not always), people are more comfortable talking with others they perceive to be similar. When communicating with others who are perceived to be dissimilar, students may experi-

ence additional apprehension. For example, an older, returning student may feel apprehension speaking up in a class full of eighteen- and nineteen-year-olds.

- Conspicuousness. When people feel like they are on display—because they are giving a speech or because they feel like they stand out in other ways—they may experience extra apprehension.
- Degree of attention. A moderate degree of attention is most comfortable. We do not want to feel like we are being ignored, nor do we want to feel like people are staring.

SIGNS OF COMMUNICATION APPREHENSION

There are a number of ways to recognize communication apprehension. The three primary realms in which you can recognize communication apprehension are physiological, cognitive, and behavioral. Table 6.2 details the physiological, cognitive, and behavioral signs of communication apprehension. Students are likely to talk about the feelings that they experience, from shaking hands to completely forgetting what they were going to say. Physiological effects are those effects on the body. People who are nervous often show elevated blood pressure, have high heart rates, and may experience sweaty palms. Shaky hands are the result of extra adrenaline in one's system. Cognitive effects have to do with both kinds of cognitive impairment a student may experience ("brain fog" or "blanking out"), and what a person thinks regarding their communication efforts. For example, a student who experiences high communication apprehension may be repeating, "I can't do this" over and over in his head. The fear of speaking may contribute to a cycle of self-fulfilling prophecies, where the fear contributes to procrastination, which in turn contributes to lack of preparation and failure. Behavioral effects are often the most obvious to the casual observer. Behaviors such as pacing and restlessness, twisting of hair, or jamming hands into one's pockets may indicate communication apprehension.

As an instructor, it is important to remember that every student will experience a different combination of effects, ranging from a student reporting, "I felt like my voice was really shaky," to a student leaving the room due to nausea. Students may also be adept at hiding the effects so they do not feel that everyone knows they are nervous. Helping your students identify the effects of communication apprehension as well as the different types of communication apprehension they may experience will help you set them on a path to dealing with the apprehension. Discussing these kinds of effects explicitly can help students normalize their experiences and realize that the feelings they have are not necessarily unmanageable.

Table 6.2. Signs of Communication Apprehension

Sign	Examples
Physiological	Fast heart rate Sweaty palms Difficulty breathing Flushed face
Cognitive	Negative thoughts about communication events Avoidance of communication experiences Negative talk about oral communication
Behavioral	Pacing Twirling of hair Filler words ("um," "uh")

LONG-TERM EFFECTS OF COMMUNICATION APPREHENSION

Communication apprehension affects people in a variety of aspects of their lives. Most important to our purposes here, communication apprehension affects people in their role as students, even when not asked to give a presentation. Students high in communication apprehension differ in the kinds of courses, activities, and classroom structures they prefer (e.g., they tend to favor larger, lecture-based courses). Additionally, high communication apprehension students tend to see consequences in their learning (e.g., lower GPAs, lower scores on assignments). High communication apprehension students tend to have attitudinal differences about school and also tend to be perceived in different ways by teachers. Table 6.3 illustrates some of the primary tendencies you might notice in your students who are experiencing communication apprehension and provides the research that has been done on these effects. As illustrated, communication apprehension can significantly influence the classroom experience—from students' abilities to learn and comprehend course content to your own perceptions of students' capabilities to the ways in which students manifest apprehension.

Table 6.3. Effects of Communication Apprehension

Compared to students with low apprehension, students with high communication apprehension tend to:	Example Sources
Sit at the back or sides of classroom	Levine et al., 1980
Be less in favor of classroom discussions	Scott & Wheeless, 1977
Have lower GPA and test scores	Richmond & McCroskey, 1997
Perform more poorly on classroom assignments	Boohar & Seiler, 1982
Have difficulty comprehending and remembering course content	Booth-Butterfield, 1988
Be more likely to drop out of school	Ericson & Gardner, 1992 McCroskey, Booth-Butterfield, & Payne, 1989
Perform poorly in participation activities	Richmond & McCroskey, 1997
Receive less attention from teachers and be perceived as lazy or distant	McCroskey, 1977 McCroskey & Anderson, 1976 Powers & Smythe, 1980
Favor large lecture classes	Richmond & McCroskey, 1997
Have more of a negative attitude towards school and less motivation to learn	Frymier, 1993 Hurt & Preiss, 1978 Richmond, 1984 Richmond & McCroskey, 1997

How You Can Help Your Students

Helping your students deal with communication apprehension can take multiple forms, depending on the needs of your students and the time you can dedicate to dealing with their concerns. Before we offer practical steps for dealing with communication apprehension, it is helpful to understand the landscape of different approaches, which draw on psychological as well as communication research. We are not suggesting that it is up to you to institute a treatment protocol for your apprehensive students, but we do think it is helpful to have a general understanding of approaches that have been taken. Table 6.4 outlines the typical treatments of communication apprehension that have been explored in research: systematic desensitization, cognitive modification, visualization, and skills training. Generally, systematic desensitization works to address the physiological signs of communication apprehension by retraining the body to handle stressful experiences differently. Cognitive modification and visualization treatments work to address the cognitive signs of communication apprehension by retraining the mind to think differently about the stressful situation. Skills training works to address the behavioral signs of communication apprehension by providing students with skills that will help them manage anxiety-producing situations. In terms of which treatment work best, research suggests that a triangulated approach (one in which you identify and teach students about multiple methods of managing communication apprehension) is more effective than any approach done individually (e.g., Dwyer, 2000; Hopf & Ayres, 1993).

Dealing with communication apprehension in the classroom may sound complicated based on these identified approaches, but even small steps can make a big difference for students. To offer specific, tangible steps to take in class with students, we suggest ways of setting up your classroom to reduce communication apprehension and ways of coaching students who exhibit communication apprehension.

Table 6.4. Communication Apprehension Treatments

Treatment	Examples
Systematic desensitization: teaching the body to respond differently to apprehensive situations	1. Walk through a relaxation process (e.g., meditation, relaxing body parts) at the same time as increasing mental focus on anxiety producing events 2. Have students focus on relaxation and breathing techniques in front of a small group, then moving to larger groups and continuing to relax body and focus on breathing 3. Use informal activities to sensitize students to communication experiences
Cognitive modification: restructuring thoughts about the anxiety producing event.	1. Walk students through every irrational thought they have about a communication event and question its probability (e.g., "I think everyone will laugh; I will probably faint"). 2. Introduce students to positive language about communication events (e.g., "I enjoy being able to make my point known to a group," "I can speak really well when I feel prepared.")
Visualization: replacing negative thoughts about anxiety producing event with visualizations of success.	1. Walk students through step-by-step visualization of the communication event, asking them to verbalize what success looks like at each step. 2. Ask students to see themselves at the end of the communication event and describe the best possible outcome.
Skills training: providing necessary preparation to reduce uncertainty about the anxiety producing event.	1. Use informal activities to teach students necessary skills for success. 2. Have students do research that will make novel, unfamiliar, or dissimilar audiences more certain.

SETTING UP YOUR CLASSROOM TO REDUCE COMMUNICATION APPREHENSION

Ideally, you can take some steps upfront to help your students manage their communication apprehension. Although not all of these suggestions will work for you and your class, we offer a variety of suggestions below that you can adapt for your needs. Some of the steps are based on the interpersonal relationships in the classroom, and others are based on skills/knowledge that can be cultivated in your students. Table 6.5 provides a synthesis of these approaches.

Table 6.5. Setting up Your Classroom to Reduce Communication Apprehension

Strategy	Example Implementations
Provide students with communication apprehension information	• Have students take the PRPSA or PRCA-24 and discuss results • Provide information about treatments and additional out-of-class resources (e.g., speaking center information)
Provide multiple opportunities to speak	• Use interactive lecture/discussion format and informal activities • Give students responsibility for housekeeping tasks (e.g., calling roll, facilitating groups, reporting out) • Scaffold activities to build skills over time (see Chapter 5 for examples)
Create familiarity with communication assignments and activities	• Discuss communication genres • Showcase models of successful and unsuccessful performances
Make grading scheme familiar	• Ask students to use a grading scheme to analyze models • Provide operational examples of criteria
Provide ungraded feedback	• Use observation sheets to give informal feedback • Use peer feedback and self-evaluations
Facilitate climate of collaboration	• Utilize peer groups • Create ground rules • Encourage interpersonal relationships between students
Reduce power distance between you and students	• Disclose your own experiences of communication apprehension
Model developmental perspective	• Engage in practice sessions • Showcase "draft" presentations
Construct safe space for students	• Provide nonverbal support • Consult individually with students

First, it is important to increase students' knowledge and skills with regard to communication apprehension and its potential treatments. Ways to do this include acknowledging that communication apprehension is very real and is not only limited to public speaking. By acknowledging what your students may be feeling (but may not want to voice), you are telling them it is OK to feel this way and that you are a partner in helping them deal with the apprehension. You can also raise students' awareness of communication apprehension by explicitly talking about it in the classroom. Administering a measure such as the Personal Report of Public Speaking Anxiety (PRPSA) or the broader Personal Report of Communication Apprehension (PRCA-24) will help them better understand their own anxiety levels (both scales available at http://www.jamescmccroskey.com/measures/). Create exercises that help students identify reasons for communication apprehension in their lives so they can more effectively deal with it (self-reflection papers, for example). Provide information about communication apprehension treatments (e.g., systematic desensitization, cognitive modification, etc.). We have also found it beneficial to have all students participate in deep breathing exercises or other activities to help them relax before speaking. Even for students who do not experience high levels of apprehension, relaxation techniques can help them focus before a presentation. Such activities can draw heavily upon published examples of visualization in order to help students reduce their fears. Finally, you can provide additional resources for your students, including referrals as necessary to other resources such as a campus speaking center or counseling center.

Second, there are several adaptations you can make to your curriculum that will help students manage communication apprehension, including providing multiple opportunities for students to speak in class. Integrating informal communication activities in the classroom can accomplish this. By consistently including communication in your class, you can help students see communication as no longer novel, which reduces apprehension. With these changes, you can also scaffold communication activities and learning by building in communication activities throughout a semester that gradually increases the stakes for students. Along with scaffolding, providing a variety of communication opportunities will reduce the novelty and uncertainty that can cause apprehension. Consider including communication events that are not graded but that still provide feedback so that students can learn about areas for potential improvement. Increase familiarity with your communication assignments. Reduce the novelty of and uncertainty about communication genres by providing models. For example, many students may be unfamiliar with the communication constraints of a poster session. Before asking students to participate in a poster session for a grade, have them attend a poster session, or create a mock poster session for them. A useful source for making posters can be found at http://guides.nyu.edu/posters. There are also various poster templates available on the web.

Curricular changes can also involve grading and feedback. One easy strategy is to make the grading scheme known. You are not going to give away any secrets by sharing with students the criteria on which they will be evaluated. Unfamiliarity is decreased by ensuring students understand what is expected of them. For example, if students are giving presentations and you are mostly interested in content, students can focus more on the content and less on delivery in preparing; see Chapter 12 for more information about preparing rubrics. Additionally, we suggest providing feedback to students on their speech material and delivery prior to the graded communication event. For example, using observation forms that list key components of the presentation or activity will allow you to jot down comments to give to the student after a practice run. Students will gain a better sense of what you are looking for and their anxiety about how to meet the requirements will be reduced.

Finally, there are several strategies you can use to build an interpersonal climate of respect, which include encouraging collaboration. Focus on having students get to know each other in class so they are familiar with their peers (and potential audience members). Set up peer support groups for your students. Although some of your students may already have friends in the class, asking students to work in peer support groups will further help them get to know classmates. Furthermore, their task as a group can be explicitly to support each other in a project. Students will then have a group of willing classmates to provide feedback before a graded event and will have friendly faces in the audience to give them encouragement during a presentation. These support groups are also another opportunity for students to build interpersonal relationships with each other. Remember that you are also part of the audience, and reducing the power distance between you and your students will help reduce anxiety. By sharing a little more about yourself throughout the semester (perhaps about your own apprehensions or even just about your background and interests), you are reducing uncertainty for your students. Sharing information also empowers students to find similarities with you, which can reduce apprehension. While sharing information about yourself can be helpful, it is also important that you keep in mind the cultural expectations of your institution, location, and students. For example, some institutional cultures are more open to personal sharing from instructors.

Your actions in the classroom will also contribute to the classroom climate. If you participate in practice sessions with your students, you showcase to your students a developmental perspective on communication performance (e.g., there is always room for improvement). You can also complete the work yourself, such as giving a practice presentation. If you ask students to talk about something with a partner, consider joining a pair. When you are grading presentations, seat yourself among the class so you are not a conspicuous observer. By reducing some of the power differences between you and your students, you can reduce the apprehension that goes along with interacting with someone of a superior status. Be aware that the decreased power difference may be uncomfortable to students, so you may need to be responsive to particular students. This reduction of power distance can also benefit from making your pedagogical choices transparent to students so they understand why you are interacting with them in particular ways. During communication events, be sure to provide positive nonverbal feedback when your students are presenting or otherwise engaging in communication event. Eye contact, nodding, and other cues that you are listening can greatly help students. Be aware of possible negative nonverbal behavior that may be unintentional. For example, if you frown because of a noise outside of the classroom, the student presenting may interpret your frown as a sign that something is wrong with the presentation. At the same time, engage your students in discussion about how to be a good audience member (or a good listener) so they can also provide appropriate feedback to classmates. Finally, provide opportunities for safe discussions with students who have communication apprehension. Consult with individual students who may be particularly apprehensive in order to better help them. Talking with individual students gives them the opportunity to reduce uncertainty by having questions answered without feeling the pressure of receiving too much attention from the whole class. Although these strategies will not eliminate communication apprehension in your courses, they will go a long way in creating a climate in which communication apprehension cannot thrive.

Coaching Students

Despite your best efforts, you may still need to take reactive steps when a student's communication apprehension comes to the forefront during a presentation, or any other activity. Whether a student runs from the lectern crying or shuts down during a group activity, you can take some steps to reactively help your students.

- If a student has an attack of apprehension (such as crying or leaving the room), you need to remain calm. Your reaction to the situation will set the tone for how the rest of the class will react.
- Avoid making the student feel more anxious. For example, you may be inclined to have the student return to the front of the class for the feedback portion of a presentation. However, the student likely needs some time and distance in which to recover.

- If a student leaves the room, ask a trusted classmate (a friend of the student, if you know of such a relationship) to check on the student. As apprehension can be related to the subordinate status, asking a classmate to check in on the student can help even more than having you be the one to go after the student.
- Make sure to talk to the student on a one-on-one basis. Talking to the student about what happened in front of the class will likely further embarrass the student and increase their apprehension for further communication events.
- When you talk to the student, make sure to listen before you try to problem solve with the student. There may have been other precipitating factors, such as a family crisis, that led to the apprehension rearing its head.
- Be encouraging with the student. Emphasize the positives of what the student accomplished.
- Provide constructive feedback. Help the student see how to further improve but don't overwhelm an apprehensive student. For example, if a student had numerous issues with the presentation, talk with the student about a couple of areas that were of highest concern rather than listing all of the problems.
- Work with apprehensive students to develop a plan for dealing with the apprehension. For example, you may be able to schedule extra rehearsal time with the student. The student may also feel better about talking in front of the class if you have vetted the content of the presentation first.
- Refer the student to outside resources as necessary. Remember, you are not a counselor and are not going to be able to solve every student's problems. Know where the resources are on campus and help students tap into those resources.
- Offer alternatives, not an out. Excusing students with apprehension from further communication events will not reduce their apprehension. Instead, work with students to determine alternatives that still meet learning objectives. For example, perhaps a student will give a practice presentation in front of you, then in front of you and a couple of classmates, then more classmates, until the student is able to present in front of the entire class. This approach utilizes systematic desensitization to deal with apprehension and will likely have a longer lasting effect than simply letting the student give the speech in front of you alone.

CONCLUSION

Students may enter our classrooms with high levels of apprehension about communicating, and apprehension may be further heightened as you introduce communication assignments. Fortunately, you can help ease students' anxiety about communication in a variety of ways, both proactive and reactive.

7 Class Discussion

S cholarly discussion has long had a respected place in higher education. Historically referred to as the "tutorial," class discussion has been
a long-standing tradition in British educational settings. Likewise,
the "seminar" format is well respected as a valuable educational format in
American classrooms. Most instructors have had mixed success with discussion. Consider the following reports from faculty members:

- It's like pulling teeth! I ask a question and they just sit there, looking
  down at their books.
- Discussion works for the people who aren't shy, but it is a nightmare
  for shy students.
- Students don't want to look like they are brown-nosing, so they don't
  volunteer anything.
- There's always someone who hogs the floor, and no one else talks because they don't want to be seen the same way.
- When someone says something wrong, I don't know how to correct
  them without embarrassing them.

As discussed previously, it is widely recognized that student talk matters to
student learning (see Murphy, et al., 2009). Yet, much of our research focuses
not on how to help students talk with students, but on how teachers ought
to talk with students, or how teachers ought to structure assignments so that
students can interact. For example, there is a substantial literature on the
"art of asking questions" focusing on teacher questioning (e.g., Bloom, 1956;
Cashin & McKnight, 1995; Dillon, 1983). Likewise, the extensive literature on cooperative learning tends to focus on teacher behaviors and classroom structuring, with less attention on helping students learn how to talk
(Johnson & Johnson, 1998). The assumption that is embedded in this work
is that, given the opportunity, students will be able to talk in productive, effective, and scintillating ways. As most instructors will attest, this is not the
case for many students.

This reality leaves a problem: We want students to talk for inquiry, but they don't necessarily know how to do so. To make matters worse, we often don't know how *we* do so. Yet, if we expect them to participate in class discussion, we have an obligation to work with them to teach them how to do so. How, then, are we to teach our students to do it? In this chapter, we will explore what research tells us about classroom participation and strategies for increasing classroom participation, with a particular focus on discussion. We will then offer recommendations for encouraging effective participation in both large class discussions and small learning-group discussions that can be adapted to the classroom.

Our suggestions regarding increasing discussion are grounded in research-based understandings of participation. To that end, we now turn to key definitions regarding participation and discussion. We will then turn to what we know from research on participation and discussion. Finally, we will provide tips for facilitating discussion, both as participants and as leaders of discussion.

What You Need to Know about Discussion

While definitions of participation vary widely, what is consistent is that students' engagement with content is considered integral to learning. Research on oral participation and learning points to the importance of encouraging student participation (see Chapter 1). Despite virtually universal agreement on participation as a positive influence on learning, the definition of participation remains murky. For example, Petress (2006) viewed participation as quantity, dependability, and quality. Often, though, participation is defined as a set of behaviors, which range from high levels of involvement (e.g., asking questions—Wambach & Brothen, 1997; Fritschner, 2000) to fairly passive (e.g., breathing and staying awake; Fritschner, 2000). Clearly, there is great variation in what is considered to be participation, ranging from simply being present in the classroom, with no qualifiers about what the student is doing, to active and vocal involvement in discussion. It is likely that you have in your mind a picture of what participation looks like in your classroom, perhaps from your own experience or from an understanding of your discipline's communicative norms. For our purposes here, our focus is on oral communication in the classroom among students and instructor that engages students with class content and/or skills. With this focus, we also recognize the variation among students, the limits of class time, and the need for multiple channels to prepare for discussion (such as asking a student to jot down notes about a topic before asking the student to share with the class).

Many instructors have experienced the difficulties associated with getting students to talk in class. Some of these difficulties may be related to the expectations of students, which are based on the experiences they have had in previous classes. The research on participation points to the typical experiences students are likely to have had with participation that could influence your discussion setting (see Table 7.1).

Table 7.1. Typical Participation Patterns

Pattern	Example sources
Typical interactions begin with teachers asking questions, which students answer	Wambach & Brothen, 1997; Karp & Yoels, 1976
Discussion among students and discussion between the teacher and multiple students is uncommon	Wambach & Brothen, 1997; Karp & Yoels,1976
When instructors are the ones who initiate interactions, there are typically more exchanges and more participants than when students initiate interactions	Cornelius, Gray, & Constantinople, 1990
Only a small percentage (e.g., 18 percent) of students participate	Fritschner, 2000
Less than 3 percent of class time is spent on student participation, although upper-level courses show more participation than lower-level courses	Fritschner, 2000; Nunn, 1996

INFLUENCES ON PARTICIPATION

What constitutes participation may vary from class to class, but the amount of research dedicated to understanding what influences participation is illustrative of its importance. A variety of factors have been connected to why students participate; from student confidence to cultural differences to instructor style to the size of the class—all have been shown to affect participation. In addition, instructor characteristics and class characteristics influence participation. These influences are summarized in Table 7.2, with more details provided in this section.

Student Characteristics

There are many reasons that students choose to talk in class. Perhaps most enlightening are the reasons students give for making decisions about participating. Howard and Henney (1998) found that the four most cited reasons for participation were: seeking information or clarification, having something to contribute to the class, feeling of learning through participation, and enjoying participation. On the other hand, reasons for not participating include a lack of interest in the topic (Brown & Prius, 1958) or lack of knowledge (Howard & Henney, 1998). Students' preparation for class as well as interest in the subject matter is related to higher levels of participation (Auster & MacRone, 1994; Fassinger, 2000; Hyde & Deal, 2003; Weaver & Qi, 2005). Other reasons for not participating include shyness and fear of being considered stupid (Hyde & Deal, 2003).

Apprehension is one of the biggest barriers to participation. Whether because of low self-esteem generally or lack of preparation, students who are afraid they will appear stupid are less likely to be willing to talk in class. People who are apprehensive often are less willing to communicate than are people with lower levels of apprehension (Neer & Kircher, 1989). For example, students apprehensive about communicating prefer to participate after getting to know classmates and are more likely to participate after gaining approval for their efforts.

Furthermore, students' communication in class is affected by language and cultural barriers. Not surprisingly, students from English-speaking countries are more likely to participate than students from non-English-speaking countries (Kao & Gansneder, 1995), and students for whom English is a second language are reluctant to speak in class (Cao & Philp, 2006). Different cultural socialization also has an impact on participation patterns. For example, Turkish students use silences as a form of participation (Tatar, 2005). Korean students may not participate because to do so is seen as a challenge to the teacher's authority, and hence, insulting (Lee, 2009; A. Palmerton, personal communication, 2006).

The age (both chronological and academic) of students also affects their participation. Nontraditional students are more likely to participate than are traditional students (Fritschner, 2000; Howard, Short, & Clark, 1996). Students in upper-level courses are also more likely to participate (Fritschner, 2000), which may also be related to course structure (i.e., more advanced students have reported feeling that they have more opportunities to participate; Heller, Puff, & Mills, 1985).

The relationship between gender and communication in the classroom is complex. Multiple studies have supported the perception that males participate more in classes than do females (Crombie et al., 2003; Levine, O'Neal, Garwood, & McDonald, 1980; Sternglanz & Lyberger-Ficek, 1977). However, Howard and Henney (1998) found that a higher percentage of women participated than did men, and individual women also participated more than did individual men. A slightly different trend comes from Fritschner (2000), who found that although the percentage of men in a class who participated was similar to the percentage of women who participated, as the level of the course increased so did the percentage of women who participated. Participation by men, on the other hand, remained stable. While gender differences in participation have been absent in some disciplines (e.g., social work; Hyde & Deal, 2003), other disciplines have had a high emphasis on male participation (e.g., biology, especially in a high-achieving class; She, 2001). Finally, institutional size may play a role; Crawford and MacLeod (1990) found that gender was related to participation at a small school but not at a larger institution.

Table 7.2. Influences on Participation

Student Characteristics	• Student confidence and self-esteem • Student apprehension, • Student interest in the subject • Student gender • Cultural background • Facility in English • Student age (nontraditional vs. traditional students) • Fear of peer disapproval • Interaction between faculty member and student
Instructor Characteristics	• Communication style (verbal aggressiveness, gruffness, sarcasm vs. supportive responses, approachability) • Incorporating ideas and experiences into discussion • Self-disclosure • Asking effective questions • Giving enough time for students to think about responses • Caring attitude (as perceived by students) • Attractiveness • Immediacy (e.g., smiling, gesturing, eye contact, relaxed body posture, using humor, encouraging responses) • Similarity (as perceived by students)
Class/Institutional Characteristics	• Class size • School size • Grade associated with participation • Emotional climate • Students' experiences with other students

Instructor Characteristics

As the instructor, your behaviors and characteristics will influence students' participation. Instructors who incorporate ideas and experience, actively facilitate the class, create a supportive classroom environment, and ask effective questions are more likely to garner participation (Dallimore, Hertenstein, & Platt, 2004; Webb & Palinscar, 1996). Students are more willing to take the risk to participate in a discussion with an instructor who is perceived as caring and as having good character (Myers, 2004). Smiling, gesturing, eye contact, relaxed body posture, attractiveness, using humor, self-disclosure, and encouraging responses all contribute to students' greater willingness to participate (Caproni, Levine, O'Neal, McDonald, & Garwood, 1977; Goldstein & Benassi,1994; Goodboy & Myers, 2008; Rocca, 2010). Instructors perceived as verbally aggressive, gruff, or speaking quickly without providing time for students to respond results in students being less likely to participate (Rocca, 2010; Fritschner, 2000).

Class Characteristics

Class characteristics, such as the layout of the room and the tools used in class time, affect students' engagement in participation. For example, Brown and Prius (1958) championed two arrangements that can encourage students to participate in class discussions: the use of panels for small-group discussions before talking in front of the class, or setting the seats in a circle with panel members guiding the discussion from within the larger group. For more traditional classroom layouts, Levine et al. (1980) found that students in the front of a lecture hall participated more. The number of students in a class has an inverse relationship with the amount of participation. Students reported that the classes in which they participated the most were smaller (Auster & MacRone, 1994), but the average number of students participating has been found to be similar regardless of class size, with a handful of students contributing more than 50 percent of the total interactions (Karp & Yoels, 1976). The use of different tools and techniques in classes can also increase participation and engagement. For example, personal response systems (clickers; Beekes, 2006; Hake, 1998), specific roles for participants in a discussion (Smith, 1996), and grades associated with participation (Lyons, 1989) have all increased participation in discussions. None of these reasons is particularly surprising, but that does not mitigate their impact. Although instructors are ultimately in charge of the classroom, students are left with relatively free will about what actions to take in the classroom and clearly there are many influences at work.

How You Can Help Your Students

You may be wondering at this point how you might help students participate in discussion. Classroom structuring, your own behavior, and students' behaviors all contribute to successful discussion. While we cannot cover all of the elements that make a discussion successful, we can offer advice about approaches that may be helpful. In this section, we make a very basic assumption: instructors and students will need to talk with each other to identify the communication behaviors that work, as well as those that don't. This assumption means that instructors must work with students to surface the embedded assumptions within your discipline about how inquiry is conducted—the kinds of questions that are asked within your discipline, the approaches to understanding and talking about texts/problems/arguments/results that are expected in your discipline, as well as the forms of and criteria for evaluation expected within your discipline. In the following pages, we first discuss some common misconceptions about how discussion works. These are beliefs often held by students and faculty alike, based on the experiences many have had in previous classes, and on models they have seen in other contexts. While keeping in mind the complexity of influences on the discussion process, we then offer advice about steps you can take in your classroom to help your students be prepared to participate in discussion. Class discussion comprises a give-and-take among all, the instructor and students. Among the problems instructors face are misconceptions about how discussion works.

- Misconception 1. The discussion leader should know all. One common misconception is that the discussion leader knows—or should know—all the answers. Instead, the discussion leader helps guide the group to discern what needs to be discovered. Sometimes the facilitator has more knowledge, particularly when the facilitator is the teacher. However, knowing more about the issue generally does not necessarily translate into knowing the exact answer to a given problem or knowing all possible ways of approaching a problem. The facilitator's job is to help the group determine how to approach the problem under discussion.
- Misconception 2. Discussion is a fishing expedition. In this view, the goals of the discussion leader are to get students to "fish for" and "catch" the "right" answer. When the facilitator is viewed as having all the answers, it naturally follows that the job of the rest of the group is to figure out what is in the facilitator's head. This approach to a class session can be useful if it is necessary to test the knowledge of the students. It is not, however, conducive to inquiry.

- Misconception 3. Participants Don't Have To Do Much Work. There is a common misconception that discussion participants can be passive—listening and guessing the "right" answers to a series of questions posed by the facilitator. This misconception is a logical progression from the viewpoint that the facilitator is the one primarily responsible for knowing the material. In this scenario, the participants sit back and absorb it; class sessions are a modified form of lecture. If students view class discussion in this light, it will fail. Discussion cannot progress satisfactorily when participants are unprepared to talk about the material. The responsibility of participants in class discussion is in many ways more demanding than in lecture classes: all participants must be thinking about the material, and thinking hard about it. All participants must be willing to pursue their thoughts, even when they do not feel confident about it. The nature of inquiry demands this openness as well as commitment.

These misconceptions may be addressed in class, but your preparation and engagement are not limited to simply telling students the "truths" of participation. Discussion is a process of give-and-take among students and instructors, and you can ease the process.

It is useful to think about an entire discussion in terms of objectives. As you design your course and the way in which you plan on using discussions, spend time thinking about your objectives for this discussion. First, what are the critical issues that you want your students to explore? What do students need to understand first, before they can move on to the deeper issues? Is there a vocabulary that needs to be clarified or concepts that need to be evaluated? What connections are there between the topic of discussion and other issues you have been covering in class? Second, during the discussion you will need to attend to the kinds of analysis taking place. Draw out the different points of view among your students. Ask students to clarify their opinions and provide their reasoning. Third, pay attention to the participation dynamics. Are all students getting a chance to have the floor? If the focus of the discussion is veering off, ask students to make the connection to the issues under discussion. Fourth, open the door for an evaluation of the texts or opinions or positions under discussion. Have students explore the strengths and weaknesses of positions. Push students to articulate their criteria for evaluation. Fifth, if you want students to share opinions and evaluations, they need to feel safe enough to do so. How will you create a climate of safety? Finally, how will you debrief the class? How will you evaluate the discussion—did the class lead to the surfacing of essential critical issues? What worked to help the discussion progress? What hindered its progress?

In Chapter 4, we provided examples of exercises that can help students become more comfortable about participating in class, and that will help set the expectation that students will participate. More structured exercises early in the term can help establish the norm for the class that students will talk, and that the instructor is not only expecting students to talk, but appreciates their contributions to the class. You can help the discussion process before, during, and after a class discussion; table 7.3 presents an overview of these processes. In the next section, we provide more detail on these processes and focus on pre-discussion preparation, how to deal with issues during discussion (implementation), and post-discussion wrap.

DISCUSSION PREPARATION

One of the most important ways to prepare for discussion is simply to talk about discussion. Both you and your students have had experiences with discussion—ask them to identify the kinds of communications that in their experience have hindered good discussions and the kinds of things that have helped. Contribute your own observations—make this discussion of discussions an example of how a discussion can work.

Establish Ground Rules for Discussion

You can list the results of the "what makes a good discussion" discussion on a chalkboard or white board—and even develop a list of class generated "do's" and "don't's" for discussion in your class. This activity is a useful first step in setting expectations for students and establishing ground rules for your class. Although we may want to assume that students know exactly what to do, the reality is that they probably have not thought explicitly about their own behaviors and the impact of their communications on the progress of a class discussion. Make sure your ground rules are not too ambiguous. For example, "Do unto others as you would have them do unto you" can be interpreted in multiple ways—and the way that some students want and expect to be treated may be dramatically different from what other students want or expect.

Table 7.3. Processes that Facilitate Discussion

Pre-discussion preparation	• Devote class time to talking about discussion with students, including how to ask questions. • Set expectations that students will come prepared, opinions should be well reasoned and all opinions should be taken seriously. • Establish unambiguous "ground rules." • Help students come prepared (e.g., clarify what readings should be done in advance). • Give students time to reflect privately on issues under discussion. • Tell students why you want them to do whatever they are required to do. • Plan what you want to accomplish with the discussion and identify what is essential.
During discussion	• Physically structure the room so that you and the students can see each other. • Encourage students to speak with each other without going through you. • Encourage students to ask the questions, paraphrase others' comments, and respond to nonverbal signals from others. • Provide an opening for the discussion that allows for multiple responses; expect and allow for continued disagreements. • Help students put course ideas, concepts, facts, or other course materials into their own personal contexts. • Clarify the goal of the discussion as a class. • Look for the insight imbedded in the incoherent or flawed statements. • Address problem dynamics as they occur. • Show your own excitement, perplexity, and general involvement in discussion.
Post-discussion wrap	• Have the class evaluate the effectiveness of their class discussions and identify specific behaviors that can make discussion more productive help individual group members participate more fully. • Have students self-reflect upon their own choices made in the discussion. • Encourage discussants (including yourself) to say when they have changed their views.

From the start of the course, it is important to set and reinforce the expectation that every student will come prepared for the discussion by doing the assigned work (e.g., will have completed the observations assigned, will have completed field notes, will have read the novel, will have completed the experiment, etc.). Students need to know why they need to participate in something that may be uncomfortable for them, or that they may think is superfluous—after all, if you are the expert, why should they discuss? Let them in on your pedagogy.

Warm Students Up for Discussion

Give students a toolbox of skills that will let them participate fully. Provide avenues for students to help them come to class prepared. For example, provide them with ways to read the text or provide a set of questions for them to answer to prepare for discussion. You might have students prepare questions for the class. Give advance notice of classroom activities they cannot do if they have not read or processed the material. Teach students how to ask questions. Don't expect that students will automatically know how to ask relevant questions. Teach students how to rephrase their own and others' comments. This rephrasing will help everyone discover new insights that may be difficult to express. You can also work with students on the importance of including reasons behind opinions and demonstrate how to discern the reasoning behind opinions. Set the expectation that it is important to genuinely try to find out why students hold the opinions they do and that it is important to take each student seriously.

Additionally, you can utilize meta-thinking to help students better understand the role of participation in their learning. Rather than thinking of discussion as something you can slip into any class period when you have a few spare minutes, plan what you want to accomplish with the discussion (see Chapter 4). Be clear with yourself about what you consider essential to cover so you will be able to guide discussions appropriately. The templates in Chapter 4 will help you do this. Be prepared to restore direction when a discussion grows aimless or disorderly (but be willing to be flexible enough to accept the aimlessness that may be needed). In the classroom, you can let students "in" on your goals, for example, by telling them why you are asking them to discuss a particular issue. You can also give students time to reflect privately on issues under discussion, for example, through writing or through one-on-one interaction or through other ways you have found that will allow them to discover what they think. Be aware that different people need different amounts of time to reflect on the questions that are raised. You can also highlight the value of particular texts or questions so students will be primed for the discussion. This information can also help students focus their energy and reduce frustrations from situations such as questions with which students need to struggle because there is no easy answer.

DURING THE DISCUSSION (IMPLEMENTATION)

Prepare the Classroom for Discussion

When it comes to utilizing participation in the classroom, instructors should have an active role but allow the students to drive the discussion. A simple step is to have the class physically structure itself so that everyone can easily see each other. You can encourage everyone to respond to nonverbal signals from members of the group (including subtle signals that may indicate withdrawal). These arrangements help students become more aware of multiple perspectives and alternative explanations of concepts. You can encourage students to speak with each other without going through you so there is truly a discussion, not a series of one-on-one discussions between instructor and individual students. Encourage and expect students to ask the questions and to paraphrase comments offered by other students to clarify and enhance understanding. Particularly for contentious issues, expect and allow for continued disagreement and lack of consensus. Encourage students to see disagreement as opportunity for deeper exploration. Emphasize the importance of disagreement, and talk about what makes disagreement constructive. Additionally, you and the students can look for the insight imbedded in the incoherent or otherwise flawed statements of the students.

Encourage Multiple Responses and Outcomes

Throughout discussion, it is helpful if you provide openings for the discussion that allows for multiple responses. That opening may be a comment, an invitation for comments, a question, a paraphrase, or any other conversational move that shifts attention from you to the relationship of students to content. Encourage and help students to put course ideas, concepts, facts, equations, or other course materials into their own personal contexts. Be open to discovering that students may discern additional essential concepts, which may lead the discussion down a path different from the one you envisioned. From the start, it can be helpful to clarify as a class the goal of the discussion. For example, are you attempting to understand course materials? To understand each other? To experience and discover the means by which to inquire into texts? To demonstrate multiple paths for solving a problem?

Engage Students as Facilitators

It is often useful to structure the class so that students are responsible for facilitating class discussion. This kind of assignment provides opportunities for students to practice leading a larger group. Such an assignment also helps students realize that the success or failure of a discussion is not just the responsibility of the discussion "leader." In most students' experience that leader is the teacher, and students have had quite varied experiences of success with instructor-led discussions. In this sense, we are operationalizing with them the concept "participation" so that they can enact the expected behaviors. The following table identifies responsibilities of both facilitators and participants in discussion, according to the general discussion objectives discussed above. You will note that the behaviors of participants do not vary much from those associated with the facilitator. Whether the discussion facilitator is the instructor, or is a student charged with leading a discussion, reviewing these behaviors with students can be enlightening.

Table 7.4. Responsibilities of Facilitators and Participants in Discussion

Goal	Responsibilities
Identify and explore critical issues	Everyone should: • Identify critical issues as well as what ideas, concepts, or issues need clarification and/or evaluation • Identify priorities: what does the class need to spend time discussing? • Consider how the material relates to other knowledge
	Facilitator should also: • Ask participants to identify critical issues for clarification and evaluation. • Guide the group to set priorities: have the group decide what they want to spend the most time discussing, with justification.
Analyze the points of view of positions expressed	Everyone should: • Ask for different points of view. • Ask for clarification of unclear remarks. • Provide reasons for opinions; ask others' for reasons behind opinions.
	Facilitator should also: • Explicitly paraphrase the areas of agreement or disagreement. • Insist that group members listen and fully understand the reasons given before evaluating them.
Allow all a chance to be heard while maintaining focus	Everyone should: • Listen to the ideas and arguments posed by others. • Ask for clarification for unclear remarks and connections for remarks that seem irrelevant. • Acknowledge the connections others make to additional spheres of knowledge.
	Facilitator should also: • Act as gatekeeper: make sure all have a chance at the floor; ask those who have not said very much what they are thinking. • Avoid taking on the mantle of "expert" who knows all the answers.

Goal	Responsibilities
Evaluate different positions	Everyone should: • Explore the strengths and weaknesses of positions and reasons under discussion. • Identify the criteria functioning among the group members in making the evaluations of the perspectives being explored.
	Facilitator should also: • Summarize the ideas expressed during discussion, with reasons given. • Open the floor to explorations of issues pertaining to the strengths and weaknesses of the arguments made. • Focus attention on the criteria being used to evaluate voiced perspectives.
Create a climate where participants feel safe enough to participate	Everyone should: • Talk with each other; ask for the opinions, evaluations, and reasons of others. • Avoid personal attacks and respect others.
	Facilitator should also: • Support every person's right to an opinion. • Resist the temptation to fill in all the quiet spots: don't fear silence.
Evaluate the discussion	Everyone should: • Review the main points of the discussion, including viewpoints that differ. • Share how the discussion affected opinions. • Evaluate how well the group integrated the material with other knowledge. • Ask what responses contributed to the discussion and which hindered progress; identify specific behaviors that will help the class during the next discussion.
	Facilitator should also: • Establish the criteria being used to evaluate. • Initiate the review of topic and main points and encourage explanation of all viewpoints. • Guide the discussion toward gaining more insight into the process of discussion itself.

Avoid Discussion "Stoppers"

It is usually easier to think of what not to do than to come up with positive alternatives—which is why we are emphasizing behaviors that are constructive. However, there are some things that you and your students should avoid. Most of these suggestions have to do with the actual discussion process:

- Don't assume that you are the one who should be asking the questions or be the arbiter of all answers.
- Don't use opening questions to which there is a single correct (or desired) answer.
- Don't try to summarize the discussion. Summarizing tends to distort or reduce the material discussed and tends to increase dependency upon the instructor to determine the ""meaning"" of the discussion.
- Avoid condescension and sarcasm, as well as highly personal or intrusive questions, such as those you yourself would not want to discuss in a group.
- Don't toy with students' ideas so that they feel tricked.
- Resist the urge to cut off a student if he or she seems to be "all wrong." Wait. Allow the discussion to continue—it may well go in a direction you have not anticipated but that is insightful. You will also provide the opportunity for students to discover their own errors.
- Do not allow students to be abusive to each other or to you. Name-calling, put-downs, nonverbal behaviors such as rolling eyes, or snickers need to be addressed clearly and openly as inappropriate and unacceptable.
- Avoid labeling ideas, particularly with pejoratives. An idea may seem bigoted, racist, sexist, "P.C.," or other "-ist," but if it is part of an honest exploration of difficult questions, even perspectives that are problematic must be open to exploration. No one said critical analysis of ideas would be easy or comfortable. Make the group a safe place to contribute and try out ideas. True inquiry only happens when it is safe enough—or important enough—to risk being wrong.

Address Problems When They Occur

In the same vein, there are several common occurrences that should be addressed when they occur in a discussion. Often, one or more students dominate the discussion. Talk with students about the two sides to the domination equation: People who tend to dominate must learn to bite their tongue while people who tend to feel dominated must take responsibility to not allow others to take up so much talk time. Additionally, someone who dominates may be a student who is unprepared for the discussion but strives to replace quality with quantity. Students may also passively or actively, consciously or unconsciously, "attack" a classmate. For example, the group may consistently ignore someone's comments or questions. Class members may also put down another student, verbally or nonverbally. Interestingly, students will often identify "respect" as a requisite to "good" discussion. What "respect" looks like when enacted, however, may vary from student to student. One person may feel "put down" when another thinks the argument was intellectually engaging. You may need to negotiate the meaning of different communication styles with students.

Post-Discussion Wrap

Allow for Reflection on the Discussion

Providing students with the opportunity to think about what happened during the discussion will help them understand the value of the activity and increase their learning. After discussion, you can have the class evaluate the effectiveness of the discussions. Students can also self-reflect on their own choices. The purpose of these evaluations and reflections can be for enhancing future discussions rather than for a grade. Furthermore, you can work with the class to identify and remove tensions that keep students from talking. You can also work with the class to identify specific behaviors the group can undertake to make the discussion more productive and to help individual members participate more fully and productively. Explore with students how their responses to disagreement may make the expressed disagreement constructive or destructive. Encourage discussants (including yourself) to say when they have changed their view.

Conclusion

Whatever your discipline or your instructional goals, you can shape the classroom experience to engage students with material in discussion with you and their peers. The implementation guidelines we have provided here flow easily into each other; together, they can help you draw your students into discussions and help them achieve their potential as critical analysts, thinkers, and problem-solvers.

8 NAVIGATING GROUP/TEAM WORK

You've heard the complaints ring from your students—the moans and groans that seem to escape from their mouths when you announce a group project. And for good cause, sometimes, as students often bring negative past group experiences with them to such an endeavor. You may have even had your own negative teaching experiences when using groups. Anyone who has had students work in groups (or who has been a group member on a work team), has probably noticed some typical patterns:

- One group member does a majority of the work, either upon the urging of the group or by that person's dominance in the group.
- The group spends more time talking about what they did last weekend than they do talking about the task.
- Group members "divide and conquer" the work rather than collaborating to complete it.
- Group members allow personality differences to interfere with group productivity.
- Group members complain about work distribution, deadlines, and individual group members.

Although many students dread the prospect of being required to work in groups and are left frustrated by the process, group work does have important benefits for students' content learning, in addition to providing a context in which they can develop communication skills. Furthermore, the ability to work productively on a team or in a work group is one of the most valued skills identified by employers (Morreale & Pearson, 2008). However, as any teacher knows, just putting people together in a group and giving them a task does not mean that the group will work well together or that the task will be done well or that the individuals in the group will learn anything but that they hate working in groups.

In this chapter, we will address the challenges and opportunities of implementing group work in your class. We will begin with key definitions, then draw on research to highlight what you might expect from your students when they are working in groups. We then provide details on how you can help students work more productively and cohesively in groups.

What You Need to Know About Groups/Teams

In order to set the groundwork for what you can expect when utilizing groups, we want to begin by defining what we mean by "small groups" and "teams." While there are various definitions of a small group, there are several common elements. A small group is a collection of 3–15 people (ideally, 3–7 people) who regularly interact and communicate with each other in order to achieve a common goal. Five basic elements are embedded in most definitions, according to Hirokawa, Cathcart, Samovar & Henmen (2003):

1. The number of people in the group matters. There needs to be a small enough number so that individuals are able to influence the others, and be influenced by them (Rothwell, 2010). The dynamic changes significantly when there is the possibility of an alliance, so two people are a dyad, not a group (Bormann, 1990).
2. There needs to be a shared sense of purpose. All members of the group need to have at least some degree of agreement on a common goal.
3. Members of the group need each other to achieve that goal (built-in interdependence).
4. Group members have a sense of who is, and who is not in the group. They identify themselves as part of the group.
5. There is regular interaction and communication among group members.

A team is generally more specifically defined as a task group with the particular organizing feature that each member of the team is chosen for a particular specialization that the member can bring to the group (Cragan, Kasch, & Wright, 2009; Rothwell, 2010). In industry, for example, a team charged with determining the feasibility of a new product may be made up of someone from research and development, someone from production, someone from marketing, someone from public relations, and someone representing management. In higher education, a team (often called a "task force") might be made up of several faculty members from different academic disciplinary areas and members of the administration such as finance, development, marketing, and representatives of faculty governance. Teams are typically given a task (that may or may not be clearly defined) by someone in authority. As Rothwell (2010) notes, the "essence of all teams is collaborative interdependence" (p. 177). For our purposes, we will primarily refer to work in "groups," whether those groups are technically "teams" or not, as the dynamics associated with group work apply to teams. No matter whether a small task group or a more specialized team, we presume two definitional criteria: interdependence and a common goal.

Critical Issues in Group Work

Just as every class is different, every group is unique. How you use groups in your teaching will vary depending on your goals as an instructor. Group tasks might include students working in group problem-solving discussions, participating in laboratory groups on a lab assignment, facilitating committees to accomplish a goal, or completing a semester-long project. Small task groups may be long-term, lasting several weeks, or short-term, lasting one or more class periods. Regardless of how you structure groups in your course, there are several issues to consider when deciding to use groups in your courses. The issues we most commonly see that concern faculty have to do with determining the membership of groups, understanding group norms and roles, dealing with the conflicts that inevitably arise, and dealing with the non-contributing group member. Table 8.1 summarizes some of the general things you can expect when assigning groups. In the next section, we will discuss these in more detail and expand on the dynamics of group interaction that influence membership, roles and norms, and emergent conflict.

Table 8.1. Critical Issues in Group Work

Issue	Example sources
Individual differences: Students will have varying degrees of expertise, experience, and motivation as well as different majors, different reasons for taking the course , and different external responsibilities.	Bormann, 1990; Cragan, Wright & Kasch,2009; Hinds, Carly, Krackhardt, & Wholey, 2000; Hirokawa & Poole, 1986; Johnson & Johnson, 1998; Rothwell, 2010
Norms: Each group will develop and reinforce unique norms, influenced by previous experiences; not all norms will be productive nor necessarily liked by all group members.	Bormann, 1990; Cathcart, Samovar, & Henman, 1996; Cragan, Kasch, & Wright, 2009; Rothwell, 2010; Shaw, 1981
Leadership: Leadership is necessary but approaches to leadership vary; emergent leadership may be inconsistent with assigned leadership.	Bormann, 1990; Cragan, Kasch & Wright, 2009; Rothwell, 2010

Issue	Example sources
Conflict: As groups work, they will need to solve problems; conflict can be productive and can help students develop life-long interpersonal skills; the ways conflict is dealt with vary by culture.	Amason & Schweiger, 1994; Esser & Lindoerfer, 1989; Hirokawa & Poole, 1986; Janis, 1972; Jehn, 1995; Johnson, Johnson, & Smith, 2007; Ting-Toomey & Oetzel, 2001
Guidance: Students need to be taught to ask the kinds of questions relevant to your discipline; discussing group processes and scaffolding assignments gives students extra support in building these skills.	Bormann, 1990; Cragan, Wright & Kasch, 2009; Hirokawa & Poole, 1986; O'Donnell & O'Kelly, 1994; Rothwell, 2010; Webb & Palinscar, 1996
Virtual groups: Virtual groups need attention to technological issues, coordination of asynchronous work, and interpersonal considerations when lacking face-to-face interaction.	An, Kim, & Kim; Elgort et al; Harvard Business Press, 2010; Rothwell, 2010

Group Membership

Not only are the contexts for group work potentially varied, but how you designate group membership can also vary depending on your goals. You might assign random groups for particular activities, or you might decide to assign membership based on particular members' skills, members' schedules, or other criteria. As you consider membership, though, take into account that research suggests individuals will tend to gravitate toward those who are similar racially, those with whom they have worked in the past (if it was a positive experience), and, if known, those who have a reputation for being competent and hard-working (Hinds, Carly, Krackhardt, & Wholey, 2000). This might be acceptable for some group activities. Yet, as a teacher, you might also want your students to learn to deal with the unpredictable and with heterogeneity. If students are exposed to varied group members, part of their learning involves determining how to help that group do its work.

Your students will bring varying degrees of experience, motivation, and expertise to the group process. In the classroom, we may not have the luxury of creating groups made up of members with specified areas of expertise. In fact, many students in many of our classes would not consider themselves an expert in any area related to our discipline, especially in courses that fulfill distribution requirements. We may have students who have never taken a course in the discipline before. Therefore, we are in a position of trying to help students learn how to work effectively in situations where some students might have more knowledge, some may be more motivated; some might be feeling quite lost or are taking three other classes that also have group assignments; some may be working thirty or forty hours per week to pay for tuition and childcare; and yet others might clearly have other priorities (an athletic schedule necessitating out-of-town commitments, for example). These kinds of challenges create potential disruptions that can be difficult to manage. Nevertheless, it could be beneficial to students to learn how to function productively and deal with such problems. At the same time, to the extent that we can minimize avoidable problems (like schedule conflicts), it is helpful to do so. Dealing with these disruptions requires being mindful of curricular choices, minimizing conflicts across classes (as much as possible), and exploring possibilities for group structures that facilitate participation by all members. Decisions about group membership include all of these kinds of considerations, and it is best to be mindful of the additional support structures that you may need to provide, given the characteristics of your particular class.

The Development of Norms and Roles

Faculty members often expect that student groups ought to follow a particular pattern of interaction, and the patterns of all groups will look approximately the same. However, every group develops unique norms and roles (Bormann, 1990; Cathcart, Samovar, & Henman, 1996; Jones, Barnlund, & Haiman, 1980; Cragan, Kasch, & Wright, 2009). This is true of any class as a whole, and it is also true of the smaller groups that you form within your class. For example, a group working in a class with one of the authors cultivated the norm of a very personable, lively interaction pattern, but when they were up against a deadline, the group turned from socializing to tasks very quickly and without needing prompting. Other groups in the same class, completing the same project, however, were more consistently task-oriented.

Roles are normative patterns specific to the behavior of individual group members. A group will develop its own unique pattern of roles, depending upon the patterns of interaction among all group members and the individual skill sets of members of the group. Most faculty members are primarily concerned with nurturing the leadership role (discussed at length below), but it is important to recognize that many different functions need to be fulfilled in a fully functioning group.

No two groups will have exactly the same configuration of norms and roles because these grow out of the interaction of the group. Norms can contribute to group productivity, or they can detract from group productivity. Roles can be functional, or there can be extensive conflict over how roles are enacted. Over time, for example, a group may develop a pattern of late arrival, leaving them without enough time to deal with the task. Another group may develop a pattern where any disagreement is avoided with a joke, impeding critical analysis of issues. Some groups develop work patterns that are highly structured, and others have low levels of structure. Neither pattern is more effective; they are just different (Putnam, 1979).

Groups not only develop norms and roles that influence productivity, these also influence creativity and participation. If a group has developed a norm where no one confronts someone who hogs the floor, this can impede the creative input from others. If the pattern is recognized, the group can reinforce the efforts of quieter people by "gate-keeping"—giving the quiet persons openings to talk—and reinforce the efforts of one person who may begin to specialize in this task. To make the most of the group effort, groups benefit from individuals who are willing to propose new ideas, activities, procedures, share knowledge, and respond to questions asked (Bales, 1949; Bormann, 1990; Cragan, Kasch &Wright, 2009; Rothwell, 2010). And if the group has established interaction norms that inhibit this, failing to reinforce those individuals taking on these role functions, there could be problems.

Individuals also bring expectations with them for how a group should function, and these expectations can also lead to conflict. For example, one of us worked with two groups of engineers who admitted that the other group drove them "crazy." The production engineers wanted to "get to the point" and "say what you mean" and were frustrated that the research and development engineers were unwilling to assert an opinion. The research and development engineers, meanwhile, were frustrated because the production engineers did not leave room for discussion or participation in decision-making—noticing that "it is their way or the highway." What became clear was that the production team worked in situations that required quick decision-making—so they often had to "get to the point" in order to get rolling and fix problems quickly. The research and development team worked in situations that required openness to ideas, careful consideration of all perspectives, and thoughtful acknowledgment of ideas that may have appeared harebrained at first. The cultures of the two parts of the same organization made it difficult for a team comprising engineers hailing from both of these areas to function. If workplace engineers had a difficult time functioning with their engineering counterparts (with whom they work on a daily basis), students are likely to need guidance working with their peers who will likely have different interpretations, experiences, and work styles.

It is tempting to believe that because students have worked in groups before, they will know exactly what to do. This is not always the case. It is true that students do enter into groups with expectations about what behaviors they (and others) ought to exhibit. These expectations are usually based upon previous experiences in similar situations and upon individual and cultural socialization. Students, indeed, carry expectations set in one class into a new class. However, expectations set in other classes may vary dramatically from what we expect of these students in our own classes, and just because something has worked for a student in one class group does not mean it will work in a different group. This is especially important to remember when working with students. They have had to conform to expectations for group work set in other classes that may vary dramatically from what we expect of them in our own classes. To be fair to our students, we need to be explicit about the kinds of expectations we have for their participation in the groups we use in our classes.

Emergent Conflict

Conflict is an essential aspect of group and teamwork. Conflict is more fully addressed in Chapter 8, but it is important here to note the presence of conflict in group work and its importance to a group's functioning. Because many groups necessitate critical analysis and evaluation of ideas, a certain level of tension is expected in a group (Bormann, 1990). Conflict may also emerge over roles and work procedures. Team members will feel this tension, and may attempt to avoid it or explain it away as "personality conflicts" with the result of ignoring essential critical insights of the party perceived to be offending the safety of the group. As we all know, disastrous events can result from this (Janis, 1972; Esser & Lindhoerfer, 1989). For example, the "slacker" is a common source of conflict in a group. Students may take over for the "slacker" and try to get through it, or get angry, or come complain to you. As with all issues groups need to address, it is important you support your students in dealing with these kinds of conflicts. In the next section we will discuss issues particular to virtual groups, then follow with recommendations about things you can do to help your students with the issues they encounter in their group work.

Virtual Groups

Increasingly, in our global society, virtual groups are being used in the workplace. Most groups now use various types of virtual communication, whether it is email, text messages, jointly working on a document in a document management system, or other technological resource. When considering virtual group work, then, it is useful to consider the extent of virtual-ness (Martins, Gilson & Maynard, 2004). In this section, we consider groups that are primarily virtual, where the separation by distance and/or time makes it more productive to use virtual media. These kinds of virtual groups differ from primarily face-to-face groups in several ways (see Rothwell, 2010; Harvard Business Press, 2010). If you decide to assign groups that will be working primarily in a mediated way, it is important to understand these distinctions. First, of course, is the lack of physical proximity. Group members are separated physically from each other. They may be on the other side of the world, in different organizations, or in the next room. Because of the potential that group members will be in different time zones, work in a virtual group tends to be asynchronous. Members may contribute to a worksite at any time in a 24-hour cycle. Group members in Senegal can meet with group members in Saint Paul and Japan in an asynchronous fashion, asking for materials, contributing materials, discussing perspectives, offering opinions, asking for opinions, and clarifying ideas—all at different times, resulting in a "meeting" being spread out over several days. This consideration will affect the timing of assignments, as well as individual students' work processes.

Working with groups that interact primarily virtually demands particular attention to the process of coordinating work, to technological concerns, and, to what is often overlooked because individuals are not working face-to-face, interpersonal concerns (Bazarova & Walther, 2009; Martins, Gilson & Maynard, 2004; Rhoads, 2010). Today's students are typically well versed in the use of technology, but they do not necessarily know how to work with others in a technological medium in any way other than socially. In the process of preparing your virtual group assignment, you will need to determine the ways in which you need to support students as they learn to interact as a task group as opposed to a social group. For example, not all individuals push emails to their phones, so will not be available to the group 24/7. Not all individuals are willing to be waked at all hours by text messages simply because another member of the group happened to be working on something in the wee hours of the morning and a question arose. Furthermore, just as in face-to-face groups, individuals have different structure needs. You can cut through some of those issues by establishing much of this structure as part of the assignment. We address some ways to help students with these issues in the next section.

How Can You Help Your Students?

As mentioned, every group develops its own culture consisting of norms, roles, and processes for doing work. It can be jarring to move from one group to another, because the cultures may be quite different. One of the marks of a competent communicator is someone who has the flexibility to adapt to the needs of the particular communication situation. One of our goals as educators is to facilitate the growth of that flexibility. Part of that involves raising these differences into awareness through processing the oral communication experiences that individuals have in our classes. In this section, we provide suggestions for structuring and supporting group work that will help your students engage in more productive group experiences.

Structure Groups According to Purposes and Outcomes

It is helpful to start by defining your own purpose: Why are you having students work in groups? What are you trying to accomplish with a group assignment? Is it the best way to achieve your pedagogical objectives? Much like our earlier discussion of objectives, the idea of orienting the nature of groups toward the ultimate goals will help ensure success. Faculty members often ask while structuring groups: What is the magic configuration of members and member characteristics (known as the "assembly effect")? There is no magic answer, whether face-to-face or virtual groups (Bormann,1990; Brilhart & Galanes, 1995; Cragan, Kasch & Wright, 2009; Martins, Gilson & Maynard, 2004). Some faculty members find that paying attention to student work and class schedules reduces tension in the group just by removing the difficulty associated with scheduling. Others are more concerned that there be a variety of skill levels, hoping to engage the learning of all through the teaching/learning exchange (Webb & Palinscar, 1996). Still others eschew the attempt to create an effective group by controlling membership and opt for random assignment. Some experiment with different approaches until they find one that seems to work for a particular kind of class. Yet others encourage students to utilize technological features that allows them to do collaborative work via web-based documents or have virtual meetings (if you do so, you will need to make sure that they have the knowledge to do so, addressed later in this chapter—Harvard Business Press, 2010; Parker, 2003; Rothwell, 2010). Think about your goals—what are the best ways to structure groups given your goals? Additionally, as groups begin their time together, help them by clarifying the group task and the expected outcomes, as well as your goals for using groups. If groups do not know what is expected of them, they are not likely to be productive. If they do not have a clear idea of the expected outcome, we cannot expect that they will learn what we want them to learn.

Help Students Identify the Norms and Roles at Play in Their Group

It is often useful to discuss norms that may be in effect when students meet as a group (or a class) for the first time. Such a discussion can be a useful exercise for students. Ask your students to consider the general question: How are people in a group supposed to act? This will help them identify their expectations for group interaction. Then ask them to identify the existing norms (if they have had a chance to establish them) or the expected norms that might be productive for their group. Once the group has identified some of the group norms or expected group norms, they can then begin to talk about whether they like these patterns, whether they are functional or not, what may get in the way of changing norms that no group member likes, how individual communication styles may interact with the expectations of the group, and so forth.

Leadership

You can also explicitly discuss the functions and roles that need to be fulfilled for a group to be productive and the kinds of communications that are associated with those functions. Three kinds of functions are typically identified in the research, each necessitating leadership: Content functions, procedural functions, and group maintenance functions (Cragan, Kasch & Wright, 2009; Rothwell, 2010). Leadership in any of these areas can be fulfilled by different group members at various times. Content-related leaders focus on providing direction related to the ideas and subject matter under discussion: The "what" of the task. Procedural leaders provide direction related to how group members will proceed, the "how" of the task. Group maintenance leaders provide direction related to the way group members interact, in order to encourage cohesiveness and commitment to the group and the group project. Whether you assign leadership roles within a group or not, students will need guidance in what comprises effective leadership. Table 8.2 provides a summary of communication behaviors associated with different leadership functions; you may find it helpful to provide your students with this information.

Students often think of leadership in academic settings as primarily content expertise. However, content leadership involves the *facilitation* of the content expertise of all group members. Content leaders focus on making sure every group member has input into the ideas, facts, materials, and critical questions related to the task. This kind of leadership may be taken on by primarily one member of a group or may be shared among several individuals. Content leaders often open avenues for exploration by asking for ideas, requesting input from others, exploring proposed ideas, and modeling openness to diverse thoughts. At the same time though, content leaders also need to critically analyze and evaluate ideas. Content leaders encourage all group members to ask questions, critically evaluate their own ideas as well as those offered by others, and encourage members to provide reasons for opposing ideas. Some language that could help your student take on the role of content leaders includes

- "What do you think about the idea that . . . ?"
- "I'd really like to know your reasons for your opinion on that."
- "Why do you think that would happen?"
- "Do those statistics really reflect the overall situation?"
- "Can you give me an example of that concept?"
- "How might that influence the larger scope of the project?"

Table 8.2. Communication Behaviors Associated with Leadership Functions

Leadership Function	Communication Behaviors
Procedural Leadership	Initiate discussion and providing direction (e.g., setting an agenda), Gatekeep; ask for input and suggestions Verbalize decisions that have been made, Summarize progress and next steps that have been decided by the group. Clarify the purposes of a group and of each meeting Helps establish goals Make sure technology is working (e.g., for virtual groups) and make decisions on what software is to be used Establish the time-frames for meetings when synchronous meetings are needed (for traditional groups and virtual)
Content Leadership	Open avenues for exploration by asking for ideas and asking for input from others. Explore ideas proposed Critically analyze and evaluated ideas by asking group members to ask questions, and to critically evaluate their own ideas as well as those offered by others. Ask for elaboration and reasoning Make abstract discussions more concrete by providing or asking for examples
Group Maintenance Leadership	Attend to participation of group members, and makes sure all members have a chance to speak Insist on respect for others and establish ground rules (e.g., no name-calling) Talk with individuals outside of the group if someone is upset, or if someone is being disruptive Encourage a healthy expression of conflicting ideas Instigate conflict if necessary, inviting disagreement, and being or asking for a "devil's advocate" Model honesty and candid expression of concerns while being sensitive to others

As you work with your students, help them understand that all members need to take responsibility for asking these kinds of questions and for content functions; a leader in this area is a guide, someone who pays particular attention to these functions but is not the only one doing them. Guidance and leadership in this area can help establish a productive and cohesive group climate where changing one's mind or position is seen as positive if there are good reasons to do so. Ideas can be abstract, and one of the functions of this role is to make abstract discussions more concrete by providing or asking for examples, analogies, and illustrations, or to expand ideas beyond one concrete example. These types of concretizations of ideas can also be built into an assignment or a check-in point.

Students often identify content expertise as the essential characteristic of leadership. Moreover, many teams are made up of individuals with specialized content expertise. While some advise a rotating leadership based on content expertise, this choice may exacerbate difficulties unless there is an individual in charge of how the group gets its work done—i.e., a procedural leader. Ultimately, such a choice about leadership is dependent on your goals for the course. For example, you may have students working in teams that reflect what they are likely to experience in the workplace. If those teams would typically be made up of a variety of content experts, perhaps your students would benefit from each becoming an expert on one aspect of the project (e.g., the historical context in which a text was written).

Although students often think of leaders as those with content expertise, it is important for them to understand procedural aspects of leadership as well. Generally, effective leadership is concerned with work procedures, and so procedural leadership is often the best fit with students' prior conceptions of leadership. Communication behaviors associated with procedural leadership include such actions as initiating discussion and providing direction (sometimes done through setting an agenda), clarifying, gatekeeping, asking for input and suggestions, verbalizing decisions that have been made, summarizing progress, and summarizing next steps that have been decided by the group. With virtual teams, this individual may also be responsible for making sure that the technical side of things is working (e.g., operating the software to be used or organizing the time-frames for meetings when synchronous meetings are needed).

One way you can help your students understand procedural leadership in groups is by providing them with language that reflects procedural tasks. For example:

- "Where shall we start?"
- "I suggest we talk about the agenda first, and then move on to the specific areas we all believe we need to explore."

- "Let's try to get a grip on what our charge is. Let's each talk about the direction we think we should go as a place to start."
- "Well, we only have ten minutes left, and we still haven't talked about ABC. How about spending the next few minutes on that just to give us an idea about what each of us is thinking?"
- "We haven't heard an update from Chris yet, so Chris, would you fill us in? And then we can set our goal for the next meeting."

Additionally, you will want to provide your students with an idea of how to manage difficulties when they arise (many student groups have gained insight from taking Putnam's Procedural Order Questionnaire, which gives group members a way to talk about difficulties over procedures that they may be facing [Putnam, 1979]). Some language you can provide to your students that focuses on keeping the group on track includes

- "Let me get this straight. Are we saying that . . ."
- "Would you talk about that idea a little more?""
- "Seems to me that three basic proposals have emerged from our discussion: that we do X, that we do Y, and that we do Z."
- "Sounds to me like we've got agreement on XYZ, but still disagree on how we should implement that proposal. Let's focus on where we disagree, and see if we can find an approach that will meet our mutual interests."
- "Looks like we have consensus on two solutions to the problem."

You can aid the procedural leadership by encouraging groups to be explicit about decisions that have been made. This sounds easier than it is. Too many groups avoid doing so because of unresolved conflict, an inability to clearly articulate what has been decided, or an inability to clarify what has been a vague discussion. Ambiguity may be used to avoid responsibility, or to justify actions that ignore group consensus. Verbalizing consensus can help avoid such problems. These are steps that are easily built into assignments or check-in days where you touch base with each group.

Group maintenance functions help ensure that individuals feel heard, and that individual contributions are valued. Groups cannot function well unless it is safe to do the hard work of questioning, critically examining ideas, and just plain slogging through the work. Group maintenance leaders focus attention on how members are participating, build the sense of psychological safety in the group, address the ways that conflict is managed in the group, and attend to the ways in which group members deal with personal needs and differences when they arise. Language you can help your students use in this leadership role includes

- "I'm really wondering what those people think who haven't said anything so far."
- "John I know you're concerned about that point. I really think we need to hear other points of view, though."
- "Remember, we are committed to mutual respect."
- "We might want to take a moment to review our group rules"
- "Let me play devil's advocate on that issue to bring up a different point of view."

Your students who are group maintenance leaders are not conflict avoiders; they are attending to the group climate in order to maintain psychological safety. Psychological safety does not mean avoiding or diffusing conflict. Rather, it means encouraging a healthy expression of conflicting ideas in such ways as to maintain personal integrity of and respect for group members. Members concerned with group maintenance try to find ways to disagree while maintaining high levels of respect for each other. If there is conflict, these members actively work to help participants address it honestly and clearly. At times this means instigating conflict, inviting disagreement, and being or asking for a "devil's advocate" to establish the expectation that disagreement will happen. A group member focused on group maintenance should be honest and candid while being sensitive to others. Other group members tend to develop a sense of trust for this individual. Again, you may find it helpful to assign someone whose focus in the group is on maintenance (for example, "the skeptic") but this role may also naturally evolve based on personality.

Facilitate Conflict Management

When groups do experience conflict, it is tempting to step in and resolve the issue for the group. Rather than being the one to do the problem-solving, you can help your students through that process. To start, simply recognizing the tension can create an opportunity to talk about what is contributing to it, and the problem-solving can begin. Additionally, it is important to help students understand that conflict might be tied to cultural expectations as group members from significantly different backgrounds bring expectations with them regarding gender, race, ethnicity, age, and disability. Chapter 10 will address this in detail, but it is important to consider it here so that you can help your students become aware of the differences that could cause conflict. Doing this gives students a vocabulary for discussing their experiences. For example, direct communication in relation to addressing conflict is no better and no worse than indirect communication—it is just different and serves different functions within the context of the cultural expectations of the group. Coming to a quick solution regarding a conflict, and not "beating around the bush," may be what is expected in US colleges and companies, but if our students come to learn that this is the only appropriate way of solving conflict, they will be at a disadvantage in the global marketplace (Ting-Toomey & Oetzel, 2001; Requejo & Graham, 2008).

Build in Considerations for Virtual Groups

Students should be briefed on not only how to use the technology but also ways to coordinate work and ways to address interpersonal concerns. Members of virtual groups do not have access to the same kinds of nonverbal and social cues that we use when meeting face-to-face. Virtual communication via texts such as email can easily be misinterpreted. Sarcasm and jokes often do not come across clearly or as intended. Cultural differences may exacerbate these difficulties. Conflicts can be heightened because of the loss of immediate nonverbal feedback, which means it is useful to explicitly discuss rules against "flaming." Conflict expressed in the virtual world takes on heightened intensity, in part because it is not modified by facial expressions and tone of voice. Disagreements often cannot be expressed in real-time, contributing to a perception of positions being locked in as opposed to simply having been offered. As with face-to-face groups, members should also remember the importance of explicitly expressing their appreciation for the work of others. This often happens off the cuff in face-to-face meetings and tends to be forgotten in virtual communications. It is important that group members know their contributions are appreciated.

Table 8.3 provides recommendations for establishing and conducting virtual groups. Just as with all groups, norms will emerge, as will roles. It is particularly helpful, however, to designate specific individuals to help coordinate interaction. There should be one person that serves as the primary contact person for questions regarding technology and coordination of work. It is also helpful to have ground-rules established and provided to all group members that indicate where the work is to be done and stored and a calendar that shows when work is to be synchronous or asynchronous. Periodic face-to-face meetings can be helpful, even if these occur only through a video/VOIP system. Some synchronous meetings, where all members can discuss concerns and questions at the same time can help with coordination and with motivation. In any fully functional group, there will be, and there should be conflict. Disagreements help groups focus on the most important elements of an idea and eliminate less constructive approaches. Establish ground-rules that welcome "devil's advocate" analyses but that also establish expectations for how conflicts will be expressed (see Chapter 9 on Dealing with Conflict and Chapter 13 on Managing Facework).

Table 8.3. Special Considerations for Managing Virtual Groups

Technological Considerations	Designate a technology coordinator as the contact person Create a specific virtual place (e.g., a blog, a content management system) where work can be done Create procedures for using the virtual space (e.g., will all members have access to all files at all time? Will there be a rotation for working on files?)
Coordination	Clarify initial roles of group members and how those roles relate to the virtual environment Create a calendar that shows deadlines Schedule times for periodic synchronous meetings
Interpersonal Concerns	Make time for members to get to know each other Make explicit efforts to acknowledge individual and team contributions Implement ground rules for communication: what is expected, what is acceptable, what is not acceptable

Help Students Self-Reflect

One way that students learn from their experiences is through self-reflection. Therefore, including self-reflection assignments—whether formally or informally—can help students process what they are experiencing. If students look at their own communication honestly and with open minds, they will gain insight into the ways in which their communication behaviors might be interpreted by others. Intended meaning is often not the meaning understood by others.

This reflection process can also be aided by providing examples and models of effective communication, such as those included in this chapter. Students may agree that certain types of communication are helpful but not know how to enact that communication. Examples, models, and discussion of their experiences with different kinds of communication directed toward them will help them identify alternative behaviors that may be more functional than those they typically employ.

Scaffold Instructional Support Throughout the Group Process

The worst thing you can do as a teacher is to assign group work or a group project on day one and then not do anything to support students. Although some groups miraculously come together to produce brilliance, many do not. Taking a small amount of time to think about how to bring in support structures throughout the process will go a long way. First, helping students understand key skills they need to develop as they work in groups will facilitate their learning about group processes and content. Also, strategically building in support for group processes throughout will minimize the likelihood of panicked members in your office on the last day of class. Although there are many pieces of advice we can offer in terms of building in scaffolded support, we have distilled research and experience on teams into a set of recommendations based on keys for effective group interactions. Table 8.4 identifies some ways to set up instructional support for groups in your course, based on keys to effective group interaction.

Table 8.4. Scaffolding Support for Group Work in Your Class

Focus	Implementation
Balance: make everyone responsible for establishing a work pattern and balancing contributions to the group	Construct ways for all group members to be accountable to each other and to the instructor Individuals are assigned tasks and left to determine the most appropriate individual approach to that task Establish an agreed upon work process for the overall project
Conflict management: keep manageable boundaries; focus on problem resolution, not being right	Build in breaks from group interaction Establish a "two-minute" conflict rule (each person has two minutes to speak during conflict so that everyone has an opportunity to be heard) Establish a norm for of listening before judging
Flexibility: help students be responsive to changing needs of the group	Utilize group members" varied expertise during different stages of the project. Build in "mid-project" assessment so students can consider procedures and roles that may be more effective

Focus	Implementation
Prioritization: groups should prioritize goals while still respecting individuals' goals	Have members of a group explicitly articulate individual goals Ask groups to establish an agreed upon group goal
Socializing: encourage cohesiveness as it enhances productivity	Build in time for non-task related experiences Have groups generate team logo and name
Responsibility: each group member should contribute so no individual carries the load; members should give credit where credit is due	Have students self- and peer-evaluate group contributions (e.g., assign members points from 1–10 on level of contribution). Establish a mechanism for individual accountability without micro-management
Individuality: group members should cultivate an attitude that individual differences should be valued and used as a resource	Consider having groups assign different tasks in terms of project management Build in opportunities to change task delegations throughout project. Group members should not try to control the behavior of other group members
Listening: keep members responsible for staying in touch with the group, speaking up if they feel strongly about something, and be conscious of silencing others	Teach students to use clarifying questions Establish group processing session (where each group member is allowed to identify concerns he or she has with group). Establish a "no interruption" rule to allow speakers to complete their contributions
Preparation: build in commitment to completing necessary tasks and coming to meetings prepared	Have groups assign pre-meeting tasks Build in accountability for preparatory material in grading

CONCLUSION

Successful group and teamwork involves leading and following, agreeing and disagreeing, contributing and questioning, exploring and expanding, focusing and evaluating, responding and crediting, and appreciating and enjoying. There is no specific recipe to follow that will result in an effective group or team, but the kinds of communication that individuals use can help create a team that works together, as opposed to working at crossed purposes, a group where members feel needed and respected as opposed to one where members feel superfluous and disregarded. Helping students see the impact of their own communication in a group context will help them become competent, ethical communicators.

9 Dealing with Difficult Interactions

Regardless of your discipline or the amount of time you've been teaching, you've probably had your share of difficult interactions. Perhaps you've even heard grumbles like these:

- "Great . . . teamwork. It always turns out that I do all the work on the team, and everyone else will get the same credit as I do. It isn't fair. I hate teamwork."
- "It is going to be the same thing, over and over. I'll do everything I can to explain my design and the prof will just tear it apart. Why should I even try?"
- "What? You are bringing people in from industry to critique our work? Last year when that happened, all they did was bring up things that we really had no idea we were supposed to do. How embarrassing."
- "I really don't like Julie, and now I'm stuck with her for our team presentation. She's likely to help our team self-destruct. I don't know how we will get along."

When you assign oral communication activities and assignments in your course, it is possible that students will face difficult interactions such as those indicated by the quotations above. You cannot escape the potential for conflict or difficulty when you ask students to speak to an audience; work with a team; or be in interpersonal interaction with colleagues, teachers, or potential supervisors. It is the nature of human interaction. Sometimes, just the anticipation of these difficult interactions causes stress—for you, for your students, and for those participating in the oral communication activity or event. Then, if there are difficulties, your students are typically untrained in how to deal with them and you probably feel you do not have the time to deal with them. Yet these difficult interactions—whether they are quick but challenging questions to a presentation, interpersonal conflict between team members, or face-threatening comments between course participants—will influence the ultimate success of the communication activity or assignment.

Therefore, it is important that you have a basic understanding of some of the things we know from research that happen in difficult interactions so that you can best prepare your students to manage them. In this chapter, we provide a summary of some of the key research in communication conflict management in order to provide you with a foundational understanding of how and why difficult interactions could occur. We then provide you with steps for managing difficult interactions. We intend this advice to be informative for you and for your students. Finally, we detail some in-class activities and provide some resources that could give students practice in preparing for and managing difficult interactions that could emerge in oral communication activities and assignments.

WHAT YOU NEED TO KNOW ABOUT CONFLICT AND DIFFICULT INTERACTIONS

Difficult interactions often take the form of conflict in the classroom. One of the most widely accepted definitions of conflict is "an expressed struggle between at least two interdependent parties who perceive incompatible goals, scarce resources, and interference from others in achieving their goals" (Wilmot & Hocker, 2010, p. 11). Central to this definition is the notion of perceived incompatible goals. Notice that conflict is not simply about actual incompatible goals but, rather, the perception of them. Two students working on a team project, for example, might have similar goals to achieve a good grade. Yet, each student might perceive the other to have different goals. The perceptions, then, lead to conflict. Additionally, conflict emerges when there are scarce resources. By resources, we do not necessarily mean tangible goods. Resources can be things like the teacher's attention, an opportunity to lead a group, time, or information. A student working on a team presentation might believe that the team has limited time to prepare the presentation. Therefore, time becomes a resource that is scarce and could lead to difficult interactions. Finally, the definition of conflict recognizes the presence of some perceived interference in goal achievement in order for difficulties to arise. If a student perceives that another teammate has the goal of "just passing" (when her goal is to get an "A") and there is very little time, that student believes the teammate will interfere with her goal (by not preparing or putting in the time).

There is a wealth of research on managing conflict in communication situations. Our goal is not to synthesize all of this research, but rather to provide you with some general information about why and how difficult interactions happen. We will discuss four typical components of difficult interactions: attribution error, the norm of reciprocity, conflict spirals, and conflict goals. In each of these discussions, we provide a general definition of the concept, a summary of what research suggests about the concept, and an example of how this concept might occur in your classroom oral communication activities. Table 9.1 presents an overview of these phenomena. In the next section we describe these phenomena more fully.

Table 9.1. Common Conflict Phenomena

Conflict Phenomenon	Sounds like
Fundamental attribution error: tendency to prioritize personal or dispositional reasons for others' behaviors while prioritizing situational explanations for own behavior	"She's a slacker" "He's just a dominating personality" "I've just had a bad day" "I'm not really that kind of person. I'm just tired"
Norm of reciprocity: tendency to respond to each other in a similar fashion or "in kind"	*Jon:* "You're lazy." *Sally:* "Me, lazy? You're just overly controlling." *Sara:* "You are really being helpful to this group by taking minutes and I know it isn't the most fun." *Martin:* "Thank you. You make it easy for me by giving me your notes."
Incompatible conflict goals: each person may have different desired outcomes or may prioritize a different desired outcome (e.g., emphasizing topic, relationship, identity, or process)	"Why did you go to the teacher and talk with him about our project behind my back? I thought we were a team." "Why do you want to present that material? Don't you think I'm good enough to do it?" "We don't have time to sit here and hash out all our disagreements. We need to get this project done!"
Conflict spirals: chained responses where interaction is managed through either avoidance tactics or through escalating responses that continue in the same fashion	*Andrea:* "I don't want to cause any problems in the group." *Steve:* "There must not be any problems because Andrea would tell me if there were. I guess I won't bring up my issues." *Andrea:* "Gosh, Steve is quiet so I'm really not going to say anything about this problem I'm having."

Attribution Error

In social psychology, the "fundamental attribution error" refers to the tendency to over-emphasize personality or dispositional explanations for others' behaviors rather than situational explanations (Jones & Harris, 1967). For example, if your students are working on a team-based project and one person is extremely quiet and doesn't participate, it is possible that other team members will say things like "he's really shy," or (less generously) "he's lazy." In this case, they are attributing this person's behavior to his personality and disposition. It is possible though, that this person is going through an extremely difficult time and does not want to bring any of these personal difficulties into the team, so he/she remains quiet. This situational explanation could be valid. Conversely, when thinking about one's own behavior, it is more likely that you would prioritize situational elements over personality traits (e.g., "I'm not lazy, I just have a lot going on!"). Research suggests that the attribution error occurs for a number of reasons. First, it occurs because it provides a quick, efficient mental shortcut that allows a person to make sense of a complex situation. Attributing a behavior to a personality is easier mental work than taking into consideration all the situational factors that could be influencing the behavior (Forgas, 1998). Second, the attribution error could occur because people do not have adequate information about the situational factors and therefore rely on the information that is right in front of them—the person (Gilbert & Malone, 1995). Although this error has negative consequences, which we will discuss momentarily, it could also provide people with a sense of control over complex social situations. The shortcut explanation and the resulting attribution could make someone feel competent in understanding and analyzing a communication event (Reeder, 1982).

In your classroom, there could be significant problems with the fundamental attribution error. If you assign students to communication tasks that require interdependence with other students or other colleagues, it is possible that they will have to deal with challenges. When they do this, they are likely to make the fundamental attribution error. The problem with the fundamental attribution error is that if students attribute other people's behavior to personality or disposition, they become stuck. If they are interdependent on this person for a communication activity or assignment and they consistently explain the other person's behavior as a personality defect, it is unlikely that they will be able to change the other person's personality (or at least it would be very difficult). So, they keep on building a perception of who the other person is without considering situational explanations for behavior. At the same time, when these teammates are attributing the other person's behavior to personality, the fundamental attribution error suggests they will tend to excuse their own behavior by using situational explanations. They might say things like "She's got a dominating personality and just took over the meeting," but when they step up and take control they might think, "No one was bringing the team together, I had to take control of the meeting." These attributions could lead to defensiveness, misunderstanding, and conflict. They will probably lead to students sitting in your office, frustrated because of "personality conflicts." The error becomes even more problematic when interacting with those who are different, such as underprivileged groups or those of different ethnic backgrounds, etc. It could lead to stereotyping that is unproductive in communication assignments. There is no way to stop the fundamental attribution error, but understanding that it will happen is a key step towards dispelling the biases that occur. We will discuss ways to manage this bias later in this chapter.

Norm of Reciprocity

The norm of reciprocity refers to the fact that people tend to respond to each other "in kind"—that is, in similar ways as they have been addressed. People tend to feel an immediate sense of obligation, for example, when treated with extreme kindness. On the other hand, when treated with attacks or judgments, people will often respond with similar attacks and/or judgment. In a team meeting for a project in your class, for example, one person could say to another teammate "Why did you do that? That was totally out of line to ask the professor. Now we look like we don't know what we are talking about." The other person is likely to respond defensively—with something like "I wasn't out of line. I was just trying to make sure we do the assignment right. Why didn't you check with the prof in the first place?" This response mirrors the original questioning with defensiveness and further questioning.

Although the norm of reciprocity has negative effects when dealing with hostile or difficult behavior, research suggests that the norm of reciprocity is quite helpful when trying to gain compliance or social influence (e.g., Cialdini, 2001). For example, advertisers will often provide something for "free" in hopes that you will take it and then feel obliged to reciprocate by purchasing their product. Examples of this tactic are widespread—from the tea or coffee given to you as you enter a car dealership to the free address labels sent with a request for a donation to the local animal shelter. Yet, we also know from research that the norm of reciprocity is time-bound; the sense of obligation seems to diminish as time passes (Burger, Horita, Kinoshita, Roberts, & Vera, 1997). Finally, the norm of reciprocity is culturally distinct; there is some evidence that suggests that certain cultures have stronger notions of familial or friendly relationships and therefore, the norm seems to hold more weight (Gouldner, 1960).

In your classroom, the norm of reciprocity could come into play in a number of difficult interactions. First, if you are assigning group-based oral communication activities that are project-driven, it is likely that students will experience some difficulty being interdependent in a high-stakes project. These students are typically unprepared to deal with these difficulties and often do not have the conflict management skills to productively diagnose and deescalate a potential problem. Therefore, one negative statement could lead to reciprocal negative statements, which then become an escalatory spiral (discussed in the next section). In a presentation-based activity, a challenging question from a critic is likely to make a student defensive and the student is likely to respond "in kind." Yet, there could also be some beneficial aspects of the norm of reciprocity. If students understand this norm, they can better influence the kinds of responses they get on a team or to a presentation. Although this is not always the case, the norm of reciprocity has been shown to be a powerful social norm that could be advantageous or potentially problematic.

Incompatible Conflict Goals

As mentioned at the beginning of the chapter, at the center of the definition of conflict is the idea of goals. When difficult interactions emerge, participants often recognize that they are trying to achieve something that is not in alignment with what the other party is trying to achieve. In a communication activity in which you are simulating a manager giving a performance appraisal to an employee (student), you might be trying to mentor the employee by providing constructive criticism, whereas the employee might be trying to advocate his or her abilities (and hide his or her faults) in order to move up in the organization. These incompatible goals tend to lead to difficult interactions.

Research suggests there are four kinds of goals that are particularly relevant in difficult interactions: Topic, relationship, identity, and process (Wilmot & Hocker, 2010). Topic goals are the goals related to the actual content of the interaction. For example, in a performance appraisal, topic goals may revolve around getting and agreeing on accurate information about an employee's performance on the job. Relationship goals refer to the goals each participant has in terms of the relationship—present and future. These goals typically focus on the amount of interdependence each party assumes and wants in the relational system. In the same performance appraisal example, the employer might try to establish a more detached relationship by asking the employee to find resources for increased improvement. The employee, who views the employer as a mentor, might expect resources to be provided, increasing the interdependence in the relationship. Identity goals are goals related to perceptions of self. In difficult interactions, these goals often emerge when participants are trying to protect their own self-image (or save face). In a performance appraisal, if an issue arises over the employee's capabilities, the employee might try to protect his/her identity by suggesting that that particular skill wasn't in the job description. Process goals revolve around the communication process that is to be used to manage the difficult interaction, once it arises. In a performance appraisal, the employer might want to table the resolution stage in order to gather information, whereas the employee might want to come to a decision in order to reduce uncertainty.

In terms of these goals, research suggests that relationship and identity goals are the most powerful in a difficult interaction (Wilmot & Hocker, 2010). Therefore, when the topic of the difficult interaction is resolved, participants often feel the issue/matter is unresolved if relational and identity issues remain. Additionally, goals often mask each other. In a difficult interaction, you might have a student team member arguing for a particular design choice when the reality of the situation is that that student wants to be seen as a team leader (identity) or wants to gain your admiration (relational) as a potential colleague. It is important to know these things because these goals characterize all difficult interactions, and these interactions can turn into conflicts if the goals continue to be incompatible. Whether you are having students participate in a one-on-one communication activity, a team-based communication activity, or a presentation-based communication activity, a difficult interaction emerging from that activity is likely to be fundamentally about incompatible goals in the interaction. Paying attention to these potential and perceived incompatibilities is essential in order to avoid further escalation.

Conflict Spirals

When difficult interactions emerge in your classroom, they often become chained and ongoing events. Sometimes the difficult interaction is bound to a time and space that has no spill-over, but often it becomes the first in a chain of interactions between interdependent parties in the communication activities. Two patterns that tend to occur (and that are not helpful in managing difficult interactions) are avoidance spirals and escalatory spirals. Avoidance spirals emerge when parties involved in difficult interactions try to manage that interaction with avoidance tactics such as withdrawal, denial of difficulty, being unresponsive or under-responsive, changing the topic or joking about the situation and not taking it seriously. We know from research that an avoidance spiral occurs when one person's avoidance tactics are responded to by the other person with further avoidance tactics, and so on and so on. The spiral is a destructive one in that the parties involved do not deal with the difficult interaction and in avoiding it; it becomes bigger and more powerful than if they had engaged with it earlier.

Escalatory spirals emerge when one person escalates the conflict with remarks that are taken as an attack, or that create a hostile climate. Some of the more overt escalatory remarks include threats, attacks, coercion, deception, or abuse of power. Subtler remarks may include sarcasm, ignoring, indifference, or condescension. The person perceiving the attack then responds "in kind" and escalates the conflict. This response, in turn, could lead to further escalation by the first person, and so on. Complementary spirals may emerge when there are complementary responses; for example, an individual talks a lot in a discussion, while others respond by being quiet, and as the talker talks more, the quiet parties get quieter. Research suggests that spirals are destructive in that the parties involved become more and more emotional about a problem that may or may not warrant such emotion. Avoidance and escalatory spirals are also destructive in that behaviors become translated into perceptions about the other person ("she doesn't care about me," or "he's just trying to blow up the team") and about the task at hand.

Avoidance and escalation spirals could occur in your classroom if you have assigned oral communication activities that involve interdependent parties over a sustained period of time. Typically, these spirals do not occur in a one-time communication event (although we have worked with some disciplines where presentations are significantly long enough to lead to negative spirals between presenters and critics). You could place students in teams, for example, and at the first sign of difficulty, the team gets into a pattern of avoidance. Over time, members continue to avoid a challenge or conflict, which then leads to more avoidance. Or you have a team that is not afraid of engagement, yet is unprepared to deal with that engagement in productive ways. Both of these situations then lead to a frustrated team in your office. Helping students understand the tendency to fall into avoidance or escalatory spirals could provide them with enough information to stop them in their tracks—or enough information to at least understand the dynamics of what is happening.

How You Can Help Your Students

If a difficult interaction does emerge in your classroom, there are several things you can do to help de-escalate it at the point of its emergence. The following suggestions will not eliminate all conflict, but they can be helpful when conflict arises:

- Remain calm and try to allow the student(s) to manage it initially.
- If you have to step in, use paraphrasing to be sure you understand and make explicit each person's issue(s) (e.g., "I want to make sure I understand. Do you mean that . . ." or "what I hear you saying is . . .").
- When possible, do not address the issues publicly. Conflicts are full of emotion, and identity and relationship concerns increase the likelihood of defensiveness. A private interaction allows you to explore the issues that may be affecting the student externally.
- If a difficult interaction escalates to the point of being unproductive, ask all involved to take a break.
- If a difficult interaction becomes too one-sided (e.g., one critic yelling at a student for a presentation; one member of a team bullying the team, etc.), initiate a back-up plan to prevent further escalation.
- Create opportunities for discussion of the difficult interaction after the fact.

There are several approaches you can take that might help your students prepare for potential conflict and deal with it should it occur. Although we cannot provide advice that will resolve all conflicts and smooth all difficult interactions, we are hopeful that these suggestions will be useful in not allowing difficult interactions to escalate beyond where they originate. We first provide four suggestions that you can use when talking with your students about dealing with conflict interactions. We suggest you provide your students with information about these issues and use this section to guide the way in which you talk with students about their difficult interactions. The four suggestions we have for preparing and dealing with difficult interactions include 1) helping students anticipate goals, 2) teaching collaborative communication tactics, 3) providing opportunities for practice, 4) creating a climate where feedback is normal, and 5) allowing for reflection and metacommunication. In this section, we provide general information about these suggestions and then provide several examples of how you could implement them with your class. Table 9.2 provides a summary of those strategies.

Table 9.2. Strategies for Setting Up a Classroom to Prevent Conflict

Focus	Implementation
Help students anticipate goals; provide opportunities to define different goals that could emerge in difficult interactions	Do "goal analysis" sheets for ongoing projects Provide cases of potential difficult interactions for analysis Have students analyze their audience's goals
Teach collaborative tactics to help students understand different ways of using language to reduce escalating conflicts	Practice analytical and conciliatory remarks Do "say it differently" exercises where students have to rephrase escalatory statements
Provide opportunities for practice and help them understand their own conflict styles	Simulate difficult audience questions Do role plays of most common team problems Have students respond impromptu to a hostile audience member Use a conflict styles inventory
Create a climate where feedback is normal and students both give and receive productive feedback	Rotate feedback responsibility Provide examples of productive feedback Do "daily feedback" sessions in which students give one substantial comment about a peer's work
Allow for reflection and meta-communication	One-minute papers on communication difficulties Create ground rules Process check-in days

Help Students Anticipate and Define Goals

Very few difficult interactions come truly out of the blue. More often, one or more of the participants have a sense that something challenging might occur—either because of past experience with the other participants, or because of an interaction that had some minor tension. When you assign oral communication activities in the classroom, it is likely that you can anticipate (as can your students) potential difficult interactions. Perhaps you know one of the critics for the final oral presentation will be particularly harsh. Or you have a sense that there are strong personalities in the classroom that could cause team problems. One way to mitigate these potential problems is to help your students anticipate the goals of all participants in the oral communication assignment.

Let's take an example of an oral communication assignment that is typical in engineering and some of the sciences: the design presentation. Typically, a design presentation is a high stakes, end-of-semester presentation in which there are sometimes external critics (e.g., industry sponsors). In this assignment, students are called upon to showcase and rationalize their design choices. Often, students dread the question-and-answer period after the presentation because it can lead to difficult interactions with faculty, industry critics, and other guests. One way students can mitigate this fear is to anticipate the goals of the critics in the audience, for example:

- Topic Goals: The topic goal of the critic is to understand the reasoning behind design decisions and to be persuaded, with evidence, that those decisions were sound.
- Relationship Goals: The relationship goal of the critic is to simulate challenging questions that often emerge in a designer-customer relationship.
- Identity Goals: The identity goal of the critic is to look credible in front of other colleagues by asking difficult and challenging questions.
- Process Goals: The process goal of the critic is to provide students with pointed questions in order to facilitate student growth and development as a pre-professional.

Anticipating these goals might help students better identify what might actually happen in a difficult question-answer period. Therefore, when a critic says something like: "We never did it that way in our company" or "What made you choose that metal over the less expensive one?" the students can recognize that the first question could be an attempt to look credible in front of the audience (identity goal) and the second question could be the kind of question a typical customer might ask (relationship goal) or the kind of question important to answer in order to justify the design (topic goal). In this way, students might be less likely to take questions personally if they understand the goals that could be motivating the question.

Teach Collaborative Communication Tactics

One of the most important skills in learning to deal with conflict collaboratively—whether on a team, in presentation format, or in a one-on-one interaction—is to listen and clarify. It is possible and likely that in a difficult interaction, participants will jump to conclusions about why people do or say particular things, presuming personality issues without understanding the full situation. These kinds of biases could color the way in which participants hear each other. Participants then spend a significant amount of time formulating a response to what they perceive to be a difficult or challenging interaction, missing the point of what others are saying and its meaning. This lack of hearing leads to misinterpretation, and could potentially lead to an escalatory spiral. Helping your students understand ways to use collaborative, active listening tactics will benefit them.

Active listening is just that—it is not a passive behavior and it does not mean simply hearing the words that someone says. It requires positioning the body and mind in a way that one can hear the complete message: what is said, what is not said, and the goals and feelings that lie beneath the words, tone and demeanor. Some behaviors associated with active listening include

- Making eye contact
- Posturing your body towards the person speaking to you
- Using nonverbal signals to indicate understanding
- Using open probes
- Asking clarifying questions
- Paraphrasing the person's ideas
- Deferring judgment
- Being aware of feelings behind statement

Active listening, therefore, is a process that requires energy and focus. Your mind cannot wander toward things you have to do; you cannot try to formulate your response as you listen. Your behavior indicates your willingness and desire to hear more and to understand beyond what you hear.

Let's take an example of a team-based project in which students are developing a product (e.g., in the sciences it could be a software program, in design it could be a webpage, etc.) and are on a time-bound schedule for finishing work. It is likely the team will have to make certain decisions about particular aspects of this product. Perhaps one member continues to assert his or her opinion forcefully, insisting the choice he or she wants is the "only way we can do it." Other members of the team can listen actively, first and foremost, by not getting defensive and by being aware that they might be making assumptions without understanding the reasons he or she might feel the need to assert forcefully. Team members could engage in active listening by using statements such as:

- "It seems like you are very passionate about this choice. Can you explain further what brought you to it so I can better understand?"
- "What do you mean when you say that other choices won't work? Can you explain further?"

- "So, if I understand you, you believe your choice is in alignment with what the teacher wants in this project."
- "I could be wrong, but you seem frustrated that we haven't jumped on board with your choice. Is this how you are feeling?"

Statements such as these indicate a willingness and desire to hear more—without bias or judgment. Clearly, these are collaborative kinds of statements: those that facilitate working with others to find solutions.

Many students do not have a sense of how to respond to conflict constructively or collaboratively. It is useful to show models of effective conflict de-escalation. You could draw on your own disciplinary models, broader models (e.g., from a movie), or your own examples from workplace or academic experience. Table 9.3 provides additional examples of constructive communication responses in a conflict situation.

Table 9.3. Statements for Collaborative Conflict Resolution

Type of Statement	Example Language
Supportive: Refer to acceptance, understanding, positive regard for the partner, support, shared interests or goals	"I can see why you would be upset." "Even though we disagree on how to do it, at least we both want to do it."
Concessions: Express a willingness to change, show flexibility, or consider mutually acceptable solutions to conflicts	"I think I could work on that more." "I'm willing to do my part if you're willing to do yours."
Responsibility: Acceptance of responsibility for self or both parties	"I think we've both contributed to the problem." "Yes, I was out of line and I'm sorry."
Description: Non-evaluative statements concerning observable events related to the conflict	"I criticized you yesterday because I didn't understand your thinking on the issue."
Disclosures: Non-evaluative; non-observable aspects such as thoughts, feelings, intentions, motivation, past history	"I swear I never thought this team would go through so much at this early stage in the project."
Qualification: Explicitly qualify the nature and extent of the conflict	"What did you mean when you said you weren't happy with the PowerPoint? I did that work—did it not meet the assignment requirements?"
Soliciting criticism: Non-hostile inquiries about events related to the conflict	"How do you feel about the fact that I haven't finished that section of the paper yet?"

Provide Opportunities for Practice

The first step towards changing conflict interactions is to be aware of them. Provide students with an opportunity to understand their own conflict styles. Even simply giving students a conflict styles inventory might help them become more self-aware of their conflict tendencies, which will allow them the opportunity to change, if necessary. See Figure 8.1 for one example of an inventory. After students are aware of their own styles, they are more likely to be able to change them.

Although you can never actually replicate the feelings and emotions that arise during a difficult interaction, it is helpful to provide students with the opportunity to practice what they would do if such an interaction were to occur. For example, you could ask students to be critics for each other on a draft presentation. Asking students to be their own critic allows them to prepare for potential difficult interactions and anticipate them. Have them role-play situations where one student is a particularly picky or even a hostile critic, and the other student must respond.

Create a Climate Where Feedback Is Normal

Difficult interactions often emerge because students do not know how to give and receive feedback in a constructive way. Therefore, create a classroom climate where feedback is regularized. If feedback becomes a natural aspect of classroom interaction and assessment, students become accustomed to hearing feedback and more in tune with hearing difficult feedback. Use feedback in a formative way before attaching a grade or summative evaluation. Put feedback in context: It is a way to help each other receive a higher evaluation in the long run.

Typically, students do not know how to give effective feedback. Therefore, it is helpful for them to hear from you what you consider to be effective feedback. You could provide them with examples of feedback from industry contexts or from other classroom contexts you find useful or not as useful. Or you could ask them to generate a list of criteria for what they find helpful in feedback, then bringing it to the larger group for discussion. Regardless of what you do, the more you talk about feedback, the more likely your students are to be willing to provide it and hear it without difficulty.

Allow for Reflection and Metacommunication

Many difficult interactions could be prevented if students had the opportunity to express frustrations before they built up over time. Therefore, create opportunities to "check in" with students on oral communication assignments that could lead to difficult interactions. This could look like one-minute papers (e.g., students write for one minute about a concern they have about a particular interaction and turn it in). Or this could be team check-in days where you schedule time for teams to discuss (briefly) their communicative process. Another way to help students deal with difficulties more proactively is to give them opportunities to communicate about how they are going to communicate when tensions emerge. For example, you could create ground rules, along with your class, for teams and classroom interactions that detail processes for managing difficult interactions. You may anticipate some common rules such as:

- Listen actively
- Empathize with others
- Be open to outcomes, not attached to a single idea
- Focus comments on the problem, not on individual people
- No pointed jokes or sarcasm

Having students identify the rules that are important to them helps students feel ownership of the class and may increase buy-in.

You may also find metacommunication particularly helpful in discussions. Perhaps you have assigned students to facilitate discussions about controversial social topics (typically occurring in social science disciplines, but which could also occur in sciences and humanities). It is likely that there will be some difficult interactions involving one or more judgmental, biased, or harsh discussants. The discussion facilitator (and other participants in the discussion) could try to reflect on and metacommunicate about the process by saying things like:

- "We all want to be able to formulate a well-reasoned opinion about this topic, let's remember this as we move forward."
- "I do not want anyone to feel threatened in this discussion—I understand this topic might make us all feel a bit nervous because we aren't sure we want to share our feelings."
- "It must feel really difficult to have to discuss this topic when you've told us that you are struggling with it in your personal life."
- "I am trying to understand your perspective and hear that you have many experiences that have led you to these beliefs."
- "It seems to me that this discussion has moved away from the topic and more towards our own personal experiences."
- "I get a sense that people are feeling a bit hostile and frustrated with the way this discussion is moving."

Statements such as these strive to create connections among participants by talking about the process itself. Those connections could serve as the foundation for de-escalating a difficult interaction.

Conclusion

If you create oral communication assignments, you will likely be faced with students who need to deal with conflict or manage an uncomfortable interaction. In this chapter, we have provided you with some essential information about managing difficult interactions. We hope this chapter has helped you think about ways to set up your classroom to prevent such interactions. Also, we hope that this chapter has given you information so that you feel more equipped to help your students when those interactions emerge.

10 ADDRESSING DIVERSITY

When you consider implementing discussion, speeches, or other oral communication activities, you may be thinking to yourself:

- My students are so different from each other; how will they work together?
- What about international students? If they can't speak English well, how can I grade them on a presentation?
- What happens if a discussion blows up in my face? What if someone says something that offends someone else?
✱• What does diversity have to do with my class? I teach math, engineering, art, etc. . . . .

Understanding more about diversity is an increasingly important part of students' education, not only because of the diversity that they will face in the classroom but also because of the diversity that they will face as they enter professional and civic lives. In this chapter, we will explore ways in which diversity issues emerge when assigning oral communication activities in your classroom. First, we discuss some foundational definitions and key research findings that could help you as you think about these issues. We then offer steps that you can take in your teaching to help your students understand and embrace diversity.

WHAT YOU NEED TO KNOW ABOUT DIVERSITY

When we talk about diversity here, we are essentially talking about difference. Difference, though, can mean a multiplicity of things. Difference may be about being raised in a different country or even a different region of the United States. Difference may be related to ethnicity, religion, gender, disability, sexual orientation, religion, age, or economic status. Students who are perceived as "different" due to any of these reasons (or several of these reasons), must confront stereotypes on a daily basis. Some are better prepared to handle the ways in which these stereotypes manifest themselves than others. Many students have never interacted with an individual with a visible disability, for example, or have actively avoided interaction with individuals they consider to be "different" in terms of socio-economic background. Yet, in a class where students interact with each other, as in a class where oral communication is a central component, they can no longer avoid it—and neither can we as faculty members.

Table 10.1. Key Definitions of Diversity Terms

Term	Definition
Diversity	Differences. Diversity in the classroom may be because of where students are from, the gender make-up of the class, ethnicity, disabilities, or sexual orientation *religion?*
Culture	"A historically transmitted pattern of meanings embodied in symbols, a system of inherited conceptions expressed in symbolic forms by means of which men communicate, perpetuate, and develop their knowledge about and their attitudes toward life" (Geertz, 1973).
Enculturation	Process of learning about the norms and values of a culture by which you are surrounded.
Socialization	Process of learning norms and values through other explicit or implicit instruction. *← inside a culture?*
Individualistic Cultures	Individuals are loosely tied to each other, but the emphasis for responsibility is on oneself and, often, the immediate family
Collectivistic Cultures	People form tight connections within communities and there is more responsibility to the good of the community than to the individual.
Race	A social construct used to identify the self or others and to signify membership in a social grouping (Nance & Foman, 2002).
Gender	Social construction of male and female (Eagly, 1987)

The wealth of research from intercultural communication provides insight into understanding the processes involved when encountering someone who is "different." Culture, for our purposes, is "a historically transmitted pattern of meanings embodied in symbols, a system of inherited conceptions expressed in symbolic forms by means of which men [sic] communicate, perpetuate, and develop their knowledge about and their attitudes toward life" (Geertz, 1973). Enculturation, then, is the process of learning about those patterns of meanings—the norms and values of a culture by which you are surrounded. A person going to a different country, for example, goes through a process of enculturation when she learns the ways in which that culture interacts. Socialization refers to an explicit process of providing experiences that help someone learn the norms and values of a new culture. For example, orientation activities help socialize new majors into a discipline.

Although there are many features of cultures that can contribute to differences, one important factor for our purposes is the continuum between individualistic and collectivistic cultures. Individualistic cultures are cultures where individuals are loosely tied to each other, but the emphasis for responsibility is on oneself and, often, the immediate family. Collectivistic cultures form tighter connections within communities and there is more responsibility towards the good of the community than towards the individual. Countries like the United States and France tend toward individualism, while countries like Argentina, Greece, China, and Portugal tend toward collectivism (Hofstader, 1991; Requejo & Graham, 2008). It is important to remember that while there is a continuum between individualistic and collectivistic cultures and that these distinctions are based on overall trends, there are certainly exceptions within any culture.

The notion of race as a biological construct has largely been discredited (Fox, 2009). Nevertheless, race is a category used within our culture to identify others and to signify membership in a social grouping. It is best thought of as a social construct with social consequences: "As scientists, there is more racially that unites us as human beings than separates us. The real issue is one of political control. The process of racial labeling starts with geography, culture, and family ties, and it runs through economics, and politics to biology, and not the other way around" (Nance & Foman, 2002, p. 36). How we identify with our "race" varies. Racial identity development theory has identified different stages for individuals who identify themselves with different social categories. What seems to be universal is that people vary in terms of their sense of their racial identity, and their acceptance or rejection of the dominant cultural majority's definitions of what is appropriate and right behavior, values, mores, and self-identity. Some individuals attempt to conform to the social, cultural, and institutional standards of the dominant ideological majority (in the US, White defined), while some are acutely aware of the problems created by those standards for their social group, and struggle to

do we mean the dominant culture?

find ways to deal with that awareness (Wijeyesinghe & Jackson, 2001; Nance & Foeman, 2002; Martinez, 2002; Fujimoto, 2002).

Finally, the definition of *gender* is vital. When we talk about gender, we are not talking about the biological differences between males and females. Instead, we are talking about the social roles of men and women that carry with them particular expectations (e.g., Eagly, 1987). Some of these expectations are related to styles of communication and interaction. While these expectations have changed and continue to change, stereotypes continue to exist related to gendered behavior (e.g., Jones & Dindia, 2004).

Regardless of your institution, you will have diversity within your class. Some aspects will be obvious while others will be subtle. It is likely that you can anticipate differences based on culture, gender, and race. Additionally, given this, it is possible that any form of diversity could bring to the fore issues of safety and cultural understanding (or misunderstanding). Finally, given that we are teaching students within a particular culture, we are, in fact, helping to socialize students into particular norms and roles (of our discipline, of the academy, and of our broader culture). This process of socialization can be threatening to students who may feel like their very identity is under attack. It is important that we recognize the challenges and opportunities we could create for our students, even when we do not realize we are doing so.

Where Differences Are Common

Differences can come from multiple sources, but we have chosen to focus on three that are likely to be the most apparent in your classes—culture, race, and gender. In this section, we will discuss these three kinds of differences so that you can get a better sense of how they might emerge in your classrooms.

Culture

During the 2008–2009 school year, over 671,000 students in the United States were international students, representing 3.7 percent of the student population (IIE Network, 2010). Students who are first-generation Americans from immigrant families are increasingly becoming part of the higher-education demographic. The challenges and opportunities for helping all students understand more about multicultural interactions abound. Although discussing ethnicity and culture conjures many complex ideas, we focus here on a subset of the aspects of culture that are particularly relevant in classroom interaction (see Calloway-Thomas, Cooper & Blake, 1999;

Hall, E.T., & Hall, M.R. 2002; Hofstede, 2002; Requejo & Graham, 2008; Ting-Toomey & Oetzel, 2001).

One particularly salient cultural construct that could influence your classroom is individualism-collectivism. As we defined earlier in the chapter, the dominant cultures of Northern Europe and North America are individualistic. Individualistic cultures emphasize the individual over the group. Individual rights are highly valued, obligations to the group being secondary. Individualistic cultures also tend to expect individuals to be treated equally (small power-distance) based on the place one has earned in the hierarchy (anyone can advance, earn a lot of money, gain status in society, etc., if they work hard enough). Collectivistic cultures, common in Asia, Africa, the Middle East, Central America, South America, and the Pacific Islands, emphasize the importance of the group (Hofstede, 2002; Requejo & Graham, 2008). The needs of the group take precedence over the needs of the individual. It is important to maintain relational harmony within the group. The differences between collectivism and individualism have several implications on using communication in the classroom. Students with an individualistic orientation will likely

- Express strong individual opinions
- Take a more competitive approach to interactions
- Expect that everyone will be treated equally based on the place earned in the hierarchy

On the other hand, students with a collectivistic orientation will likely:

- View the success of an individual as deviant until that success is credited to the entire group
- Show concern for their own face as well as the face of others
- Make points indirectly to allow agreement without backing down from a previous position; this approach also allows disagreement without strong threats to face (Palmerton & Bushyhead, 1994; Jordan, Au, & Joesting, 1983; Philips, 1983 ;Ting-Toomey & Oetzel, 2001).

Additionally, faculty and student orientations may come into conflict. For example, faculty members socialized in collectivistic cultures sometimes have a difficult time with individualistic US students because of the different interpretations: questions about content or structure may be perceived as challenges to authority, when for the student they are simply questions.

Awareness of these elements can be particularly important during class discussion or during interaction in groups for group projects or labs. The frustration that students feel when encountering approaches to communication that vary from their own can result in significant conflict. Helping students understand more about cultural variables—even the fact that cultural variables exist—can help reduce tensions significantly.

Another area in which ethnicity and culture might emerge as important in your classroom communication activities is with regard to emergent conflict. Based on the work of Blake and Mouton (1964), scholars recognize five predominant conflict styles in Western culture: avoidance, accommodating, compromising, competing, and collaborating. Typically, the collaborative style is seen as the most productive, with concern for others' and one's own interests being taken into account. Competitive styles are venerated by those concerned with obtaining a positive result for oneself, with little concern for the impact on the other. Ting-Toomey and Oetzel (2001) point out that cultures concerned about face (collectivist cultures) are likely to approach conflict in quite a different way, with avoiding and accommodating being of high value when one's concern is primarily for saving the other's face and concern for one's own face can be placed as a lower priority. Both of these approaches are likely to be expressed in highly indirect ways and would be expected in many cultures, especially from those in lower-status positions. Competitive approaches are reserved for those times when one's own face is of high priority but concern for another's face is low. Collaborative approaches are likely to be handled by third parties who can manage the face issues of both parties when face is of concern to both parties.

When considering classroom dynamics, where discussion of difficult issues may be taking place, differing communication styles, especially when it comes to conflict, may result in serious misunderstandings. An individual interpreting competitive styles as selfish may be traumatized by another individual with a more aggressive, direct manner. An individual interpreting indirectness as manipulative or sneaky, may become even more aggressive in attempts to "get you to say what you really mean," resulting in more withdrawal. The cycle can escalate fairly quickly. While Ting-Toomey and Oetzel focus on differences across international boundaries, similar style differences occur regionally as well. One of us has seen these kinds of dynamics develop in classrooms with students from New York (using an aggressive, "in your face" communication style) interacting with students from rural Minnesota (known for "Minnesota Nice"). Raising cultural variables into awareness also helps prepare students for their work once they leave the university. For example, as Requejo and Graham (2008) point out, individuals in the United States are insulated to the extent that we tend to think that everyone approaches the world in the same way we do. When involved in global business negotiations, this perception can put unprepared US negotiators at a significant disadvantage. US business people tend to value the ability to make independent decisions (individualism), believe that informality makes *good example* {

for a better negotiating climate (small-power distance), and get frustrated when the other seems to "beat around the bush" (high context), but these are all characteristics of a different cultural style. A US negotiator may interpret someone who will not make a decision in a negotiation, deferring decision-making to a higher authority (collectivist, high power-distance), as attempting to "pull a fast one" rather than simply deferring to authority. A US company welcoming a foreign competitor may not understand why offense would be taken at informal "friendly" backslapping (large power-distance). Failing to understand and adapt to cultural expectations can result in failed or disadvantaged negotiations (Requejo & Graham, 2008). Students might experience these misinterpretations of expectations in the classroom as well. Helping them look carefully at different cultural patterns illustrates self- and other-awareness. Raising these into the awareness of students is one way of preparing them for the work they will do not only in the classroom, but also once they leave the university.

While it is impossible to list all the different characteristics of communication styles, being aware that there are different approaches to communication, different expectations about how one should communicate, and different interpretations attached to the ways in which people communicate, can help both faculty members and students realize the importance of listening to discover what the other is really saying. In addition, surfacing the dynamics—that is, talking about the fact that there are different styles and helping students discuss their interpretive expectations—helps students gain a better understanding of the differences they are encountering and will encounter in the future.

Race

Dealing with racial and ethnic diversity inevitably raises the question of racism and prejudice. Tatum emphasizes the importance of the distinction between the two, with racism being defined as "a pervasive aspect of US socialization" based on "a system of advantage based on race" and prejudiced as "a preconceived judgment or opinion, often based on limited information" (Tatum, 1992, p. 3). She notes that prejudices occur across all color lines: we all have cultural stereotypes, regardless of our racial or ethnic backgrounds. However, "it is only the attitudes of Whites that routinely carry with them the social power inherent in the systematic cultural reinforcement and institutionalization of those racial prejudices" (p. 3). Prejudices are problematic no matter who holds them, yet what are more problematic are the ways those prejudices emerge in power differentials.

Whites are the problem? →

How we identify with our "race" varies. Some individuals attempt to conform to the social, cultural, and institutional standards of the dominant ideological majority (in the US, White defined), while some are acutely aware of the problems created by those standards for their social group and struggle to find ways to deal with that awareness (Wijeyesinghe & Jackson, 2001; Nance & Foeman, 2002; Martinez, 2002; Fujimoto, 2002). There has been much work done on attempting to identify the stages of racial identity development—that is, how people come to accept or reject their racial identities and the processes they go through to do so (Tatum, 1992, 1994; Wijeyesinghe & Jackson, 2001)—but those developmental stages are not set in stone. In your classrooms, then, you might have some students who are well aware and connected with their racial identity and others who are not. In these cases, students who have not thought about the significance of their racial group or who have internalized negative stereotypes about their own racial group, may find interacting with others who challenge societal assumptions about race extraordinarily difficult. The ensuing angst is not simply related to learning about difference—it challenges the self-concept at its core (Fox, 2009; Tatum, 1992). Students who are experiencing anger often associated with rethinking and reinterpreting experiences in the context of more complex historical racial understandings may have little time for those who have not "seen the light." In fact, Tatum (1992) identifies three sources of resistance to talking and learning about race and racism that are useful for this discussion. First, especially in mixed race groups, discussing race is taboo. Second, the United States is seen by many students of all races as a "just" society and the injustices associated with race do not square with this view. Third, it is easier to see racism and prejudice by others, not as something practiced by oneself. Even in classes where discussing race and racism is not the central focus of the class, these forms of resistance will potentially influence attempts to address dynamics of interaction that may be perceived as related to race. Anger may in turn push some students away and contribute to their decision to withdraw from active participation in the course. Despite these potential responses, it is worthwhile to acknowledge, be aware, and sometimes openly discuss these issues in your classroom. While it is beyond the scope of this book to detail the dynamics at work relative to racial concerns in the classroom, we highly recommend the work of Beverly Daniel Tatum (1992, 1994), Helen Fox (2009), and Charmaine Wijeyesinghe and Bailey Jackson III (2001) to gain further insight into classroom dynamics related to race, prejudice, and racial identity development.

Gender

Research studies on gender and language have identified several characteristics of language use that are gender-linked (see Chapter 7 for a discussion
of the influence of gender in class discussion). Many of these findings are
controversial (see Canary & Dindia, 1998; 2006). Many of these characteristics are related to power and status, regardless of gender. Historically, gender
differences in language use were interpreted as being primarily about power,
with the language associated with women contributing to and reaffirming
a power differential between men and women (Lakoff, 1975; Sattel, 1983).
Analyses of power, gender, and language affirm the complexities in understanding the relationships between gender, language, and power (Spender,
1984). For example, some work has highlighted the importance of language
patterns associated with women in establishing and maintaining relationships. Other research has shown that women attend to conversations in ways
that encourage the other to talk more (Tannen 1990; Wood & Inman, 1993).
This talk often involves higher levels of self-disclosure, elaborations from
personal experience, and responsiveness to the other participants in the conversation (Tannen 1990; Wood & Inman, 1993). In addition, women appear
to respond to supportive situations and communications differently than do
men, thinking more deeply about those messages, a difference that holds
across ages, ethnicities, and cultures (Burleson et al., 2011). In sum, women
tend to be associated with a more relational communication style than that
used by men. Of course, there are always exceptions to this research, but we
want you to be aware of the existing research so that you can understand how
it might influence your classroom.

As a learned characteristic, gendered language styles will change with
time, and the more information we have about particular styles, the more
likely it is that stylistic variables will shift. The meaning given to an utterance characterized by a particular style also varies, depending upon the individuals' understandings of the logic embedded in that style. Just as with stylistic variables related to culture, so too with gender communication styles:
what may seem a problematic utterance by speakers of one style, may be seen
as a highly functional stylistic characteristic for speakers socialized to that
style. Just as with culture, it is essential to remember it is not appropriate to
evaluate one style as "good" and the other "bad." Both are functional. The
patterns that signal inclusivity (often associated with women) invite participation by others. Yet to some, this style seems to signal lack of confidence
and indecisiveness. The patterns typically associated with men function to
signal assuredness and certainty, as they are more commanding and direct
communication styles. Yet to some, this style can seem to indicate a lack of

caring, arrogance, and selfishness. Even more complicating, because of expectations related to gender, is the fact that the same communication by a man or a woman may be perceived differently—hence the problem cited by many women that when they signal assuredness and certainty they are seen negatively. On the other hand, a man signaling inclusivity may be seen as wishy-washy. Table 10.2 provides additional insights into perceived differences between men and women.

Table 10.2. Common Language and Perception Differences between Men and Women

Men are more likely to . . .	Women are more likely to . . .
Use declarative statements to get straight to the point	Use tag questions at the end of declarative sentences (don't they?) and use a questioning tone of voice.
Use "I think" as a modifier.	Use qualifiers, modifiers, hedges, mitigators (kind of, I guess), and fillers (um, ah, ok)
Use casual grammar and imprecise pronunciation (e.g., thinkin' instead of thinking)	Use proper grammar
Avoid self-disclosure	Be self-disclosive
Emphasize empirical support	Emphasize personal experience as support
Be direct: phrase requests, suggestions or commands as directives	Be indirect: phrase requests, suggestions, or commands as questions or observations
Be called on in class; be allowed more time to respond	Be viewed negatively when interrupting; be more likely to be interrupted
Be judged higher in dynamism, strength, and aggression in public speaking	Be judged higher in intellectual status and aesthetic quality in public speaking
Receive higher ratings in professional evaluations (e.g., student evaluations, physician satisfaction)	Receive lower professional evaluations (e.g., student evaluations, physician satisfaction)
Be seen positively when forceful	Be seen negatively when forceful (as abrasive) when in an out-of-role occupation

Categorizations of language use by gender are not absolute: there are differences within groups as well as between groups. As such, there may be greater differences between certain men or certain women than between men and women. In addition, cultural practices shift over time, and gender role differentiation and changes over the last half-century have had an impact on these language patterns. Despite these general cautions, findings about language style have been consistent enough to assert that certain language patterns tend to be expected of men in our culture, while other patterns are more likely to be expected of women. In your classroom, you may find that explicitly discussing the experiences that your students have with different kinds of communication styles can raise some of these issues into awareness.

ISSUES OF SAFETY AND UNDERSTANDING

Concerns about safety and vulnerability run through the literature on diversity in the classroom. For example, sometimes White students often fear being labeled as a bigot and offending students of color (Bonilla & Palmerton, 2000). They sometimes express concerns about not knowing how to interact with students of other races or ethnicities, given a lack of exposure and knowledge about the difference in question (Bonilla & Palmerton, 2000; Fox, 2009). Other times, students of color bring with them their experiences with stereotypical assumptions, and are often tired of having to explain their experiences to White students. They are tired of making themselves vulnerable. They are tired of having to respond to the discomfort of White students and faculty, often expressed subtly and nonverbally (Bonilla & Palmerton, 2000). While some students have become adept at ignoring the responses of others, or at hiding their reactions, it is more difficult to hide when engaging in intense discussion or when engaged in group work. When we ask students to engage in oral discussion and participation, we are asking them to make themselves vulnerable yet again. Faculty feel vulnerable too, wanting to do the right thing and often not knowing what that "right thing" is. If a student isn't talking up in class, should I call that student into my office to encourage that individual to participate? If someone makes a comment that could be construed as racist, should I ignore it or call it out? Should I do so in public, or privately? Students want faculty to be role models of how to address issues of race and ethnicity, disability and difference, and are disappointed when faculty do not live up to their expectations (Bonilla & Palmerton , 2000; Fox, 2009).

Instructors often do not feel capable of addressing issues related to diversity when they arise. There is a tendency to ignore what is happening and hope things will work themselves out. If difficulties are egregious (and evident) enough, an instructor may ask to speak with a student in private. If the concern is for a student who may not be participating in class, or who may have been offended by something that happened in class, asking the student to come to a faculty member's office may have results contrary to the instructor's intent. If the student is from a collectivistic culture with a strong emphasis on face, that student may feel shamed by such a request and drop the course, for example. The threat to face that such a request holds is simply too much to handle. If the instructor requests to meet with the offender, even if there is behavior change, the rest of the class does not benefit from the explication of the issues. Students turn to faculty members to help them learn how to respond to difficult interactions.

- did this tell you what to do?

Students come to our classes with very different backgrounds, needs, and levels of understanding. We know this when preparing to work with students relative to the content of our courses. The same is true for working with students relative to their experiences with diversity. Some students have had little to no exposure to those not of the same race, religion, or social class. Others have had multiple experiences. Some students have worked through issues related to racial, gender, and ethnic differences, while others are in deep denial that there are any such issues to work through. Faculty members have different levels of comfort with teaching styles preferred by some students, and students have different levels of comfort with teaching styles preferred by faculty members. There will be collisions.

Socializing Students

Finally, we know that by the nature of our communication instruction, we are, in fact, helping to socialize students into particular cultural norms— those of our disciplines, of the academy, and of our broader cultures. Just as it is important to prepare students for careers in a global workplace, it is also important to recognize that when teaching oral communication skills, we are engaged in socializing students to a particular style of talk. In doing so, we are privileging that style of talk, as well as certain ways of thinking. Students already socialized to such a culture are not as likely to be aware of this fact. In fact, they are likely to consider communication styles that do not conform to the dominant standard as inferior, bad, lazy, or not "right." It is therefore beneficial to think about the oral communication skills that we are teaching as providing students with access to the "codes of power" within our society (Delpit, 1988). At the same time, the codes that we teach are not the only functional communication styles, nor are they the most functional in every circumstance or in every culture. Even in the world of academics, we can see these differences as we move from discipline to discipline. The addition of diversity results in even more complexity.

Students socialized in non-dominant US culture (that is, not White, Western, or Eurocentric culture) are likely to be socialized to communicate in ways that do not conform to the standard power structure of our society. They, in turn, find it unsettling to try to conform to our preferred academic communication styles. Some students feel their very essence is under attack and that if they conform they will lose their own identity. One of us (the authors) has worked closely with Ojibwe students who struggled with the expectation that arguments follow a linear structure. The problem for them was that much of the necessary context was lost with the linear structure, so argumentation in the Western linear style did not make sense. Within their cultural context, such an approach to argument was certainly not likely to be effective. Furthermore, the protections for face embedded in highly contextual indirect argument are limited in linear forms, increasing vulnerability and the potential for offense exponentially. The demand for a clear thesis, for example, may be antithetical to a concern for showing respect to the other and for preserving face (Palmerton & Bushyhead, 1994). Potential solutions may never be stated explicitly, and evidence may be embedded in contextual references known to the individuals participating in the argument. For those in lower power positions in a social hierarchy (women and minorities, historically), face preservation can mean the difference between having influence or being ignored. For students with these concerns, which they are likely to not even realize consciously, resistance to our preferred academic forms is embedded in the knowledge that what we are asking them to do is inadequate for what they want to express—our style simply will not do the job. Others find our requirements at odds with cultural values and identity.

Further examples illustrate how our socialization of students into the academy could come into conflict with students' backgrounds. For example, Carbaugh told the story of a young woman student who simply could not do a public speaking assignment. To do so would have placed her in the position of the traditional elder male in the Blackfoot community. "In effect, the course was addressing her as one who must perform in a social position that she respectfully reserved for 'elders,' especially 'elder males.'" (Carbaugh, 2002, p. 144). This tension is also reflected in stylistic differences encountered between African-American students and students from other cultural backgrounds: "Some African-American students feel that a heated exchange shows that students 'care about the issues,' while silence or polite generalizations reveal their lack of investment . . . [but] international students from Africa may have more in common with some Asian students who feel that too much clash of opinion is divisive and that respectful listening is preferable" (Fox, 2009, p. 77).

Clearly, there are students who have difficulties adapting to the communication styles and codes within our academic community. These students might be in your classroom and might illustrate such difficulties. On the other hand, those students who learn the multiplicity of styles and develop flexibility in adapting to different cultural styles will be more likely to have the skills necessary to succeed in the global workplace. Often the very students who have the most difficulty adjusting to a classroom that is different than their background develop the abilities to recognize that there is need for adaptation and to work to determine how to effectively conform to the communication demands of the situation. Increasingly, students not so prepared will be at a disadvantage. Ironically, those students who may excel in a traditional academic environment may see no need to learn to adapt and will ultimately be disadvantaged in the workplace.

Students who have been socialized in the styles of the dominant US culture present other difficulties. These students may be unprepared to listen to instructors with an accent or who have "different" classroom styles (Rubin, 2002). Individuals doing group work who are unprepared to consider diverse communication approaches may reject inputs from a group member based on that member's style. Regardless of background, students often fall into the belief that everyone will interpret behaviors and communication in the same way. Different interpretations, arising from different socializations, are often also associated with differences in race, gender, and ethnicity. The confusion surrounding differing communication styles may therefore be interpreted as racism, sexism, or ethnocentrism.

Dealing with diversity means learning to identify the cultural rules in a given setting and coming to realize that not all people interpret communication behaviors in the same way. The interpretations we make of others' communication are bound up in our own experiences, expectations, and socialization. Students bring with them many experiences related to responses they have encountered based upon others' perceptions of their race, ethnicity, gender, disability, and any other category that may inspire expectations about behavior. These experiences contribute to additional expectations about how others will respond. When a response is puzzling or offensive people seek explanations and turn to those explanations that make the most sense. All of us—students as well as faculty members—are influenced by our own expectations and biases that influence the interpretations we make of others' behaviors and communications. In the classroom, these expectations influence the classroom dynamic.

we are assuming it is cultural misunderstanding when it could just be a failure in the hearts of the individuals.

true?

Every communication is a transaction between the individuals communicating, with each communication influencing and being influenced by every other communication. As Bahktin notes, "Any utterance is a link in a very complexly organized chain of other utterances" (Bahktin, 1952/1986, p. 69). How a faculty member and how students respond to each other helps shape the character of the classroom. Based on this background, we have several suggestions for what you can do in the classroom to help deal with diversity issues.

How You Can Help Your Students

Whether addressing diversity specifically as part of course content or addressing it because it has become an issue in the class, there are several pieces of advice that may be helpful. The following suggestions are based upon recommendations from Helen Fox (2009), Beverly Daniel Tatum (1992) and Bonilla and Palmerton (2000).

First, learn how to deal effectively with racist, sexist, and ethnocentric behaviors in the classroom. Look for faculty development opportunities. Ask your institution to provide faculty development to help faculty members learn how to deal with diversity in the classroom. There are no magic answers and no great phrases that will work in every instance. The more you learn, the better prepared you are to deal with the problems that arise. You are the role model; students look to you for insight into how to deal with difficult behaviors. Table 10.3 presents several steps you can take to deal with these behaviors. One way to proactively deal with diversity is to be clear that intolerance will not be accepted. Language you could use on the first day or on a syllabus includes

- "We will be discussing concepts and issues that are difficult, and that may make you angry, upset, sad, or humble. Realize that we are all here to learn, and learning cannot happen if we are not willing to take the risks to make mistakes. None of us can grow if we expect that all of us should have it all figured out already."
- "We need to establish some ground rules for our discussions. These are mine: 'Listen, don't judge. Focus on understanding. Don't use sarcasm. Don't make jokes at your own or anyone else's expense . . . .'"
- "This is a place of learning. That means we all need to feel safe enough to learn. Bullying, putting others down, side remarks and snickering, and similar behaviors will not be tolerated in this class. If you are disruptive, or if you engage in behavior that is harmful to the class, I will ask you to leave."

Table 10.3. Ways to Deal with Racist, Sexist, and Ethnocentric Behaviors in the Classroom

Action	Examples
Explore difference.	Do not be afraid of opening up discussion about difference. Assume that everyone wants to learn and understand about others.
Don't be afraid to admit your limitations.	While you are a faculty member, you are also an individual who has to deal with the same issues. Telling your students "I am still learning, and I know I will mess up too" will help reinforce that you are all in this together.
Gatekeep.	Make sure everyone has a chance to participate in discussion. Be watchful for those who may feel silenced (because of their gender or race or background or personal style) and invite them into the discussion. "Ka, you haven't said anything for a long time. I'm wondering what your perspective on this is."
Ask students to speak from their own experience.	Encourage students to draw on their own experience rather than make generalizations based on observations or stories told by others. "You are talking about what others have told you they saw—what about you? What have you experienced?"
Provide opportunities for greater exposure to different racial and ethnic groups.	Consider developing assignments that will require students to interact with individuals different from themselves. For example, students might complete an oral history assignment where they must interview someone from their own ethnic background and someone from a different ethnic background, and report their findings to the class.

Next, provide and maintain a safe environment for all. As noted above, a proactive approach sets the stage for maintaining a safe environment. Setting ground rules for discussion is a good place to start. Tatum suggests establishing an ethic of confidentiality. Students need to know that their confidentiality will be maintained when discussions get intense and difficult. She also discourages the use of "zaps," which can be defined as overt or covert put-downs that may be used jokingly. When a student oversteps the line, the instructor might say something like, "Hey, we agreed, no zaps!" If a student uses inappropriate language, call out the student or refer to the common ground rule. Language that might help you create a safe environment includes

- "That language is not acceptable in this classroom. There has to be a better way to say what you want to say. I'm finding myself completely distracted from your point because of the language you used!"
- "Sounds like you really disagree with the point Patrice is making. Take us through your thinking, but let's agree that Patrice has a right to lay out her ideas too."
- "Josh, you are rolling your eyes, which isn't helpful to discussion. I take it you disagree. What are you thinking?"
- "You are making many judgments and generalizations about all Muslim women, but your assumptions don't seem consistent with what I know. Can you do some additional research to see what the Quran says?"
- "You are raising important questions, and many people disagree on these issues: How must you go about finding the answers to these questions?"

Emphasize that all learning involves making mistakes. Students need to know that they can make mistakes without being labeled racist, sexist, ethnocentric, or other "-ist." If everyone knew everything, there would be no need to learn. Tell stories on yourself; it can be very powerful for students to know that you are not perfect, that you have messed up, and that you are still learning.

Finally, model sensitive intercultural interaction. Fox emphasizes the importance of showing personal respect by learning how to pronounce unfamiliar names. The best way to do this is by asking students how to pronounce their names. This step shows respect and interest in the individual student. Many of us have seen the delight in a student's face as we struggle to pronounce something that is very difficult for a native English speaker. The struggle itself begins to establish a degree of empathy and shows students that you also struggle with new experiences. Express interest in each student's home country or neighborhood. Take time for introductions and activities that help students get to know one another. Language that models sensitivity includes

- "How have your religion or beliefs affected your opinion about X topic?" (leaving the prompt open to a variety of belief systems)

- "What are some other possible perspectives on X?" (providing an opportunity for students to respond from personal experience or from other knowledge)
- "How did you learn to handle X when you were growing up?" (providing an opportunity for all students to respond and being open to international, regional, and familial diversity.

CONCLUSION

When it comes to oral communication, the choices, patterns, and struggles are out in the open for all to see. Classes where oral participation is expected and valued bring issues of diversity to the surface. While intimidating, oral communication focused classes may also be a unique place to begin to address these issues. While addressing diversity explicitly is often difficult, helping our students understand more about diversity will not only help them function in the academic setting, but will prepare them for careers in a workplace increasingly characterized by diversity.

SECTION IV: EVALUATING ORAL COMMUNICATION IN YOUR CLASSROOM

E arlier sections in this book introduced you to a framework for implementing oral communication in your classroom and gave you insights into dealing with common concerns. In this section, we will address one of the biggest concerns we hear: How to assess oral communication. We begin by discussing the nature of evaluation and provide steps to follow in creating a system of evaluation in Chapter 11. In Chapter 12 we discuss rubrics and provide suggestions for developing rubrics. Finally, in Chapter 13 we discuss the impact of evaluation in terms of the individual and ways to help students see evaluation as something that will be useful to them, rather than as a threat.

11 Evaluating Oral Communication Assignments and Activities

The most common question we get from faculty who are considering using oral communication in their classroom is about evaluation. In fact, grading oral communication tends to be one of the reasons many teachers decide not to use oral communication activities in the classroom. Concerns we hear include

- I'm not an expert speaker. How can I grade presentations?
- I don't want to spend all my time grading presentations.
- How do I grade teamwork?
- I can't lead a discussion and grade during it. But if I don't grade discussions, will students take it seriously?
- I'm more interested in what students learn during communication activities, not how well they communicate. How do I grade this?
- I can't let students grade each other. They won't provide good feedback, will they?

These concerns are just some of the issues we hear faculty raise about evaluating oral communication activities and assignments. And these concerns are legitimate. The last thing we want is for you to spend time grading oral communication if you do not believe the grading process will help you accomplish your course goals and help students achieve desired outcomes. But we also do not want you to give up on grading oral communication simply because it seems daunting. Depending on your goals, grading oral communication can take some time. We want that time to be well spent. In this chapter we provide you with some of the basics of evaluating oral communication in order to help you make decisions about how you want to spend your evaluative time. We first discuss our philosophy on evaluation—that it should be situated and discipline-specific. We then walk through an overall framework you can use for making decisions about grading oral communication that includes prioritizing your goals, considering particularities involved with grading different types of oral communication activities and assignments, choosing from various overall evaluative frameworks, and choosing different response structures.

SITUATED NATURE OF EVALUATION

Before we discuss the various decision-points you will need to address when grading oral communication, we would like to underscore one of the themes of this book—context. We believe evaluation is a contextual activity and should be done as such. We do not advocate for assessment that uses generic evaluation tools and we do not argue you "borrow" assessment tools from public-speaking courses. Rather, we believe assessment needs to be driven by the distinct nature of your discipline, the types of communication valued in that discipline, and the expectations for performance that hold weight in that disciplines.

Take, for example, the discipline of design as an illustration of the contextual nature of communication (and hence the need for situated evaluation of that communication). In design, students are expected to give "critiques." Critiques (also referred to as "juries" or "reviews") are an integral part of design classes (Anthony, 1991). During critiques, students take a set amount of time (often ranging from 4–30 minutes) to talk about their projects. Then, they participate in a feedback session that includes comments and questions from critics, which include faculty and outside professionals. The interaction described above illustrates the distinct nature of critiques as performative, interactive, emotionally laden, and at times uncomfortable. Most design literature that addresses communication skills in critiques uses what Morton and O'Brien (2005) termed a "public speaking" approach (e.g., a generic approach), when instruction is given at all (Nicol & Pilling, 2000). For example, Anthony advises students to dress appropriately for the occasion, prepare in advance, and emphasize key points—all advice that could be garnered from any public speaking course and that says nothing about communicating like a designer. Yet critics, such as those in the above scenario, are quick to identify design-specific communication successes and failures during critiques and rarely address those generic skills identified in some of the design literature. Literature emerging from the communication in the disciplines (Dannels, 2001) framework, though, suggests there are discipline-specific competencies that are important to explore in design. In a study that explored critics' feedback in order to derive design competencies, researchers found five competencies vital for design students: systematic demonstration of design evolution, comprehensive explanation of visuals, transparent advocacy of design intent, credible staging of presentation, and appropriate interaction management (Dannels, Housley Gaffney, & Norris Martin, 2008).

Additionally, other research emerging from the communication in the disciplines framework suggests that critiques (along with all oral genres) have important relational elements, in addition to those content or performance-focused elements. These relational elements—termed "relational genre knowledge" (Dannels, 2009) include the real and simulated, present and future relational systems that are invoked in the oral genre teaching and learning. In practice, relational genre knowledge calls upon teachers to attend to relational systems that are important to the oral genre event. These relational aspects of oral genre learning, while often lying beneath the surface of the instructional space, can often be a significant factor in the perceived and actual success of the event.

Given the disciplinary nature of design communication competencies, and the complex relational elements present in the critique, the question of assessment looms large. In this setting, how can teachers hold students accountable for being a competent communicator and relational partner in the design critique? Also, can generic assessment tools provide useful data for teachers, students, and scholars when looking to explore the critique as a teaching and learning event? We suggest that they cannot. Rather, we argue that communication competence is contextual and disciplinary and therefore necessitates situated assessment practices that attend to the actual and desired relational systems that are valued within the oral assignment and to the specific design competencies that are warranted in the critique itself. Design is just one discipline—in your discipline there are similar complexities and disciplinary particulars that warrant attention in assessment and evaluation.

STEPS IN EVALUATING ORAL COMMUNICATION

You can mitigate many of the headaches associated with grading by some strategic planning prior to the oral communication activity or assignment. In this section, we discuss five steps for you to consider, provide basic recommendations for each step, and identify questions for you to answer that will help you construct an evaluative plan that will accomplish your goals in a manageable way. Table 11.1 presents an overview of planning questions to start the process.

Table 11.1. Planning Questions: Evaluating Oral Communication

Prioritize goals and outcomes: What are your primary learning outcomes for the assignment? Secondary learning outcomes? Which are most important and which are peripheral?
Translate outcomes into evaluative measures of success: What teachable, measureable, and observable criteria will help you recognize whether students have achieved outcomes? How will you know the outcomes when you see them?
Create rubrics: What kind of rubric will you create for students—categorical? Holistic? Combined?
Account for genre-based considerations: What particular evaluative issues might you need to consider for presentation, team, or discussion-driven genres?
Choose Forms of Response: What medium(s) of response will you use in addition to the rubric? Oral? Technological? What other evaluative forms will you need to create? Who will provide feedback in addition to you? Self-reflection? Peers?
Tone: What feedback structures might help you manage face issues?

Prioritize Goals and Outcomes

In the earlier section of the book we discussed several general objectives that could be driving your decision to incorporate oral communication in the classroom, such as helping your students become more professionally competent, helping them critically think about course material, and helping them learn to be active public citizens. Within those broad objectives, we encouraged you to consider multiple student-learning outcomes for your oral communication assignments that are teachable, observable, and measurable. If you have done that, you have made considerable headway on the first step in evaluating oral communication assignments. Evaluation begins and ends with objectives and outcomes. If your objectives are not focused on particular aspects of an oral communication assignment or activity, do not waste time evaluating that aspect! For example, let's presume your broad goal is to increase the professional competence of students in your software engineering course, and you have written student-learning outcomes that include the following: students should be able to argue, with statistical evidence, how their design benefits a prescribed customer. In order to do this, students might have to master multiple aspects of the oral communication assignment, but they might not need to be able to construct an emotional appeal. Therefore, you should not grade them on their ability to construct an emotional appeal.

Therefore, the first step in evaluation is to go back to your objectives and outcomes and prioritize them for evaluative purposes. In the above example, delivery issues such as eye contact or vocal projection might be of huge importance to you. Therefore, you might have an outcome that reads, "Students should be able to maintain a confident, professional interaction with the customer that is characterized by consistent eye contact, vocal variety, and professional language." If this is important to you, you would prioritize this. If it is not, perhaps you place this outcome beneath the earlier outcome having to do with statistical evidence. We suggest you prioritize your outcomes along three general categories:

- Essential: These are the outcomes of the assignment that sit at the core. If students cannot do this, they have not achieved the overall goal of the oral communication assignment. Of note: these are outcomes you have the most responsibility for providing instruction about as you support students in preparing for this oral communication assignment.
- Important: These outcomes are important to the assignment, but students do not need to fully master them in order to be successful at achieving the core goal of the oral communication assignment.
- Peripheral: These outcomes would be the icing—they are not central to the core elements of the oral communication assignment. If students achieve them it would be nice, but you might not necessarily provide instruction on them nor would the assignment be considered a failure without them.

The key here is that you get to decide which outcomes are more important and which are less important.

On that note, we often get asked—where does performance or delivery or style fit? Shouldn't that always be in the "essential" prioritization? Not necessarily. You might have an oral communication assignment or activity in which you want to focus solely on the ways in which students display critical thinking. In this case, you might not be invested in whether students use filler words or nervous gestures because your focus is on the critical thinking. On the other hand, for high-stakes pre-professional presentations, delivery might be an essential aspect of achieving the goals of the assignments. You get to decide.

As you prioritize your outcomes, you might find a nagging desire to rewrite them. This is completely natural. The instructional design process is iterative—thinking about objectives in terms of evaluation often helps you clarify them further. Creating evaluative frameworks often helps you realize that some objectives are not necessarily manageable. This is absolutely fine and this is why we suggest you begin thinking about and strategically planning for evaluation as you are designing your assignments. As you do this, you will find you have a much better understanding of what lies at the core of what you want to achieve and what lives on the edges. This understanding not only benefits your evaluative process, but also the ways in which you work with your class on the oral communication assignment or activity.

Account for Genre-Specific Considerations

Depending on the kind of oral communication assignment you have decided to use, there are the genre-based considerations you will need to address when thinking about evaluation. First, you will need to think about the relative formality of the genre you are assigning. The level of formality and focus of your evaluative framework is directly tied to your objectives and the kinds of assignments you have designed to meet those goals. Broadly speaking, if your objectives revolve around professional competence and you have designed high-stakes, formal assignments to help students meet those objectives; the evaluation will tend to be more formal and focused on professional competence. If your objectives focus on the learning of course content and your assignments are more activity-driven (instead of high-stakes, semester-long assignments), then you do not need to do formal evaluation of communication competencies, but rather need to find a way to quickly hold students accountable for their learning. More specifically, the level of formality of the evaluation also influences the need for support. More formally evaluated assignments typically need more instructional support than less formally evaluated assignments. For low-stakes group work (for example), you might only incorporate a quick ten-minute module on group norms. For higher-stakes group assignments, you might bring in a number of the suggestions from Chapter 7 on group work.

Below are some characteristics of formal and informal evaluation processes. Know now that we see these as a continuum, rather than a toggle switch, but it is often helpful to define the two ends of the continuum clearly. As we illustrated in Chapter 4, informal assignments do not need extensive evaluation. Rather, the focus is on holding students accountable for their learning. At this stage of evaluation, it is important to revisit the level of formality of your assignment so that you can match the evaluative method to that level.

Also, depending on the nature of the assignment, there are several evaluative considerations that could emerge and that need attention prior to the evaluative period. Each type of oral communication assignment comes with its own particular "sticking points" for evaluation. By sticking points, we mean the points where students are most likely to be anxious or the points where faculty are most likely to experience evaluative angst. We bring these sticking points up now so that they do not surprise you and so that you can make strategic decisions about how you will manage them as you proceed in your evaluation. We organize these sticking points loosely according to the type of oral communication assignment you are doing (presentation-based, team-based, discussion-based, and interpersonal-based assignments). You might find that your goals provide you guidance with these sticking points, but we highlight them because they merit attention. Table 11.2 summarizes these sticking points and our recommendations for managing them.

Presentation-Based Assignments

For presentation assignments, the two key sticking points that often emerge are, 1) distinguishing performance (delivery) from content; and 2) supporting both confidence and competence. First, many faculty like to evaluate the performance of a presentation separate from the content of a presentation. Yet, as you can probably guess, it is often difficult to distinguish the two—as poor delivery at times muddies fairly good content and makes the content seem worse or slick delivery often masks poor content and makes the content seem fairly good. So while it seems natural to separate the two, it is often difficult in practice. When it comes down to it, both the content and the delivery influence the overall effect of the presentation. If delivery is important to you (and is one of your essential goals), our recommendation is that you make that clear. Just be prepared that it is often a challenge to extricate performance (delivery) from content and you might find it difficult to comment on each separately. In order to deal with this, we provide the following recommendations:

- Decide early how important delivery (performance) is to achieving the goals of the assignment.
- Show students sample presentations that illustrate the ways in which content and delivery can influence each other (for the better or for the worse).
- If you want to evaluate delivery as its own measure, also include (in your evaluative framework) a section that articulates the ways in which content and delivery work together in the presentation.

Table 11.2. Genre-Specific Considerations for Evaluation

Considerations	Recommendations
Evaluating delivery and content of presentations	Show students sample speeches; discuss how content and delivery influence each other. Decide weighting of content and delivery in rubric.
Competence and confidence with presentations	Incorporate self-report measures of students' confidence levels. Consider incorporating process into rubric.
Evaluating processes and products of group work	If weighting product heavier than process, build in ways for students to informally account for process. If evaluating both process and product, incorporate distinct evaluative measures in rubric.
Evaluating individual work vs. team work	If you plan to evaluate individual contributions to a team, decide how to track those over time. If primarily evaluating the team product, provide opportunities for students to comment on their own and their teammates' contributions.
Evaluating frequency and quality of participation in discussion	Create discussion ground rules with the students. Discuss examples of productive and unproductive discussion comments. Include a self-evaluation rubric.
Managing roles of evaluator and participant in discussion	As evaluator, remove yourself from facilitating or participating. Ask other students to be discussion evaluators.
Balancing individual and relational lenses in interpersonal communication	Provide separate sections on rubric that address the quality of the student's individual performance and the overall relational interaction. Use the relational interaction feedback to encourage reflection.
Mitigating the observer effect for interpersonal interactions	Create a random schedule of teacher evaluation of interpersonal-based assignments. Rotate peer evaluators.

Second, it is often difficult when evaluating presentation-based assignments to balance support for confidence with support for competence. Often, one of the best things you can do for the novice presenters in your class is to increase their confidence and desire to speak in public. For some, this is a huge success. Yet sometimes, increasing confidence does not equate to increasing competence. For example, a student who suffers from moderate communication apprehension might, as a goal, want to manage that apprehension better. Sometimes doing this means that students will look calmer, use fewer nervous gestures, and not rely on filler words during difficult times. Other times this means that students change their internal state and become calmer and more relaxed, which might not necessarily translate into behavioral changes. Yet, a student who has a better handle on apprehension is one step closer to becoming more competent. The point is that sometimes increasing confidence (or decreasing apprehension) is difficult to measure because it does not translate into behavioral events easily. There are a number of ways to understand how students are building their confidence, but more traditional measures of public-speaking competence might miss important learning processes your students are going through. We recommend that you:

- Discuss confidence and competence as separate, interrelated aspects of presentations
- Incorporate self-report measures of students' confidence levels (e.g., reflection papers, net forum discussion, etc.).
- Decide how to emphasize process (e.g., building confidence) and product (e.g., competence) in rubric.

Dealing with these sticking points ahead of time will not eliminate their presence—the challenges involved in balancing performance and content with confidence and competence are age-old. Considering your own goals and thoughts on these issues will help you work with your students ahead of time, so that you are not left making difficult decisions during the stress of grading.

Team-Based Assignments

When assigning team-based oral communication assignments, there are two primary sticking points that we have seen come up for faculty trying to evaluate those assignments: 1) how to evaluate team process and team product; and 2) evaluating individual performances on a team and overall team performance as a whole. First, you have probably had the experience of being on a team that worked terribly together, without any organizational structure or communicative logic. Yet somehow you managed to produce something that was quite good. Conversely, you have probably worked on a team that was smooth sailing in terms of team process—everyone communicating well with all deadlines being met. Yet despite this, what you produced was not necessarily up to par with expectations. These samples illustrate the differences between team processes and team products. In most situations, a good team process facilitates a good team product. This is why you should spend time helping your students understand what makes a good team process. Yet, there are times when process and product are not necessarily logically connected. In these cases, you need to decide how to weight process and product in your evaluation. Some believe that process is irrelevant and prefer to simply evaluate the product. Others believe that process is entirely relevant and weight it heavily. Our recommendations are as follows:

- Decide early on whether team process counts for anything in your evaluative framework
- If you prefer to weight product heavier than process, build in ways for students to informally journal or log about process (this will provide them with an outlet).
- If you prefer to evaluate both process and product, incorporate distinct evaluative categories on rubric (e.g., weekly team meeting logs for process; rubrics for product) and build in opportunities to discuss how the two influence each other
- Discuss your process/product philosophy with your students.

Second, you will need to decide how to evaluate individual performance in teams and team performance as a whole. If you have ever assigned a team process, you have probably experienced the "one person is doing all the work" phenomenon, as well as the "team slacker" phenomenon. In these cases, it seems unfair that the entire team should receive the same grade when there are members who have not contributed. On the other hand, when students enter the workplace they are often judged on their team performance, regardless of their individual contribution. You need to decide if it is important to you to evaluate both individual participation on a team and team performance as a whole. We suggest first looking at your objectives to help you make this decision. If one of your objectives, for example, for including a team-based oral communication activity is to help students learn to delegate and communicate responsibilities in a team atmosphere, then you will need to find a way to evaluate individual performance. If your objectives focus more on the ways in which a team sells a product to a client, then the focus might be more on the team performance as a whole. Our recommendations for dealing with these issues are as follows:

- Decide where your evaluative emphasis will land—on the individual contributions to a team, on the team as a whole, or on both.
- If you plan to evaluate individual contributions to a team, build in ways for students to track those over time (e.g., self-reflection logs, team meeting notes).

- If you decide to minimize individual contributions in the evaluation, provide opportunities to give feedback on their own and their team-mates' contributions.
- If you are uncomfortable dividing up the evaluative process, use informal feedback discussions to provide students with the opportunity to metacommunicate about individual contributions to team processes.

Again, we emphasize that one of the most important ways of mitigating these team-based assignment sticking points is to discuss your evaluative framework on these issues with your students ahead of time. This way, students have a clear understanding of how their team process and individual performance will be evaluated in the team-based setting.

Discussion-Based Assignments

Discussion-based assignments bring up their own evaluative sticking points, and it is especially important to consider these ahead of the discussion because during a discussion event, it is difficult to be both the teacher (and think about these sticking points) and to be engaged in the discussion. The two sticking points that often emerge in evaluating discussion-based assignments are 1) evaluating frequency of contribution as well as the quality of the contribution and 2) managing roles of evaluator and participator in the discussion setting. First, it is probably not difficult to remember or imagine a classroom discussion in which one person talks a lot but says nothing important. On the other hand, we've all had students who say very little, but when they do talk, they say something quite important. If you simply evaluate contribution frequency, it is likely that you will open the door for students to try to speak without thinking in order to get their time in. Evaluating the quality of a contribution is difficult, as well, because there are so many issues that influence participation (see Chapter 6), including issues of gender and diversity (see Chapter 9). It might be difficult, for example, for particular ethnic groups to challenge you or their classmates, and if "challenging others" is a measure of discussion competence for you, they will suffer. In order to deal with these issues, we recommend the following:

- Create discussion ground rules with the students (see Chapter 6 for a sample of how to do this) and use those ground rules as part of the rubric.
- Articulate (and provide to students) samples of productive and unproductive discussion comments
- Ask students to evaluate their own contribution frequency and quality through self-reflective processes

The second sticking point that often emerges when trying to evaluate discussion-based assignments is managing the multiple roles of "evaluator," "teacher," and either "discussion facilitator" or "discussion participant." If you want to evaluate the discussion itself and be part of the discussion, these two roles are often difficult. As a participant or facilitator, you attend to where the discussion is going, how to link comments from earlier in the discussion to current comments, how to transition to the next discussion topic, etc. As a grader, you attend to who is participating, how well their comments meet your evaluative standards, and other issues that might be influencing students' participation. These are both intellectually difficult processes to manage together. Our recommendations in dealing with this are as follows:

- If you want to evaluate the discussion itself as it is happening, remove yourself from facilitating or participating in it.
- If you choose to facilitate or participate, incorporate indirect evaluative measures of the discussion (e.g., student reflection papers).
- Ask other students to be discussion evaluators (and rotate them) and have them sit outside the discussion and provide evaluative feedback.

One of the key elements to remember in discussion-based activities is that you are probably most concerned with creating a climate for learning. Therefore, evaluation should follow from that. It is unlikely, then, that you are concerned with students' delivery abilities in discussion formats. Rather, as an evaluator, you can consider ways to provide students with feedback on the extent to which their discussion participation reflects good, critical thinking and learning of course content.

Interpersonal-Based Assignments

Interpersonal-based oral communication assignments bring to the fore several evaluative sticking points. Two that we see frequently involve, 1) balancing individual and relational evaluative lenses and 2) mitigating the "observer" effect. First, the interpersonal-based communication assignments you would most likely use work towards helping students understand how to be in a one-on-one relational system (typically mimicking the workplace but not always). Sometimes these assignments are purposefully set up to simulate difficult and challenging relational spaces. At other times, you ask outsiders to interact with students in order to give them practice in these relational interactions. Yet, when evaluating these assignments, it is difficult to separate the evaluation of the individual student from the evaluation of the relational interaction. You might have a critic doing a face-to-face critique of a student's poster, for example, and the critic does not exhibit good communication skills in this process. The student, then, has very little to work with. The student can still respond appropriately, but the relational interaction could be off-track at this point, given the critics' communicative style. Can you hold both relational interactants accountable? This issue becomes less critical when asking students to engage in interpersonal-based assignments with each other, but the question still remains—what is the unit of evaluative analysis (similar to the issue of team vs. individual performance)? Our recommendations are as follows:

- Ask students to self-reflect on both their individual performance and the relational interaction as a whole.
- Provide separate comments on rubric that address the quality of the student's individual performance and the quality of the overall relational interaction
- Use the relational interaction feedback to encourage reflection and future change, not necessarily to provide a grade on the activity or assignment.

Second, interpersonal-based assignments are typically completed in a smaller context than many of the other types of assignments. Yet, if you want to evaluate a one-on-one assignment, your presence creates an "observer" effect that might be difficult for students (of note, your presence will do this in any evaluative setting, it is just extremely obvious when you are the third-wheel grading). Students involved in a mock interview, for example, might feel distracted having you sitting next to them evaluating their interview. This approach is complicated by the sheer difficulty involved in sitting in on "x" number of one-on-one interpersonal-based assignments. Yet if you do not sit in and evaluate, will students take it seriously? Our recommendations for dealing with this sticking point are as follows:

- Create a random schedule of teacher evaluation of interpersonal-based assignments (e.g., you will grade them twice during the semester and they do not know when)
- Rotate peer evaluators to get students' accustomed to being "watched" in interpersonal-based assignments.
- Incorporate self-reflective evaluative measures to avoid the need for you to bear the full burden of evaluation

As with discussion-based assignments, some interpersonal-based assignments are focused more on the learning than on the competence. Yet others are designed to simulate interpersonal communication competencies that are necessary for the workplace. The evaluative framework should clearly reflect whichever of these is relevant to your course and assignment.

TRANSLATE OUTCOMES INTO TEACHABLE, MEASURABLE, AND OBSERVABLE CRITERIA

If you have written student-learning outcomes in a teachable, measureable, and observable manner, it is likely you have accomplished this step. Yet, we find that many faculty have to translate the outcomes they have written into a form that can be used on a rubric. It is important to ask yourself: "How will I know it when I see it?" It is even more important to be specific. Why? Because you might completely understand what an "organized" presentation is, but you probably have a different understanding of organization than does a faculty member in another discipline. Take these three anecdotal accounts of what makes an "organized" presentation:

- "An organized presentation is one that starts with the results of the design and does not waste time going through the design process." (Mechanical Engineering)
- "Critiques are organized if they go through each design decision and provide a rationale for what is chosen and what is not chosen, leading up to the unveiling of their concept." (Architecture)
- "An organized presentation is repetitive—hitting the main points in a number of different ways so that the audience will remember them." (Psychology)

Not only do we, as faculty, have different ways of understanding various criteria, but students also come to interpret our criteria in different ways. Take these anecdotal statements, from students, about their perceptions of what it means to be "professional" in a speech:

- "I think when she says 'professional' she means that I have to dress up in a suit and use PowerPoint." (Political Science)
- "My teacher doesn't want me to use any slang or to mumble. That would not be professional in my speech." (Crop Science)
- "Being professional means that I have to sound like a real engineer instead of a student. So I have to use big, technical words." (Software Engineering)

Given these issues, it is critical that you spend some time articulating what you mean about particular outcomes or criteria. One "test" to help you push your thinking on this is to ask yourself, of each criteria: "How will I know it when I see it?" In the next chapter, we will provide additional information on how to translate your outcomes into teachable, measurable, and observable criteria using descriptive and detailed language.

DESIGN RUBRICS

The third step in evaluating oral communication is to create a rubric and other evaluative forms you will use. In creating a rubric, you will need to decide whether you will use a holistic or categorical framework for evaluating oral communication assignments and activities. Holistic evaluation relies on your overall impressions of an oral communication activity or assignment, while categorical evaluation relies on your desire to provide feedback on distinct categories of performance. Both evaluative frameworks are widely used, and decisions about which to use are typically dependent on your course structures and goals.

Chapter 12 will discuss creating rubrics in detail, but we wanted to give you a preview here so you could begin thinking about which of the available approaches might fit. Holistic rubrics are best used when you want to articulate the overall impressions that make up different levels of competence (e.g., A, B, C, etc.) for the assignment. You can then match your assignment against those descriptions to see where it fits. Holistic evaluative frameworks allow you to render a decision on the oral communication assignment as a whole. Often, holistic frameworks are used with multiple graders (in large classes where there are teaching assistants) because you can work with graders to reach agreement and internalize what makes up an "A" presentation or a "B" discussion participant (i.e., find a "norm") Of note: teachers often think holistically about oral performances (e.g., watching a presentation and being able to say "that was an 'A' presentation," etc.) but many are less comfortable actually grading using a holistic rubric.

The other option is to work from a categorical framework. Categorical rubrics rely on your desire to evaluate and make separate comments on distinct categories of performance in an oral communication assignment. Categorical evaluation usually involves creating a rubric with lists of criteria that are weighted and scaled separately and then providing feedback on each of those criteria. Criteria often include overall structural headings of "introduction," "body," "conclusion;" but also include performative criteria: "evidence," "validity of sources," "professional delivery." Categorical evaluation provides students with information on how they accomplished different parts of the oral communication assignment, often giving them particular areas for improvement. As you will see in Chapter 12, you can choose one or the other of these styles of rubrics, or you can choose to create a combined rubric that brings in both kinds of evaluative frameworks.

CHOOSE RESPONSE STRUCTURES

The final decision point you will need to address in evaluating oral communication assignments and activities is how you will respond to students' work. There are four different items for you to consider in this process: the medium of the response, the source of the response, the timing of the response, and the tone of the response. In this section, we address the first three items (medium, source, and timing). Given the importance of the tone of the response, we devote all of Chapter 12 to this issue.

Medium of Response

We have already alluded to one particular response medium—rubrics. Rubrics are the most common medium to use for responding to students' oral communication assignments and activities. They can be formal (e.g., holistic or categorical) or relatively informal (checklists or exit slips). Although we will discuss the creation of rubrics in more detail in Chapter 12, we have three overall recommendations when using rubrics for oral communication assignments:

- Give the rubric to students ahead of time and encourage them to use it formatively to prepare for their oral communication activity or assignment.
- Practice using the rubric (if possible, practice using it while observing a similar oral communication assignment or activity).
- Supplement the rubric with other forms of response that provide immediate feedback to students on oral performance.

Another medium of response (that will provide immediate feedback) is oral response. Given oral communication activities often generate anxiety, it is extremely helpful to incorporate various other forms of response. You could incorporate some form of oral response immediately after the assignment. This response does not need to be grade based and usually is best given from a general impressions perspective. This kind of response is very good for students to practice giving to each other, as well. Additionally, oral response does not need to take up too much time. Some samples of ways to use oral response are as follows:

- Following each presentation, have one student provide a "pat on the back" and a "recommendation for improvement" to the presenter.
- After a discussion, provide general impressions of what went well in the discussion and what you would like students to concentrate on for the next discussion.

- Following a team meeting, ask one team member to provide a summary of his/her perceptions of the team process and one thing to focus on to improve the process for the next meeting.

Additionally, you might choose to create additional evaluative forms to supplement the rubric. You could, for example, create a peer revision guide that students could use during a practice presentation. Depending on the type of assignment you are using, these additional types of forms might prove extremely helpful. In particular, when your assignment is team-based or discussion-driven, it is often helpful to use self or peer observation forms to guide students towards becoming peer- and self-evaluators. Figures 11.1–11.3 provide samples of forms students can use when self- or peer-evaluating teamwork or discussion activities.

Evaluation of Class Discussion

Circle the description that best indicates your reaction to the discussion and your assessment of your own performance.

1. To what extent did classmates listen to each other?
    Not at all   Somewhat   Very much

2. To what extent did classmates express ideas clearly?
    Not at all   Somewhat   Very much

3. To what extent did classmates respect others' ideas, even when they disagreed?
    Not at all   Somewhat   Very much

4. To what extent did you listen to others?
    Not at all   Somewhat   Very much

5. To what extent did you express clear ideas?
    Not at all   Somewhat   Very much

6. To what extent did you respect others' ideas, even when you disagreed?
    Not at all   Somewhat   Very much

What did you like best about today's discussion?

What could you personally due to improve our next discussion?

Figure 11.1. Form for Students to Evaluate Discussion Performance of Themselves and Their Peers.

Evaluation of Discussion Leader

Name of leader:_____

Name of evaluator:_____

        1 = Unsatisfactory
        2 = Adequate
        3 = Average
        4 = Good
        5 = Excellent

- Organization/Clarity of purpose   1 2 3 4 5

- Comments and questions   1 2 3 4 5

- Adaptability/responsiveness to others   1 2 3 4 5

- Imagination/risk taking   1 2 3 4 5

- Authority/Confidence/commitment   1 2 3 4 5

- Class involvement   1 2 3 4 5

What comments/questions furthered your understanding of
_____?

What did the leader do that made this discussion go well (be specific)?

What could be improved?

Figure 11.2. Evaluation Form for Students to Provide Feedback on a Classmate as Discussion Leader. Used with permission from Diane Clayton, Asian Studies, Hamline University.

Group Member Feedback
Due: Tuesday

Directions: Complete one evaluation for each group member, including yourself. Make additional copies as needed.

Completed by:

Group member:

This group member....

	Strongly disagree	Disagree	Neutral	Agree	Strongly Agree	Not Applicable
Actively participated in our group's activities	Strongly disagree	Disagree	Neutral	Agree	Strongly Agree	Not Applicable
Contributed to a supportive group climate	Strongly disagree	Disagree	Neutral	Agree	Strongly Agree	Not Applicable
Contributed to critical thinking within our group	Strongly disagree	Disagree	Neutral	Agree	Strongly Agree	Not Applicable
Appropriately articulated disagreements	Strongly disagree	Disagree	Neutral	Agree	Strongly Agree	Not Applicable
Met the group's expectations for contributing to the group	Strongly disagree	Disagree	Neutral	Agree	Strongly Agree	Not Applicable

Figure 11.3. Peer Evaluation Form Asking Students to Evaluate Each Group Member's Contributions to a Group Project.

Another increasingly popular medium for responding to students' oral communication activities and assignments involves technology. Technological response may or may not be available to you, but if it is, we encourage you to think strategically about what it will add to the evaluative process. As with any technology, do not incorporate it simply because it is technology—think about your evaluative philosophy and decide if technology could fit as a medium of response. Several technological possibilities are as follows:

- Word "comment" function on any written work that accompanies students' oral communication assignments (e.g., presentation outlines or team meeting agendas)
- Audio responses to any written work that accompanies students' oral communication assignments (e.g., using a program that will record your voice and send the students' an audio file)
- Wiki, Blog, or net forum discussion responses with summary feedback to students' in class performances
- Pod/vidcast responses to videotaped students' performances

Given the growth of new technologies, these response structures are bound to expand exponentially over time. What we would like to stress is to consider them carefully and within the goals of the assignment and your own teaching philosophy.

Source of the Response

You do not have to be the only one providing a response to students' oral communication activities and assignments. In fact, it is often helpful to create a classroom culture that supports frequent feedback from many sources. When considering who should provide response and feedback, first start with your goals and assignment structure. If your assignment depends on "expert" feedback, then you and/or other experts will need to provide that feedback. If you believe students could benefit from getting and giving peer feedback, incorporate that into the evaluative structure. Here are some recommendations we have when considering peer feedback:

- If building in peer feedback to oral presentations, ask peers to provide content feedback while you provide feedback on performance. This will make peers focus on what their colleagues are saying and will make them less likely to tune out and rely on statements such as "you need more eye contact."
- Support and acknowledge good peer feedback (either through participation points or praise).
- Consider whether peer feedback will be incorporated in the grade and if so, weight it only partially.
- If using peer feedback, incorporate multiple opportunities for it in order to get students in the habit of doing it.

- Teach students to give effective feedback—they probably don't know how to.

We highly recommend providing students with opportunities to practice giving feedback. One approach is to begin with a discussion about what makes good feedback, and use the fruits of that discussion as criteria for evaluating the feedback. You could also consider having students practice providing feedback with samples that represent common missteps in providing feedback (e.g., overly nice or overly harsh, too broad). Ask students to rewrite the feedback in a way that would encourage the author/presenter to make changes. Working with the provided feedback statements gives students the opportunity to practice before providing feedback to a classmate. An excellent opportunity for students to provide feedback is to do a gallery walk. Have each student bring a draft of an oral communication assignment (such as a poster draft or a speech outline). Place the drafts around the room by either pinning them to the wall or placing them on desks. Have students walk around the room and for each draft, write one piece of feedback on an index card that is then placed in an envelope next to that draft. At the end, discuss with students the most helpful feedback.

Timing of Response

Another consideration when thinking about responding to oral communication activities and assignments is the timing of the response. There are two broad options for this—grading in real-time and grading after the fact. What you decide to do will depend largely on the kind of oral communication assignment you have and the classroom structure. Grading in real-time essentially means that you are an evaluator during the oral communication performance (regardless of whether it is a presentation, discussion, etc.) and by the end of the performance; you have arrived (more or less) at a grade. You might not have time to fully write a response on a rubric, but your decision-making is nearly complete. Grading after the fact means that you spend your time during the performance taking notes about the performance, but save your decision-making until you have a chance to review the notes. Sometimes, you have the benefit of having an artifact to look at (e.g., an outline, meeting notes, or even a videotaped presentation) as you are making the decision.

We advocate that you work toward grading in real-time, saving your post-grading time for creating a response that attends to face issues (that will be discussed in the next chapter). We advocate for this because it is consistent with the ephemeral nature of oral events—they exist and make impressions in real-time and those impressions are typically the ones that last (rarely do you leave a presentation thinking "I'll wait until I think about it more to see if I like it."). Helping students understand that oral events are typically one-shot opportunities that require attention and care is important. Additionally, evaluating in real-time will hone your evaluative skills and allow you to focus your time on the tone of the response, which is critical in terms of whether it will be successful as feedback intervention. This does not mean that you have to have everything figured out by the end of the oral assignment. What this means is that you take short handwritten notes that will trigger your memory about particular parts of the presentation (for later use in providing feedback) and you register you "in the moment" evaluation (whether holistic or categorical). As you do this more often, you will find less and less of a nagging need to go back and change these evaluations. If you feel uncomfortable doing this at the start, we suggest you begin by taking detailed notes and waiting to render judgment. What you will find is that you will begin to internalize the criteria in habitual ways (if you have created detailed enough criteria) and after some time, you will be able to rely less and less on post-assignment sense-making and more and more on "in-the-moment" evaluation.

CONCLUSION

In this chapter we have outlined steps for you to take when thinking about evaluating oral communication assignments. Given the complicated nature of evaluation, we do believe it is important to spend extra time discussing two of these steps in more details: creating rubrics and managing facework. Chapters 12 and 13 will address these two issues.

12 Using Rubrics

Most instructors have had the experience of a student questioning a grade or demanding an explanation. At times these questions seem out of place, as we often assume students should know what we expect of them in terms of performance on a task (Goodrich Andrade, 2000). Yet, often they do not. Therefore, they come to us anxious and sometimes frustrated, and if you are like us, those are conversations that can be somewhat difficult. Using clear criteria in the form of a rubric can help alleviate some of the stress of these situations. Rubrics provide an opportunity for teachers to make their judgments about students' performances clearly captured and communicated to students (first and foremost) and to other pertinent audiences (e.g., administrators).

Rubrics not only provide a means for making instructors' evaluative judgments clear, they can also help students as they prepare for and complete assignments. According to Moskal (2000), rubrics are beneficial for evaluating the extent to which students meet specified criteria, as well as provide feedback to students on performance. It can be instructive to give rubrics to students before the assignment (don't worry, you aren't going to give it all away). Students should know what they are going to be assessed on and should have the opportunity to use the rubric formatively as they plan for their communication assignment.

For our purposes here, it is helpful to clarify what a rubric is not. A rubric is not a checklist. Checklists allow for the determination of whether a feature is present or absent. For example, a checklist for a presentation outline may require confirmation that a student included a title for the speech. The checklist, however, would not provide any qualitative assessment of that title. Furthermore, a rubric is not a performance list (Arter & McTighe, 2001). A performance list provides a list of things to rate and a scale. While there are more options for scoring in a performance list than in a checklist, there is still a lack of qualitative explication of criteria. By contrast, rubrics include a measure of quality—providing students with an assessment of degree of competence they have achieved on particular outcomes.

In this chapter, we will first describe the two main types of rubrics. We will then articulate steps for designing rubrics, and finally, we will provide samples of different versions of criteria that typically appear on an oral communication assignment rubric.

Types of Rubrics

Rubrics designed to assess a specific assignment can be divided into two types: holistic and categorical (or analytical). Although both types of rubrics are valid means of providing feedback to students, they vary on the logistics of use and the information they provide to instructors and students. It is important to note here that you get to decide which kind of rubric makes sense, given your goals, outcomes, students, and course constraints. It is also important to note that many faculty we work with choose to use different kinds of rubrics for different assignments, or a combination of the two types. To help you make this decision, we provide you with a general idea of the kinds of rubrics and the situations in which they are most used.

Holistic Rubrics. Holistic rubrics provide a "quick snapshot of overall quality or achievement" (Arter & McTighe, 2001, p. 21). As such, holistic rubrics are best to use when you see an oral communication assignment as a combination of overlapping features and outcomes that can be assessed as a whole, rather than in particular, distinct parts. Holistic rubrics use what is called a "single descriptive scale" (Brookhart, 1999) that identifies what counts as a strong, average or weak performance. This kind of scale provides students with broad feedback on their performance. For example, Boettger (2010) described a holistic rubric used to evaluate a timed writing assignment. At the highest level:

> A superior response—defines and describes the above content areas in detail but also provides vivid and particular descriptions arranged for a clear purpose. It has a personal voice and uses words with attention to their tone as well as their meaning; it has a discernable organization and is focused. Response discusses both content areas with clear, specific language.

The lowest level on this holistic rubric included:

> The incompetent response—conveys ineptness at handling the assignment: it reflects failed attempts to begin the task, inability to produce the written dialect, unwillingness to undertake the writing assignment, and the like.

As illustrated, these holistic descriptions provide the students with the instructor's overall reaction to the performance. They typically do not provide details on different aspects of the performance (e.g., strengths and weaknesses). Therefore, two students could receive the same score but have very different performances; both could, however, overall represent (for example) "average" work.

To describe in more detail, holistic rubrics include descriptive statements of strong, average, and weak performances (or A, B, C, etc.). These statements incorporate all-important aspects of the performance and illustrate how they differ based on the level of performance. Here is a sample of some holistic criteria for a final research presentation:

> "A" presentations illustrate a clear thesis and purpose statement reflective of the study's main contribution; provide a focused (yet succinct) synthesis of the literature on the topic; detail a clear and specific methodology; give a sophisticated analysis (with sufficient data supportive of the results); illustrate insightful and data-based interpretation(s); and advocate with a strong rationale about the importance of the study. In terms of evidence of competence in research design, "A" presentations do not illustrate any problems in design, analysis, or presentation of research. "A" presentations are well delivered, with few, if any stylistic issues that detract from the presentation content.

You can use holistic rubrics for a number of different oral communication activities. Here is a sample of holistic criteria for an ongoing in-class discussion on psychological controversial topics:

> "Weak" discussion participants do not fully engage the major psychological principles involved in the topic of the day. They often present opinions without data and/or present data that is experientially based, rather than based in the reading. "Weak" discussion participants do not question or interrogate the assumptions emergent in the discussion—either taking the discussion off-track or staying quiet and saying nothing.

Making the distinctions among criteria can be helpful for students. For example, one set of general, holistic criteria used in an introductory course reminded students that a "C" grade means that you have completed the assignment in an acceptable manner, whereas "A" work reflected completion of the assignment in a truly exceptional and extraordinary manner. Specifically, the rubric outlined the details for A, B, and C grades:

1. "A" assignment—Superior, exceptional work
   a. Meets all assignment requirements.
   b. Addresses concepts in a focused manner, using course concepts accurately.
   c. Show exemplary reflective thought and analysis.
   d. Probes beneath the surface in addressing questions and analyzing information.
   e. Appearance, spelling, grammar, and organization of the assignment are college-level work.
2. "B" assignment—good work
   a. Meets all assignment requirements.
   b. Addresses concepts in a focused manner, using course concepts accurately.
   c. Attempts reflective thought and analysis; however, analysis could have been more in-depth.
   d. Overall strengths in appearance, spelling, grammar, and organization of the work outweigh the weaknesses.
3. "C" assignment—acceptable work
   a. Meets all assignment requirements.
   b. Provides basic responses to reflective questions with limited evidence of reflective thought or analysis.
   c. Course concepts are accurately referenced but not elaborated.
   d. Could have used further proofreading prior to submission.

You see in this example that the holistic criteria rubric looks more like a list. Although holistic rubrics are often more narrative in style, they can be written in a list form such as illustrated in the above example. Figure 12.1 provides an example of a full holistic rubric that could be used when a group presents a pitch for their chosen topic. Such a presentation may be brief and more focused on providing students guidance than on fully developed presentational skills, so a holistic rubric can provide succinct evaluation.

If your desire is to provide feedback on specific, independent elements of an assignment, a categorical rubric (also referred to as analytical) may be of most use. Different than holistic rubrics, categorical rubrics allow the instructor to provide independent judgments on different categories of performance. Typically, numerical weights are assigned to each category and the grade then becomes a sum of those judgments. For comparison, let's look at categories from an analytical rubric described by Boettger (2010), developed to evaluate a job letter written by students. The criteria for the assignment included: formatting, salutation, goodwill, introduction, education narrative, employment narrative, action, and closing. Within each criterion, the rubric included descriptions for five levels of success. For example, the introduction criteria ranged from "Applicant includes 4 functions, appearing in any order: names the source of the job ad, identifies the position, asks to be considered for the position, and forecasts the letter with no mechanical errors" to "None of the 4 required functions included."

Criterion	Successful	Unsatisfactory
Attention to all aspects of presentation	Addresses the full scope of required information.	Required information is missing or unclear.
Accessibility to listeners	Content is accessible to listeners; introduces and defines any terms and topics that are unfamiliar to a general audience.	Repeatedly uses technical concepts or jargon without definition or explanation.
Professional nonverbals	Group presents a professional image without distracting behaviors.	Group presents itself in unprofessional manner with distracting behaviors.
Group involvement	All members of group contribute to the presentation.	One or more members of the group does not speak in the presentation.

Figure 12.1. Sample Holistic Grading Rubric to Evaluate a Group Proposal of Project Topic

CATEGORICAL RUBRICS

As illustrated, categorical evaluation relies on your desire to evaluate and make separate comments on distinct categories of performance in an oral communication assignment. Categorical rubrics typically include lists of criteria that are weighted and scaled separately. Criteria often include overall structural headings of "introduction," "body," and "conclusion" but also include performative criteria "evidence," "validity of sources," and "professional delivery." Categorical evaluation provides students with information on how they accomplished different parts of the oral communication assignment, often giving them particular areas for improvement. Sample categorical criteria include the following:

- Results-Oriented Organization
    - 5 = presentation was organized in a way that illustrated a logical connection between design results
    - 4 = presentation was organized according to design results but connections between results were not clearly articulated

> 3 = presentation generally followed design results but results did not follow in logical progression
>
> 2 = presentation was minimally organized around to design results
>
> 1 = presentation was not organized around results of the design

Another example of categorical criteria for a discussion could be:

- Supporting opinions with evidence
    3 = Discussion participation provided clear description of personal opinion that was supported by specific references to course readings
    2 = Discussion participation illustrated personal opinion with general references to course material
    1 = Discussion participation included personal opinion but did not draw on course materials as evidence

These examples illustrate one category of performance for each assignment. Presumably, there would be others (e.g., connecting opinions with other students' comments, using audience-sensitive examples, etc.). Although the scales we illustrate here are specific to that category of performance, categorical scales can be more general, providing a measure of quality for several categories of performance. Figure 12.2 provides an example of a categorical rubric for a group presentation in a physics course aimed at pre-service teachers. In this example, students work in groups to conduct an experiment on a topic related to light (e.g., shadows) and prepare a science-fair style display and presentation. Groups then present an explanation of the experiment and the underlying principles. Of note, as you look at this sample rubric (and the ones we present later in the chapter) we recognize you will probably see things that you would not use in your own rubric. These are meant to spur your thinking—all rubrics have benefits and drawbacks. You need to decide how to create a rubric that has minimal drawbacks for your course and students.

How Do I Choose?

The type of rubric you choose to use will depend on your purposes and constraints. According to Nitko (2001), holistic rubrics can result in quicker grading than can use of categorical rubrics. Categorical rubrics, on the other hand, provide evaluation when a focused type of response is desired. While they take longer to use, categorical rubrics provide feedback on the individual criteria. Ultimately, the use of one type of rubric over the other will depend on your goals for the class and assignment. A combination of the two types, such as providing detailed feedback about different aspects of an assignment but providing a holistic grade, is also a possibility. For example, a presentation assignment could articulate various categories of performance, each of which having descriptors of "excellent," "proficient," and "limited" illustrations of that performance:

Light Science Fair Presentation

Group #: _____   **Topic:** _____

	Score
Setup	
All required items present and appropriately prepared (as noted on your project assignment sheet)	/10
Some optional additional items from project assignment sheet prepared.	/5
Presentation	
Accurately interprets experiments and cites correct theories	/10
Visual aids are easy to understand and interpret	/5
Explanation follows logical structure, and is clear and easy to follow	/10
Used clever modes of presentation, resulting in memorable delivery	/5
Total Score	/40

Other comments:

Figure 12.2. Sample Categorical Rubric: Presentations about Light in Physics for Teachers. Used with permission from Jon D. H. Gaffney, Physics and Astronomy, Eastern Kentucky University.

- Explanation of technical terms:
   Excellent: Technical terms are explained accurately and at appropriate detail for technical audience (e.g., not too much time).
   Proficient: Technical terms explained accurately but presenter spend too much time on detailed definitions for this audience.
   Limited: Technical terms are not explained accurately
- Vocal variety:
   Excellent: Presenter varies vocal tones and maintains appropriate volume throughout presentation.
   Proficient: Presenter varies vocal tones and maintains appropriate tone during almost all of presentation.
   Limited: Presenter is monotone and/or cannot be heard during most of the presentation.

This example illustrates that you can combine the two kinds of rubrics based on your goals and outcomes. Figures 12.3 and 12.4 provide examples of combined categorical and holistic rubrics.

Theory Oral Presentation (50 points)

"A"	"B"	"C"	"D"	"E"
Context is clear and succinct, providing details necessary for audience to understand the context choice (5 pts)	Context is mostly clear, providing most details necessary for understanding (4 pts)	Context presented in a general and/or somewhat confusing manner (3 pts)	Context presented in a general or confusing manner (2 pts)	Context only tangentially addressed (1 pt)
Provides a summary of previous research that reflects both a breadth of studies and a depth of understanding (9 pts)	Summarizes previous research with some minor gaps (8 pts)	Summarizes previous research with clear gaps in the research (7 pts)	Uses broad or vague allusions to previous research (6 pts)	Provides no details about previous research in relation to topic (5 pts)
Summary of theory is accurate and highlights the key aspects of the theory (9 pts)	Main ideas covered, demonstrating a general understanding (8 pts)	Covers majority of key points but shows shallow understanding (7 pts)	Misses key points of theory or shows little understanding (6 pts)	Summary addresses little of relevance to the theory (5 pts)
Theory and context were clearly related (7 pts)	General theory-context connection made (6.25 pts)	Theory-context connection fairly appropriate with some ambiguity (5.5 pts)	Theory-context link questionable or unclear (4.75 pts)	Theory-context link not made or not appropriate (4 pts)
Clearly articulated research questions/ hypotheses connect to context and theory (5 pts)	Understandable but misses minor information (4 pts)	Somewhat vague or missing important information (3 pts)	Vague, unclear, or incomplete (2 pts)	Lacking or irrelevant (1 pt)
Verbal delivery enhances content (volume, rate, inflection, minimal vocal pauses, appropriate word choices)(5 pts)	Verbals generally strong with few distracting behaviors (4 pts)	Verbals understandable but do little to enhance the material for listeners (3 pts)	Verbals generally detracts from content (2 pts)	Verbal delivery is unintelligible (1 pt)
Nonverbals enhance content through the use of gestures and eye contact and the lack of distracting behaviors (5 pts)	Generally uses appropriate nonverbals with small exceptions (4 pts)	Nonverbal behaviors neither enhance nor detract from presentation (3 pts)	Nonverbal behaviors are somewhat distracting (2 pts)	Nonverbal behaviors consistently distract from content (1 pt)
Handles audience questions and comments with poise; responds appropriately (5 pts)	Appears open to comments/questions but shows hesitation (4 pts)	Not responsive to feedback but does not overtly resist (3 pts)	Appears disinterested in feedback (2 pts)	Shows resistance to feedback from audience (1 pt)

Figure 12.3. Sample Combined Rubric for Theory Oral Presentation

Design Critique Rubric

Criteria	5	4	3	2	1
Concept	Identifies overall concept of the design; organized description of work addressing both the beginning and end.	Identifies concept; addresses both beginning and end of process with only minor points of confusion.	Identifies concept, but vaguely; process explanations are clear/confusing at approximately equal rates.	Does not address concept in obvious ways; organization and connections are difficult to follow.	Does not address concept and presents no understandable sense of design process.
Credibility	Physical and spoken performance consistently enhances credibility.	Credibility generally supported by physical and spoken performance with small exceptions.	Physical and spoken performance support and detract from credibility approximately equally.	Physical and spoken performance generally detracts from credibility with small exceptions.	Physical and spoken performance consistently detracts from credibility.
Argument	Argues convincingly for how design addresses site and constraints, using supporting evidence.	Overall solid argument(s) with evidence but missing minor evidence.	Key aspects of the argument (e.g., evidence or connections) missing or confusing.	Little, vague, or incomplete support for how design choices address the site.	No convincing support for how design choices address the site.
Visual	Oral content is coordinated with visual material in a logical manner.	Discusses most of displayed visual material in logical fashion with few notable exceptions.	Often matches oral and visual content; connections are inconsistent/disorderly.	Consistently lacks oral-visual links; connections that are made are disorderly.	Visual material and oral content are not matched.
Audience	Values feedback, embraces alternative perspectives, gives overall positive reaction to audience.	Shows some interest in audience feedback, generally considers alternative perspectives.	Interest and reactions are approximately equally positive and negative.	Demonstrates little interest in audience feedback, including resistance to suggestions.	Shows no interest in audience feedback or alternative perspectives.

Figure 12.4. Sample Combined Rubric for Design Final Presentation

STEPS IN CREATING RUBRICS

In creating rubrics for use in your class, the same basic process will apply across assignment types and disciplines. Although the details of what will be assessed and how it will be assessed will vary by discipline, the mechanics remain constant. As you probably can guess from the last chapter, we situate the creation of rubrics within the larger evaluative framework. We begin, in this section, with the second step of that larger framework (step 2: translate outcomes into teachable, measurable, observable criteria). We revisit this step here to provide you with additional information on how to use descriptive language to accomplish this task. We then provide several steps to follow when designing rubrics (step 3 in a larger framework).

1. Create categories of performance or holistic descriptors
   a. Categorical: Operationalize categories, create anchors and weightings for each category
   b. Holistic: Write descriptors of strong, average, and weak performances
2. Decide how to translate descriptors or categorical judgments into grades.
3. Practice using the rubric.

Translate Outcomes into Teachable, Measurable, Observable Criteria. Descriptive, concrete language in a rubric helps convey your expectations while easing your grading. Ideally, rubrics will use descriptions of work rather than judgments about work (Brookhart, 1999). Phrases such as "good" require fairly subjective judgments. Instead, the terminology in your rubric should clearly define the criteria, whether the rubric is holistic or analytical. Table 12.1 provides several examples of criteria that may initially appear in rubrics, alongside rewritten criteria that more fully explains the intention of the criteria in a teachable, measurable, and observable form.

Table 12.1. Translating Outcomes into Teachable, Measureable, and Observable Criteria

Vague Criteria	Rewritten Criteria
Good use of sources	Integrates and cites appropriate sources consistently
Group worked together	Group cooperatively developed project, with all members contributing to the design and final version of the project
Easy to follow organization	Organization provided guideposts to listener about what would be addressed in the presentation and followed through with the promised organization.
Included a thesis	Speech offered a clear thesis demonstrating the argument to be made in the speech
Audience adaptation	Language use and level of explanation appropriate for the target audience
Makes eye contact	Consistent eye contact made with all areas of audience
Attention-getter catches audience interest	Presentation begins with an attention getter that attracts audience attention and leads into the rest of the introduction; attention getter is relevant to the rest of the presentation.
Visual aids well-chosen and presented	Presentation aids are incorporated smoothly into the presentation in order to enhance the audience's understanding of presentation; presentation aids appear professional and are relevant to the presentation
Use of vocabulary	Word choice is appropriate to topic and audience; jargon is defined in meaningful terms for audience; chosen words are correctly pronounced and used
Appropriate use of gestures	Nonverbal behaviors (e.g., gestures, posture) consistently reinforce and add to the verbal message; nonverbal behaviors are not distracting

CREATE CATEGORIES OF PERFORMANCE OR HOLISTIC DESCRIPTORS

This is the point in the process where you have to decide whether to create a holistic, categorical, or combined rubric. Remind yourself of the distinguishing features of these rubrics as you make this decision: Do you want to provide feedback on individual criteria, or are you more interested in providing students with an overall (holistic) impression of their assignment? The choice you make here is going to be informed by how the assignment fits into your overall course, as well as the logistics of the assignment. For example, if you are grading students' engagement during an in-class discussion, a detailed rubric comprising ten distinct criteria is going to be unwieldy for even the smallest class. However, you could more easily manage a holistic rubric that provides students with a description of what different levels of discussion participation look like. Your superior (or "A") category may look something like: An "A" participant in discussion is a student who comes prepared to class with the material read. This student consistently participates in the discussion, offering questions, insights, and/or extensions of ideas. The student builds off the overall conversation with contributions and demonstrates respect for others' thoughts and opinions (e.g., does not interrupt, put down, or otherwise diminish the contributions of classmates and instructors). Based on this description, then, you can derive the different levels of participation.

When creating holistic categories of performance, be sure to incorporate each attribute in the overall description. Begin by writing the highest level of performance and lowest level of performance, followed by filling in the details for other levels in the continuum. Holistic descriptors can be nominal (e.g., "excellent," "average," "needs improvement") or numerical (e.g., 1–5, where 1 equals incoherent and 5 equals clearly excellent). For example, imagine that in an education class, students present case studies of how a current education law affects teaching decisions. Criteria focus on explication of the law and specific cases, development of connections among materials, use of supporting material, organization of material, and delivery. The "excellent" or "5" (excellent or superior) presentation could be one where:

> Student's explication of law provides listeners with necessary breadth and depth of relevant materials in an intelligible manner appropriate to audience. Case study is presented in sufficient depth to help audience understand the situation, and a clear and appropriate connection is made between the law and the case study. Content is supported by the use of specific details and at least three scholarly sources orally cited. Material is organized in a clear manner, made transparent from early in the presentation and followed throughout. The material is presented with appropriate tone of voice, volume, and inflection. The speaker appears confident (e.g., good posture and poise) and utilizes body movements such as gestures to emphasis points.

When creating a holistic rubric, keep in mind that you are painting an overall picture of the student's performance.

By contrast, if you are creating an analytical rubric, address excellent work and poor work for each individual attribute such that you can evaluate students in particular attributes. Complete the other levels in the continuum for each attribute individually. Campbell et al. (2001) offered an example of how a criterion such as "eye contact" can be broken into five levels for business presentations (p. 41). The levels focus on having the anchors of highest achievement, lowest achievement, and a midpoint, which are then used to fill in the additional levels:

- Eye Contact:
    5 = continuous eye contact. Faces audience and refers to notes or slides for less than once a minute. Rarely glances at slide screen or at part of room away from audience
    3 = moderate eye contact. Either faces audience but refers to notes or slides occasionally . . . or turns body sometimes at screen
    1 = no eye contact.

As you create categorical rubrics, you will need to decide how to scale, anchor, and weight your categories of performance. When deciding on these anchors, it is important to use parallel, consistent descriptors (Wiggins, 1998). Table 12.2 provides a summary of various anchors that can be used to measure the categories of performance. Of note: these anchors can be used for both categorical and holistic rubrics—you would just be attaching them to distinct categories of performance in categorical rubrics. In categorical rubrics, you can also weight your categories of performance. If you decide that "use of logical evidence" is a critical category, you can have that worth twice the score as other categories. When weighting the categories, it is helpful to consider, though, the next step—translating those categories or descriptors into grades.

Table 12.2. Example Anchors for Rubrics

Novice, Apprentice, Master, Expert
Emerging, Developing, Achieving, Extending
Needs Improvement, Fair, Successful, Exemplary
Limited, Proficient, Excellent
Poor, Acceptable, Exceeds Expectations
Never, Rarely, Sometimes, Often, Always
Inadequate, Minimal, Adequate, Superior

Translate Descriptors or Categorical Judgments into Grades

A concern about utilizing rubrics is translating the rubric marks to grades. For holistic rubrics, this translation is a bit clearer. If you have five holistic categories (whether you use nominal or numerical categories) that translates easily in to an A–F grading scale. You will want to consider whether you will be giving +'s and –'s though, and decide if you will create holistic descriptors for each grade. Additionally, if you have three holistic descriptors, you will need to decide how those three translate into your grading scale. The important point is to make those decisions clear to the students and explicit in your syllabus. For categorical rubrics, the easiest translation happens when you have numerical anchors that can be added up to a certain point total that can then be translated into a grade. Yet, there are some cautions. We work with many faculty who, after adding the points together, realize the presentation point total is not necessarily the grade they believe the student has earned. Therefore, think about a logical translation (Arter & McTighe, 2001; Trice, 2000). For example, on a presentation with a 1–6 scale (6 being the highest) and 10 categories of performance, the following logical rules could apply for the high and low end of the scale:

A = no less than 10 percent of the scores lower than 4, and at least 70 percent of the scores 5 or above

D = 40 percent of scores were below a 3, 10 percent of the scores at a 4 or better

Again, the point here is you get to decide how to make this translation. We suggest being proactive about it and articulating to your students what the equation is ahead of time so that they are clear about how you will go about the process.

PRACTICE USING THE RUBRIC

Before launching this rubric into the world of grading, you should try it out for yourself. Use samples of previous student work (or related projects) and evaluate them according to the rubric you have developed. Make note of any problematic areas and be cognizant of the additional information you are applying in evaluating the assignment. Ideally, someone else should be able to use your rubric in evaluating assignments with results consistent with your own assessments. Trying out the rubric with colleagues will highlight areas of concern, and asking students to apply the rubric to a sample assignment will bring to light areas of potential confusion or conflicting criteria. Be certain you can apply the rubric consistently. The rubric is intended to make your life easier as the grader and to help your students understand what is important in the oral communication event.

Chances are your first attempt at a rubric will need revision. You may need to go back to some of the steps, perhaps even multiple times. Don't think of rubrics as carved in stone from semester to semester. Although you should not change criteria in the midst of an assignment or during grading, rubrics will likely evolve as you adjust assignments and realize new possibilities in grading. When practicing with your rubric, consider using the following guidelines for revision (Arter & McTighe, 2001):

- Content (Does the rubric clearly illustrate the content you are evaluating?)
- Clarity (Does the rubric reduce the interpretive possibilities others could use?)
- Practicality (Can you use the rubric given your time and course constraints and can those receiving it understand it?)
- Technical soundness (Do the anchors and descriptors accurately measure the outcome being assessed?)

Of note, it is difficult to assess the technical soundness of a rubric unless you engage in reliability measures. If you are able to do that, great! If not, we believe you can gain insight on all of these measures from colleagues who are well-versed in your discipline, course, and assignment. Additionally, past or current students can provide insight that might be useful as you revise your rubrics.

SAMPLE EVALUATIVE CRITERIA FOR RUBRICS

We want to take a moment here to acknowledge the work involved with creating detailed, specific, measurable language for your rubrics. As we have noted through the various chapters here, one size doesn't fit all when it comes to communication in the disciplines. Not all assignments have the same goals, so not all grading criteria apply to all assignments. Because the task of developing solid, reliable rubrics for each assignment seems daunting, you may be tempted to rely on generic rubrics. There are clear benefits to generic rubrics. Your time and energy spent developing rubrics is reduced because the same rubric can be recycled for multiple assignments. Your effort in grading is also reduced because you will be familiar with the criteria. Students may gain a broader perspective on what "quality" work looks like in your discipline because they are seeing the same basic criteria applied to multiple settings. However, all of these advantages are tempered by the disadvantages of generalized rubrics.

Highly generalized rubrics do not provide enough depth to be able to provide meaningful feedback to students. For example, the use of vocabulary, such as what is appropriate for the audience, will be very different in literature and biology. Rather than adopting broad, generic rubrics, we suggest you either work from the ground up and design highly specific rubrics that make sense given your course and discipline or, adopt the vision of the Association of American Colleges and Universities (Rhodes, 2010) and use the Oral Communication VALUE rubric (available at http://www.aacu.org/value-rubrics) as a starting point for your own rubrics. The VALUE rubrics have no content-focused categories. Presumably, you would incorporate your own categories focused on the discipline-specific content of the presentation. Additionally, you might adapt the category descriptions in ways that are more consistent with your discipline. We encourage you to use these kinds of generic rubrics to familiarize yourself with the language of oral communication so that you can begin thinking about ways to adapt that language so it fits in your discipline—rather than simply using a generic rubric that might or might not be applicable to the situated nature of your assignment.

As you begin to design your rubric, you will want to consider the situated expectations that live in your disciplinary world. As illustrated in Chapter 11, language like "organization" or "professionalism" can have many different meanings. Therefore, it is important to give your students an idea of how your course and discipline assign meaning to these criteria. To illustrate this, Table 12.3 provides samples of the five most commonly used criteria for oral communication assignments and illustrates different disciplinary instantiations of those criteria. Of note, although we illustrate these criteria from particular disciplines, they do not necessarily have to represent those particular disciplines. Rather, the point is to get you thinking about disciplinary ways of writing criteria.

Table 12.3. Criteria and Possible Descriptions in Different Disciplines

Criteria	Design	Engineering	Psychology	History
Organization	Uses inductive organizational structure; addresses beginning and end of process	Uses deductive structure focused around results of design	Uses problem-solution structure to orient audience to key issues and potential outcomes	Uses narrative structure to tell story of people during particular time period
Visuals	Oral content is coordinated with visuals in a logical manner	Visuals serve as critical illustrations of design claims, ideas, and products	Visuals provide a map of possible solutions to proposed problem	Visuals add depth beyond the narrative
Argument	Provides convincing argument(s) for how his/her design choices address the given site	Sells an idea or product to a public; argument is made in a numerically-rich way	Provides fair description of benefits and drawbacks of each solution	Showcases particular contribution of historical people through examples and stories
Audience	Demonstrates that he/she values feedback and embraces alternative perspectives	Uses simple terms appropriate for a lay audience	Uses audience-specific examples to illustrate problem and potential solutions	Illustrates importance of historical people to particular audience
Evidence	Supported with precedents and client's needs	Supported through numbers as primary form of evidence	Supported with statistical research and/or expert testimony	Supported by stories from time period

CONCLUSION

As you can see, creating rubrics is a process that takes some time. But we contend that the time you spend considering these evaluation decisions will be time well spent. Why? Because it gives you the opportunity to clearly think through what you want and to present that in a way that is understandable to your students. Your students will probably not all achieve the pinnacle of success in these assignments, but at least you will have set the bar so that they know what to aim for.

13 Managing Facework in Oral Communication Evaluation

W e have all had the experience of spending hours upon hours writing comments to students' work only to be dismayed that some seem to focus solely and completely on the grade. Amidst these few who focus only on the grade, there are many who attend to the comments we provide in important ways. Yet, the way in which students attend to our comments is entirely dependent on the way in which we provide those comments. Sometimes in the fury of grading, we lose sight of the impact of our response to students. If we buy into the "all they care about is the grade, it doesn't matter what I say" philosophy, we are neglecting one of our primary opportunities to effect change in the teaching and learning environment.

If you are unconvinced, just think about the way in which you hear feedback. Remember the last time someone gave you feedback—either positive or negative—on something you had produced. The content of the feedback is just the tip of the iceberg. The tone of the feedback, the relationship you have with the person giving the feedback, and the style of the feedback all influences your desire and ability to hear the feedback clearly and use it constructively. Even the most constructively critical feedback is difficult to hear. If that feedback is colored with tonalities of disrespect, challenge, or relational tension, it becomes even more difficult to hear. This chapter deals with these issues and focuses on a central construct important to the feedback process—facework. Of note: we feel this chapter is a fitting end to the book because facework is not only central in feedback and evaluation, but it is also central to any teaching and learning of oral communication.

The concept of face refers to the desired self-image you present when interacting with other people. We first introduced you to face-related issues in the diversity chapter when illustrating how different cultures have varied face-related norms. Facework refers to the communicative strategies you use in order to maintain or rescue your own or other's self-image in interactions (Goffman, 1967). Face threats are those communication strategies that challenge the self-image you desire to share with others. Facework issues emerge in all teaching and learning settings, even outside of the feedback and evaluation process. In discussions, students often try to "save face" in order to look good in front of their peers. Teachers can feel threatened if students challenge their credibility (their "face," if you will). When oral communication performances are involved, facework is paramount because oral communication is an embodied, performative act. Therefore, in every oral communication activity or assignment, students' self-images are on the line.

In particular, facework plays a significant role in feedback interactions with students. The double-edged sword is such—our role as teachers is to provide corrective advice and recommendations to students. That is, at core, what we do. But because it is corrective, our recommendations and advice often feel like face threats. When students feel face threats, they are less likely to hear our recommendations clearly. In these cases, the feedback intervention probably will not achieve its goals (of facilitating change in students' learning and/or performance).

In this chapter, we provide you with a summary of information about facework, as it could potentially influence the ways in which you provide feedback to students on their communication activities and assignments. We first review general research on facework and then discuss several strategies for managing face in evaluative processes. Subsequently, we provide several examples of face-supportive feedback to oral communication and include exercises that could help you and your students learn to give feedback that will achieve its goal.

What You Need to Know about Facework

Most of the research on facework in the classroom builds on politeness theory (Brown & Levinson, 1987), which suggests that there are two consistent needs that drive social interactions—the need to be socially affirmed by those we value (positive face) and the need to be autonomous and unimpeded by others (negative face). Teaching, ironically, inherently becomes a face-threatening process because as teachers, we evaluate what students do and hence constrain and restrict their freedom (Cazden, 1979). Evaluative feedback, in particular, could be heard as disapproval (threatening positive face) and constraining of future possibilities (threatening negative face). When evaluating oral communication, in particular, face threats are likely because oral communication is embodied and personal in distinct ways from other modes of communication (Ong, 1982; Sprague, 1993). Additionally, as we mentioned in Chapter 9, research on facework suggests that it is a cultural phenomenon—being culturally universal and culturally distinct (Ting-Toomey,

1994). Therefore, students come to our classrooms not only having to deal with face issues that emerge within the classroom and feedback interventions but also with the cultural history that influence their conception of face.

Facework and Teaching/Learning

As mentioned, the teaching and learning relationship is one riddled with potential face threats. When the communicative aspects of teaching threaten positive and negative face, there is potential for the teaching and learning relationship to be equally threatened (Kerseen-Griep, Trees, and Hess, 2008). And when the teaching and learning relationship is threatened, there are multiple consequences. The ways in which students' feel about their teachers and classrooms will influence their abilities to integrate new ideas and be open to guidance (Daly & Vangelisti, 2003; Do & Schallert, 2004). When feedback threatens face, or is poorly communicated, it can reduce students' motivation (Cazden, 1979; Kerssen-Griep, Hess, & Trees, 2003) and damage their self-image (Smith & King, 2004).

Not only can teachers influence the context with face threatening communicative strategies, but students, as well, attend to face issues in the teaching and learning context. We know from research that when the relationship between the participants in interaction is distant and when the speaker has minimal power in relationship to the recipient, face threatening acts are seen as more of a threat than in close, equal relationships (Brown & Levinson, 1987). This makes the evaluative setting even more sensitive in terms of face issues. According to politeness theory, facework involves three kinds of needs—two needs addressing positive face (the need to belong, "fellowship face," and the need to be respected, "competence face") and one need addressing negative face (the need to act without impediment, "autonomy face"). When these needs are threatened, the interaction becomes less focused on its content and more on the identity of the participants (Lim & Bowers, 1991).

Feedback Intervention Theory (FIT) helps explain how this happens in feedback situations. In the past, research has suggested that feedback interventions (while generally assumed to increase performance) actually decrease performance in many cases. Feedback intervention theory attempts to explain why this happens. According to FIT, the overall success of a feedback intervention depends on a number of variables; one of the more significant of these variables being whether the feedback includes any perceived threats to identity (Kluger & DeNisi, 1996, p. 267). If a student is focused on maintaining his or her identity, he or she does not have the cognitive attention on the task itself. Therefore, FIT suggests that feedback focused on meta-task features (e.g., focused on the identity of the receiver of the feedback—face threats) limits performance (directing students' attention away from the task itself and necessitates cognitive focus on identity issues). By contrast, feedback that focuses on the learning of the task and reducing the feedback standard gap (the gap between performance and the ideal standard) is more likely to change performance and enhance learning.

Yet, ironically, research suggests that mitigating face is a central component to students' perceptions of feedback (e.g., Kerssen-Griep, Hess, & Trees, 2003; Kerssen-Griep, Trees, & Hess, 2008). Students claim that feedback that acknowledges face issues (either the need for affirmation or the need for autonomy) is helpful, easier to attend to, and easier to process (Trees, Kerssen-Griep, & Hess, 2009). Given this, teachers face a challenge—focusing students on the task while attending to face issues. Teachers who are skilled at managing face in feedback interventions—who can successfully manage task-related goals (e.g., sharing corrective information) and face-related goals (protecting students and their own self-image)—contribute to a more productive learning environment (Jameson, 2004; Jussim, Soffin, Brown, Ley, & Kohlhepp, 1992), satisfaction within the perceived mentoring relationship, and a more supportive classroom climate (Kerssen-Griep, Trees, & Hess, 2008).

Yet, attending to face issues in feedback interventions is a challenge. Research suggests that students prefer and respond better to more elaborative feedback than to non-specific and impersonal feedback. Elaborative feedback tends to be more detailed, though, and can be more face-threatening for students. Therefore, the challenge for teachers is to provide feedback that is both elaborative and specific and that mitigates face threats. Positive and negative facework tactics can do this. For example:

- Positive facework tactics (e.g., expressing approval, verbally or nonverbally showing solidarity) and negative facework tactics (e.g., less direct statements, hedges, etc.) can reduce the threat felt in facework interventions and allow a space where the learners can focus on the task itself.
- Instructors who use skilled facework (in the eyes of students) are viewed as giving more fair and useful feedback and having greater character and competence (Trees, Kerssen-Griep, & Hess, 2009).
- Positive and negative facework that attends to fellowship face (desire to belong), competence face (desire to be respected), and autonomy face (desire to act independently and without impediment), all contribute to students' intrinsic motivation to learn new things, students'

tendency to ward off apathy, and students' attentiveness in school and orientation towards schooling (Kerssen-Griep, Hess, & Trees, 2003).

- Positive and negative facework feedback that is "buffered" (e.g., feedback that acknowledges both high standards and the learners' ability to achieve those high standards, hence attending to both face and task) is more productive than feedback that is unbuffered (e.g., simple praise, criticism, etc.) in terms of invoking change (Cohen, Steele, & Ross, 1999).

- Facework messages of solidarity increase learners' desire to seek out and use learning resources (Piorkowski and Scheurer, 2000).

As illustrated, attending to facework in feedback interventions in your classroom is critical for all evaluative purposes. But, as mentioned, when those feedback interventions are connected with oral communication, facework becomes even more critical. When students are speaking, whether in front of a large group or in a team setting, they are essentially putting their identity on the line. Creating a space that supports that identity while still achieving instructional goals is critical. So what kinds of strategies can you use to manage and attend to facework in your class? The next section will address three strategies for managing facework in your classroom that emerge from the research on positive and negative face: Tact (addressing the need for autonomy), solidarity (addressing the need to be included), and approbation (addressing the need to be respected).

STRATEGIES FOR MANAGING FACE

In this section, we will review three primary strategies (tact, solidarity, and approbation) that will address many of the positive and negative face issues that could emerge, both in the teaching and learning of oral communication and in an evaluative process between you and your students. Essentially, these three strategies help create a supportive communication climate that can be focused on the learning instead of identity issues. We know from research that communication climate does make a difference. In his foundational work on communication climate, J. R. Gibb (1961) identifies strategies (based on an eight-year study of small groups) that contribute to both supportive climates (ones in which participants do not feel threatened) and defensive climates. Strategies that contribute to a supportive climate include providing descriptions, maintaining a problem orientation, spontaneity, empathy, equality, and provisionalism. Defensive communication climates are more likely when evaluation, control, strategic manipulation, indifference, superiority, and dogmatism are present. Subsequent research suggests that, in educational settings, supportiveness is more salient than defensiveness and that classes students report liking were viewed as more supportive than defensive (Rosenfeld, 1983). Furthermore, teacher behaviors such as humor (Darling & Civikly, 1987; Stuart & Rosenfeld, 1994), affinity-seeking (Myers, 1995), and self-disclosure (Mazer, Murphy, & Simonds, 2007) influence the ways in which students perceive the relative supportiveness of the classroom climate. Therefore, it seems clear that the way teachers act will influence students' perception of the climate of the classroom.

The three strategies in this section—tact, solidarity, and approbation—will provide you with some concrete ways to address students' primary needs that emerge in inherently face-threatening situations (such as evaluation)—being included, respected, and autonomous. In managing positive face, you can mitigate the needs of being included and respected through strategies of solidarity and approbation; in managing negative face, you can mitigate the need of being autonomous through strategies of tact (Lim & Bowers, 1991). Of note and as a reminder, these strategies are intended to manage face issues in a way that allows for cognitive energy to be focused on the oral communication task. Ideally, using these strategies will allow you and your students to prevent face issues from derailing the evaluative setting (as they otherwise could). These are strategies you can incorporate within the design of your assignment and evaluative structure, as well as within your response systems. For each of the strategies, we present general guidelines for adopting the strategy, evaluative structures that could foster that strategy, and language that could illustrate that strategy in interaction. Table 13.1 summarizes the strategies and teaching and learning structures and language to illustrate these strategies. The subsequent sections provide more detailed explanations of these strategies.

Tact

Tact strategies work to address students' need for autonomy in feedback intervention situations. Essentially, tact strategies presume that if students feel autonomous and without impediment, they will be more able to hear feedback in ways that produce change. General tact-based guidelines to consider while designing and responding to oral communication assignments include

- Providing students with the ability to choose how to respond to feedback
- Not forcing students to feel pushed into agreeing with your feedback suggestions
- Allowing opportunities for students to propose their own ideas in light of your feedback

- Creating an evaluative dialogue, where your response begins a conversation (whole class, individually, or electronically) instead of ending a conversation

Table 13.1. Implementing Tact, Solidarity, and Approbation in Instruction

Strategy	Tact	Solidarity	Approbation
Definition	Preserve students' autonomy in the teaching and learning setting	Help students feel included and invested in the teaching and learning setting	Respect students as individuals in the teaching and learning setting
Evaluative Structures	Response sheets Evaluation Dialogue Brainstorming Session	Letter writing Process feedback Contribution roundtable	Product-based review Effort/outcome assessment Pat-on-the-back
Language	Open-ended questioning Choice-consequence language Experience-based language	Future-oriented language Connective language "What struck me" language	Expectation-driven language Descriptive language Experience-based language

Some evaluative structures that could help accomplish these items include

- Response sheets: For each oral communication assignment, incorporate a "response sheet" in which students write their response to your feedback in the form of a short memorandum. Response sheets are best used with the 24-hour rule—encouraging students to wait to fill out their response sheet until 24 hours after receiving the evaluation, in order to allow for time to digest, understand, and remove the emotional element out of the response.

- Evaluation dialogue: Incorporate a face-to-face or online dialogue in which you and the student have a brief exchange about the evaluation. This could mimic performance reviews that could occur in industry.
- Brainstorming session: Build in (either in class or out of class, online) a brainstorming session in which students take your evaluation and generate several ideas of how to improve (you could market this as a team activity in which students begin with coming up with their own ideas and the team then contributes).

Some examples of language that illustrates tact-based strategies include

- Open-ended questioning: When talking to students about their oral communication assignments and activities, use questions that illustrate that you are interested and invested in the independent choices they have made. These questions could look like: "Could you explain to me your rationale behind presenting that particular visual for this project?" Or, questions could be focused on choices student will make: "As you look forward to your next assignment, what areas of my feedback do you want to primarily focus on in your learning process?"
- Choice-consequence language: As you discuss your evaluative framework with students, help them to understand their role as a decision-maker in the learning process. Students don't "have to" do anything in your class. They have choices and those choices have particular consequences. They are allowed to make any choice they want if they are willing to accept the consequences. Helping them understand this before the oral communication assignment could place them in more of an autonomous role.
- Experience-based language: Framing your evaluative statements as an experienced viewer can help students understand your role differently. Language like: "When you presented the statistical table from this design decision, I was confused about which numbers I should attend to," can help students understand that their actions/choices have influences on a viewer.

As illustrated, tact-based strategies work to address students' needs of autonomy in evaluative settings. They allow you to recognize students' independence and provide guidance in helping them make individualized and unimpeded decisions about their work.

Solidarity

Solidarity strategies work to address students' need to feel included and involved in the evaluative process. These are strategies that work to individualize evaluation and to help students know you understand the work they have put into the project. Some general guidelines for using solidarity strategies include

- Showing concern for the feelings students express in the evaluative setting
- Indicating understanding of the evaluative stress or the preparation process students have used in accomplishing the oral communication assignment or activity
- Expressing care about the students' learning and evaluative experiences
- Helping students to feel they are important members of the class
- Attending to students as individuals

Evaluative structures that could help accomplish these tasks include the following:

- Letter-writing: Writing the evaluation in the form of a letter, addressed individually to each student.
- Process feedback: Build in a structure (online, in class, or one-minute notes) in which students provide reflective feedback about the process of preparing for the oral communication assignment. You will want to include specific prompts and provide some incentive for completing this. Prompts such as, "what was the most difficult part of preparing for this team presentation?" or, "describe the biggest challenge you had with this assignment" can help students think more clearly about the process.
- Contribution Roundtable: Following oral communication assignments (especially those that are presentational in nature), incorporate quick feedback that illustrates the distinct contribution the student has made. You can do this or you can ask peers to do this (e.g., "What is one thing you know now that you didn't know before the presentation that is beneficial to you?").

The kinds of language that support solidarity strategies include the following:

- Future-oriented language: Framing the evaluative setting as one where you are a mentor, helping students achieve a larger goal in becoming better communicators, could help achieve solidarity with the students. Language such as: "As you work towards your goals of becoming an expert communicator in chemical engineering settings, I would like to provide you with input that will help . . ." can help students understand you are working with them to achieve their goals.
- Connective language: In evaluative situations where this is appropriate, incorporate language and experiences from your own evaluative

setting to help students know you understand. This could look like: "When I prepare for conference presentations, I often worry about balancing the data with the theory. When I have an audience of potential 'stars,' I want to look good, so I often will lean towards trying to include as much theory as possible. I understand how you might have done this."

- "What struck me" language: Beginning the evaluation with language that shows the students you appreciate the role they play in the larger classroom can illustrate your solidarity. Language such as "I first want to tell you, I was struck by the way you maneuvered the discussion around difficult topics with ease and appreciate the impact that had on the other students' willingness to participate" can help students understand that they play an important role in the class.

The above strategies all work to help address students' need of belonging/fellowship in evaluative settings. They help acknowledge that students' work contributes in distinct ways to the classroom and help students' understand your interest in supporting them in bettering their work.

Approbation

Approbation strategies are those that address students' needs to be respected in evaluative settings. These strategies also work to separate criticism of the student (as a person) from criticism of the product—illustrating respect for the person even if the product is below standards. Some general guidelines for using approbation strategies include

- Illustrating you think highly of students' abilities to meet your expectations
- Separating disapproval of the product from disapproval of the student
- Avoiding blunt criticism of students' capabilities
- Maintaining privacy in difficult evaluative instances so that students do not look bad in front of peers
- Praising both the product and the student

Some specific evaluative structures that could help accomplish these things include

- Product-based review: Build into the evaluative structure draft reviews of whatever product emerges from the oral communication event. If it is a presentation, have students review the outline. If it is a team-based activity, have students review the meeting notes. Be sure the product is in the center of the physical space and that evaluative comments are written on the product. This will symbolically focus the review on the work, not the person.

- Effort/outcome assessment: Build in the opportunity for students to reflect on the effort they put in and the outcome they produced. Illustrate how evaluations of each could be different and model encouragement of effort.
- Pat-on-the back: After oral communication assignments (specifically those focused on presentation), have another student provide the speaker with a "pat on the back"—a statement of praise about the assignment.

Language that illustrates approbation includes

- Expectation-driven language: In evaluation, clearly indicate your belief that students can fill in the gap between where they are and where they need to be, and provide them with potential action items that will support their progression. Language such as "the expectations for performance are high—I expect you to be able to translate these technical specifications in a way that is persuasive to a lay audience—but I believe you can achieve these expectations. Some possible strategies you could use to do this include . . ." could accomplish this.
- Descriptive language: Instead of using evaluative language such as "good" or "bad," use language that describes the oral communication assignment. Examples could be: "This was a well-argued topic," an "insightful presentation," or a "sophisticated visual representation of your design."
- Encouragement-based language: Instead of blanket praise, use language that helps students feel respected for the processes they have undergone to complete the oral communication assignment. Examples could include "I can tell that you've put a lot of effort into leading this discussion because the questions are specific and push us toward new insights in the reading," or, "you've come a long way since your last presentation in terms of dealing with the performance issues you were struggling with."

These strategies will address students' need for respect in evaluative settings. They illustrate your approval for those aspects of the assignment they have done well and distinguish your criticism of the product from that of the person.

Facework in the Disciplines

Although many of the strategies we present in this chapter are generic and can be used in any classroom, we encourage you to take the evaluative pulse of your discipline in order to understand how to tailor these strategies to your own disciplinary cultures (or to understand which of these strategies might need some attention given your own disciplinary culture). We know from research that many variables influence facework in multiple contexts. For example, Holtgrave's (1992) face management theory suggests the following about variables that influence facework interactions:

- Power, distance, imposition, and other interpersonal variables influence the interpretation of the level of threat perceived in an interaction.
- Individuals may be different in their assessment of face threat and these differences may be related to cultural and subcultural assumptions.

Given this, it is important to understand the variables that might come into play in your discipline as you manage facework in evaluative interventions. We propose you do this by 1) understanding the nature of the evaluative culture in which you are responding to students, 2) exploring the norms associated with praise and criticism in your discipline, and 3) acknowledging the teacher-student relational variables that could influence face issues in your discipline. We will now provide several questions to help you do this and encourage you to interrogate these questions as you plan and implement oral communication assignments.

First, understanding the nature of the evaluative culture in which you are responding to students requires a keen sense of who your students are and how they approach evaluation. Although individual students embrace evaluation differently, we have found that communities can define their evaluative culture. For example, one of the authors teaches in a large state institution in which many students are first-generation college students. Other students in this institution live a fairly traditional college life—fraternities and sororities, parties, roommates, etc. This author once taught in an institution in which many of the students had families, worked full time, and were not living in the traditional college script. These different kinds of students approach evaluation differently. Another one of the authors worked in an institution where there were a number of students from varied ethnic backgrounds. In some of these cases, certain ethnicities had higher sensitivities to face issues—and we know from research that face sensitivities vary among individualistic and collectivist cultures (Ting-Toomey & Kurogi, 1998). In order to understand the emergent patterns within your evaluative culture, ask yourself the following questions:

- What explicit messages does your institution give about evaluation of students?
- What implicit messages does your institution give about evaluation of students?
- What is the cultural lore about students' evaluative framework at your institution and/or department?
- What ethnic or cultural considerations do you need to address based on the students at your institution?
- What departmental messages do you receive about evaluation of students?
- What disciplinary or institutional constraints influence your evaluative framework?

As you answer these questions, you should get a better sense of the scene within which you will be enacting these evaluative frameworks. It is possible that this scene will make some of these face management techniques difficult. Or it is possible that you will need to tinker with some of these face management techniques based on the constraints within which you are evaluating students.

Second, we encourage you to explore your disciplinary or departmental norms associated with praise and criticism. Two of the authors have completed a large amount of research with the disciplines of architecture and landscape architecture. In these disciplines, criticism (often harsh) is part of the norm of the critique (the standard oral event in classrooms). Faculty enact it, individually, very differently, but students come into the culture expecting that norm. Another author has worked with faculty in education for whom praise holds very clear and complex meanings given work with children. Bottom line: It is important to understand the cultural norms associated with praise and criticism in your context. Some questions to help you do that include

- What counts as acceptable criticism in your context?
- How do students in your context typically respond to criticism?
- What would teachers in your context consider out-of-bounds in terms of criticism?
- What do teachers in your context consider as acceptable praise?
- How do teachers in your context typically balance criticism and praise in evaluating students?
- What disciplinary or institutional constraints influence the notions of praise and criticism?
- What do you believe about praise and criticism that might influence your face management strategies?

Understanding the institutional and individual understandings of praise and criticism does not mean you have to adopt them. We encourage you to better understand them so that you can either work within them or work to change them, should you be inclined. Regardless, the constructs of praise and criticism can be historically, personally, and culturally laden with meanings that influence whatever facework strategies you adopt. It is important to understand those meanings.

Third, it is important that you acknowledge the teacher-student relational issues that could influence face management strategies in your discipline. For example, in some institutions and departments, there is a clear hierarchy—students never call teachers by their first names and the thought of any socializing with teachers is unheard of. In other institutions and departments, there is less of a formal hierarchy—teachers regularly ask students to call them by first names and often hold final classes at coffee shops or restaurants. Some institutions have a culture of open dialogue and challenge. Others have a culture where this kind of dialogue and challenge is rarer. These relational issues are important to explore when thinking about face management strategies in your classroom. Some questions to consider are:

- What hierarchical structure typifies the teacher-student relationship in your department or discipline?
- What messages does your department or discipline give about the ways in which teachers and students should interact (specifically in terms of evaluation)?
- To what extent do students challenge teachers and evaluation outcomes in your discipline?
- What is your belief about the structure of the teacher-student relationship as it relates to evaluation?

Evaluation begins and ends with the teacher-student relationship. The ways in which that is instantiated—departmentally and disciplinarily—will influence the extent to which particular face management strategies will work.

CONCLUSION

In this chapter, we have provided you with information about face and facework, with the hope that you will spend some time considering ways to manage facework in your instructional settings. Although it might seem like extra work, it will benefit you and your students by allowing the focus to remain where it should in the classroom—on learning.

Epilogue

Chris M. Anson

Epilogue: a final section or speech after the main part of a book, play, or musical composition.
                    —*Merriam-Webster's Learner's Dictionary*

As reflected in the definition above, an *epilogue* has both an oral and a written history. Both are designed to sum up a longer act of communication, such as a book or a play. But each also requires attention to the unique features of its genre. When a student with ample writing experience and instruction is asked to write an epilogue, she will draw on her prior knowledge and produce something that meets the requirements of the genre. But without parallel experience and instruction in speaking, she may flounder when asked to give an "epilogue-like" oral synthesis of several articles in a course in her major or progress summary of a panel of conference talks in her chosen line of work. For students to gain the relevant experience to address these kinds of oral communication events (as well as any others they might encounter), they need instruction. As this book argues, oral communication needs to gain prominence as an educational tool and as a crucial skill for students' success in college and in their careers.

With its genesis in the 1960s, the writing across the curriculum movement (WAC) was designed to respond to widespread concerns about the state of students' writing abilities. For decades, writing had been systematically pushed off into the domain of its presumed experts—those who taught literature, grammar, and language arts. Consequently, teachers of other disciplines felt less and less inclined to attend to students' writing development or even include writing in their courses. Increasing enrollments and class sizes only made matters worse, leading to educational practices in which students listened to lectures about content and took objective tests that could be scored with scanning machines. Dismayed by what they often saw when they did assign writing, discipline-based teachers asked why students hadn't learned to be effective writers in their one or two required first-year writing courses, which often focused on reading and analyzing literary essays (Lindemann, 1993). A predominant ideology of learning in which students should have been "inoculated" against poor writing masked the actual source of the problem: a lack of sustained writing experience across all courses and curricula.

The movement to incorporate oral communication across the curriculum (CAC or CXC) developed in the wake of the WAC movement, supplementing and, as amply illustrated in *Oral Communication in the Disciplines*, eventually enhancing it. Its roots were similar in theory: instead of assuming that a single public-speaking course could prepare students to be effective oral communicators, CAC is based on a richer set of principles: that students need multiple experiences speaking in both formal and informal ways, to groups small and large, across a multitude of contexts if they are to demonstrate gains in ability and, as Chapter 1 documents, meet the expectations of employers. Like writing, genres of oral communication also vary considerably across disciplinary and professional settings. Consider, for example, a speaking event in chemical engineering: a poster presentation at a professional conference. In this case, the presenter is working between two computer screens, each of which contains different graphical, verbal, and statistical information. The audience is transient, moving from installation to installation in a large room. The presenter needs skills of oral synthesis—to be able to capture the essence of a research study in a brief summary. But as people move into and away from the scene of the presentation, attention to the shifting knowledge of the audience is also required—the introductory material has to be reframed for newcomers without leaving behind those who have already heard it. Meanwhile, the audience may be asking questions whose responses need to be artfully woven into the material. While planning and readjusting this flow of information, the presenter also needs to manage information on two screens, locating relevant slides for display.

As demonstrated in this book, paying attention to oral communication in every course has can be beneficial for three primary reasons. First, doing so will help students acquire both general and discipline- or situation-specific abilities (like the dual-screen scientific poster presentation). Although teachers of general public speaking lay a crucial foundation, they don't have access to all the varieties of speaking that students will encounter in their majors and in their careers (see Anson, Dannels, Flash, & Housley Gaffney, 2012). Those varieties are most appropriately supported by teachers who have expertise in the specific fields where they are instantiated. A nursing student will constantly face situations where certain skills will be required, such as addressing the concerns of patients in a comforting but non-patronizing or infantilizing way. Those same field-specific abilities will not be required of a student planning a career in marketing, which assumes a different kind of audience awareness. Both students will find it helpful to have learned the generic skill of "being able to translate complex information into concepts and language that a less informed audience will understand," but each also needs specialized oral communication skills to be successful. Giving students the relevant practice and experience in the context of the courses in the major, as this book suggests, is the only way they will leave their college or university prepared for their careers.

But learning field- and job-specific abilities is not the whole story. A second important reason for paying attention to oral communication concerns the quality of students' learning and the nature of the instruction that fosters it. When carefully integrated into classroom instruction, both oral and written communication change the classroom dynamic, turning students from passive receivers of knowledge to active participants in their own learning. Although the genre of the "class discussion" is ubiquitous, many varieties of oral communication can be employed to realize specific learning goals, as described in this book (Chapter 7). This requires a shift in instructional ideology from objectivism—"information in/information out"—to constructivism, in which students actively participate in the restructuring of existing knowledge with new concepts, ideas, perspectives, and information.

Taking a constructivist perspective toward oral communication in the classroom also means moving beyond conventional beliefs and practices. When oral communication is invoked in educational settings, many teachers conjure up the image of students standing at a lectern and delivering a formal presentation to the class. Limiting speaking to this narrow experiential bandwidth militates against its broader use across different courses of different sizes with different modes of delivery: any class larger than, say, 10-15 students will not be amenable to "speaking" because such presentations will take far too much time away from covering content (and in very large lecture classes, speaking is considered to be a moot point). Writing experts have long argued for the incorporation of frequent low-stakes, informal writing into even large courses, where copious attention to the formal characteristics of the writing (its structure, style, adherence to grammatical conventions, the presence of a thesis, etc.) is not needed, giving way instead to the use of the writing interactively in class. As shown in Chapters 3 and 4, parallel uses of less formal speaking activities can likewise engage students far more productively in their learning than lecture. These modes of speaking—pair-and-share, micro-presentations, small-group communication, etc.—don't require teachers to formally evaluate students' abilities but to attend to the meaning they are wrestling with and creating. Instead of telling a student who makes a comment in class that she has used "like" four times and made a subject-verb agreement error, the teacher can ask for clarification or elaboration of a statement or elicit responses from other students. Although the feedback isn't designed to formally teach public speaking, students are tacitly learning crucial skills of oral interaction, including turn-taking, face-negotiation, diplomacy, clarity of expression, and affective response. While for many students these kinds of activities are not "low-stake" in the same sense that they may be for writing, they prepare students for the multiplicity of oral communication situations they are likely to encounter in the future.

In addition, many kinds of speaking exist along a continuum from the least formal (such as a pair-and-share or free-floating discussion) to the most formal (such as a rehearsed, formal presentation to important stakeholders). Gently increasing the formality of a speaking genre can help students to practice without all the constraints and fears of a full-fledged presentation (which, as Chapter 6 of this book discusses, can engender high degrees of apprehension, fear, and avoidance). Even formal oral presentations can be designed in various ways (as illustrated in Chapter 5), each of which helps students to practice different but related skills. The pecha kucha or ignite presentation, for example, requires heightened attention to the use of concise language, artfulness in the design of visuals, and intense rehearsal to be sure that the spoken text is timed effectively alongside the automatically advancing slides. The collaboratively delivered presentation demands attention to the balanced sharing of information, carefully cued transitions between speakers, and careful timing to avoid undermining the different speakers' remarks.

The skills of effective oral communication are highly valued in the workplace, which offers a third compelling reason to take the excellent advice in this book seriously and put it to work in instruction. Ask virtually any business leaders what abilities they hope for in new hires, and inevitably writing, speaking, and teamwork will come up first. All the content knowledge in the world won't help a new employee to succeed until they have excellent communication abilities and can put them to work in written text, in a variety of oral situations, and in working in teams. But those abilities extend beyond single genres, such as the business memo or the orally delivered sales update. New hires are expected to demonstrate *adaptability*—being able to figure out what's required of a less familiar genre and start producing it effectively. Such adaptability involves metaknowledge—standing back from a situation and mindfully asking what existing knowledge can be deployed or transferred and what else needs to be known or discovered (see Yancey, Robertson, & Taczak, 2014).

The importance of integrating oral communication into the classroom cannot be overstated. And while doing so may require some retooling and some new attention to course structure, the design of class activities, and the creation of clear evaluation criteria, with the help of this book it doesn't mean that the teacher of cell biology, music history, macroeconomics, or organic chemistry needs a degree in communication or extensive workshopping in teaching and learning. The common-sense advice provided here will go a very long way toward creating classrooms where students are dynamic, active participants in their own learning and along the way become effective, confident oral communicators in the many genres they will be expected to perform in their other courses, on the job, and in their participation as responsible citizens.

REFERENCES

Anson, C. M., Dannels, D. P., Flash, P., & Housley Gaffney, A. L. (2012). Big rubrics and weird genres: The futility of using generic assessment tools across diverse instructional contexts. *Journal of Writing Assessment, 5*. Retrieved from http://journalofwritingassessment.org/

Lindemann, E. (1993). Freshman composition: No place for literature. *College English, 55*, 311-316.

Yancey, K. B., Robertson, L., & Taczak, K. (2014). *Writing across contexts: Transfer, composition, and sites of writing*. Logan, UT: Utah State University Press.

REFERENCES

Amason, A. C., & Schweiger, D. M. (1994). Resolving the paradox of conflict, strategic decision making, and organizational performance. *International Journal of Conflict Management, 5*(3), 239–253.

An, H., Kim, S., & Kim, B. (2008). Teacher perspectives on online collaborative learning: Factors perceived as facilitating and impeding successful online group work. *Contemporary Issues in Technology and Teacher Education, 8*(1). Retrieved from http://www.citejournal.org/vol8/iss4/general/article1.cfm

Anderson, L.W., Krathwohl, D.R. (Eds). (2000). *A taxonomy for learning, teaching, and assessing: A revision of Bloom's "Taxonomy of Educational Objectives."* Boston, MA: Allyn and Bacon.

Andrade, H. G. (2000). Using rubrics to promote thinking and learning. *Educational Leadership, 57*(5), 13–19.

Anthony, K. H. (1991). *Design juries on trial: The Renaissance of the design studio.* New York, NY: Van Nostrand Reinhold.

Arter, J. A., & McTighe, J. (2001). *Scoring rubrics in the classroom: Using performance criteria for assessing and improving student performance.* Thousand Oaks, CA: Corwin Press.

Auster, C. J., & MacRone, M. (1994). The classroom as a negotiated social setting: An empirical study of the effects of faculty members' behavior on students' participation. *Teaching Sociology, 22*, 289–300.

Bahktin, M., & Emerson, C., & Holquist, M. (Eds.)(1986). *Speech genres and other late essays* (V.W. McGee, Trans.). Austin, TX: University of Texas Press. (Original work published 1952)

Bales, R. F. (1949). *Interaction process analysis: A method for the study of small groups.* Cambridge, MA: Addison-Wesley Press.

Bargh, J. A. & Schul, Y. (1980). On the cognitive benefits of teaching. *Journal of Educational Psychology, 72*, 593–604.

Barnes, D. (1980). Language across the curriculum: The teacher as reflective professional. *The English Quarterly 13*(3), 9–20.

Bazarova, N.N. & Walther, J.B. (2009). Attributions in virtual groups: Distances and behavioral variations in computer-mediated discussions. *Small Group Research, 40*(2), 138–162. doi:10.1177/1046496408328490.

Bazerman, C., Little, J., Chavkin, T., Fouquette, D., Bethel, L., & Garufis, J. (2005). *Reference guide to writing across the curriculum.* West Lafayette, IN: Parlor Press and WAC Clearinghouse.

Begel, A., & Simon, B. (March 2008). Struggles of new college graduates in their first software development job. *Technical Symposium on Computer Science Education.*

Bickford, S. (1996). *The dissonance of democracy: Listening, conflict, and citizenship.* Ithaca, NY: Cornell University Press.

Blake, R. R., & Mouton, J. S. (1964). *The managerial grid.* Houston, TX: Gulf Publishing.

Bloom, B. S., Engelhart, M. D., Furst, E. J., Hill, W. H., & Krathwohl. (1956). *Taxonomy of educational objectives, the classification of educational goals: Handbook 1 cognitive domain.* New York, NY: David McKay Company, Inc.

Boettger, R. K. (2010). Rubric use in technical communication: Exploring the process of creating valid and reliable assessment tools. *IEEE Transactions on Professional Communication, 53*(1), 4–17.

Bonilla, J. F., & Palmerton, P.R. (2000). Hamline faculty and student voices: Race, ethnicity, & gender in the classroom. *The Hamline Review, 24,* 72–94.

Boohar, R. K., & Seiler, W. J. (1982). Speech communication anxiety: An impediment to academic achievement in the university classroom. *Journal of Classroom Interaction, 18,* 23–27.

Booth-Butterfield, S. (1988). Inhibition and student recall on instructional messages. *Communication Education, 37,* 312–324.

Bormann, E.G. (1990). *Small group communication: Theory & practice.* New York, NY: Harper & Row.

Brilhart, J., & Galanes, G. (1995). *Effective group discussion* (8th ed.). Dubuque, IA: W.C. Brown & Benchmark.

Brookhart, S. M. (1999). *The art and science of classroom assessment: The missing part of pedagogy.* ASHE-ERIC Higher Education Report (Vol. 27, No.1). Washington, DC: The George Washington University, Graduate School of Education and Human Development.

Brown, P., & Levinson, S. C. (1987). *Politeness: Some universals in language usage.* Cambridge: Cambridge University Press.

Brown, C. T., & Pruis, J. J. (1958). Encouraging participation in classroom discussion. *Speech Teacher, 7*(4), 344–346.

Burger, J. M., Horita, M., Kinoshita, L., Roberts, K., & Vera, C. (1997). Effects on time on the norm of reciprocity. *Basic and Applied Social Psychology, 19*(1), 91–100.

Burleson, R.B., Hanasono, L.K., Bodie, G.D., Holmstrom, A.J., McCullough, J.D., Rack, J.J., & Rosier, J.G. (2011). Are gender differences in responses to supportive communication a matter of ability, motivation, or both? Reading patterns of situation effects through the lens of a dual-process theory. *Communication Quarterly, 59*, 37–60.

Byrd, M. L., & Sims, A.L. (1987). Communication apprehension among Black students on predominantly white campuses. *The Western Journal of Black Studies, 11*, 105–110;

Calloway-Thomas, C., Cooper, P.J., & Blake, C. (1999). *Intercultural communication: Roots and routes.* Needham Heights, MA: Allyn & Bacon.

Campbell, K. S., Mothersbaugh, D. L., Brammer, C., & Taylor, T. (2001). Peer versus self-assessment of oral business presentation performance. *Business Communication Quarterly, 64*, 23–40.

Canary, D. J., & Dindia, K. (Eds.) (1998). *Sex differences and similarities in communication: Critical essays and empirical investigations of sex and gender in interaction.* Mahwah, NJ: Lawrence Erlbaum.

Canary, D.J., & Dindia, K. (Eds.) (2006). *Sex differences and similarities in communication: Critical essays and empirical investigations of sex and gender in interaction* (2nd ed.). Mahwah, NJ: Lawrence Erlbaum.

Cao, Y., & Philp, J. (2006). Interactional context and willingness to communicate: A comparison of class participation of behavior in whole class, group and dyadic interaction. *System, 34*, 480–493.

Caproni, V., Levine, D., O'Neal, E., McDonald, P., & Garwood, G. (1977). Seating position, instructor's eye contact availability, and student participation in a small seminar. *The Journal of Social Psychology, 103*, 315–316.

Carbaugh, D. (2002). "I can't do that!" but I "can actually see around corners": American Indian Students and the study of public "communication." In J. N. Martin, T. K. Nakayama, & L. A. Flores, (Eds.), *Readings in intercultural communication: Experiences and contexts,* (2nd ed., pp. 138–149). Boston, MA: McGraw Hill.

Carmean, S.L., & Weir, M.W. (1967). Effects of verbalizations on discrimination learning and retention. *Journal of Verbal Learning and Verbal Behavior, 6*, 545–550.

Cashin, W. E., & McKnight, P.C. (1995). *Answering and asking questions.* Center for Faculty Evaluation and Development, Kansas State University. Retrieved from http://www.tamuc.edu/facultyStaffServices/centerForFacultyExcellenceAndInnovation/documents/Idea%20Paper%20No.%2015.pdf

Cathcart, R.S., Samovar, L.A., & Henman, L.D. (1996). *Small group communication: Theory & Practice*. Dubuque, IA: Brown & Benchmark

Cazden, C. (1979). Language in education: Variation in the teacher-talk register. In J. Alatis & G. R. Tucker (Eds.), *Georgetown university round table on languages and linguistics* (pp. 144–162). Washington, DC: Georgetown University Press.

Cialdini, R. B. (2001). Harnessing the science of persuasion. *Harvard Business Review, 79*(9), 72–81.

Cohen, G. L., Steele, C. M., & Ross, L. D. (1999). The mentor's dilemma: Providing critical feedback across the racial divide. *Personality and Social Psychology Bulletin, 25*, 1302–1318.

Collegegrad.com. (2008, March 27). Survey results detail what top entry level employers want most. Retrieved from https://collegegrad.com/press/what-employers-want

Cornelius, R., Gray, J. M., & Constantinople, A. P. (1990). Student-faculty interaction in the college classroom. *Journal of Research and Development in Education, 23*, 189–197.

Cragan, J.F., Kasch, C.R., & Wright, D.W. (2009). *Communication in small groups: Theory, process, and skills*. Boston, MA: Wadsworth Cengage Learning.

Crawford, M., & MacLeod, M. (1990). Gender in the college classroom: An assessment of the 'chilly climate' for women. *Sex Roles, 23*, 101–122.

Crombie, G., Pyke, S. W., Silverthorn, N., Jones, A., & Piccinin, S. (2003). Students' perceptions of their classroom participation and instructor as a function of gender and context. *The Journal of Higher Education, 74*, 51–76.

Cronin, M., & Glenn, P. (1991). Oral communication across the curriculum in higher education: The state of the art. *Communication Education, 40*(4), 356–367.

Cronin, M. W., Grice, G. L., & Palmerton, P. R. (2000). Oral communication across the curriculum: The state of the art after twenty-five years of experience. *Journal of the Association for Communication Administration, 29*(1), 66–87.

Dallimore, E. J., Hertenstein, J. H., & Platt, M. B. (2004). Classroom participation and discussion effectiveness: Student-generated strategies. *Communication Education, 53*, 103–115.

Daly, J. A., & Vangelisti, A. L. (2003). Skillfully instructing learners: How communicators effectively convey messages. In J. O. Greene & B. R. Burleson (Eds.), *Handbook of communication and social interactions skills* (pp. 871–908). Mahwah, NJ: Lawrence Erlbaum Associates.

Dannels, D. P. (2001). Time to speak up: A theoretical framework of situated pedagogy and practice for communication across the curriculum. *Communication Education, 50,* 144–158.

Dannels, D. P. (2001). Time to speak up: A theoretical framework of situated pedagogy and practice for communication across the curriculum. *Communication Education, 50,* 144–158.

Dannels, D. P. (2009). Features of success in engineering design presentations: A call for relational genre knowledge. *Journal of Business and Technical Communication, 23,* 399–427.

Dannels, D. P., Housley Gaffney, A. L., Norris Martin, K. (2008). Beyond content, deeper than delivery: What critique feedback reflects about communication expectations in design education. *International Journal for the Scholarship of Teaching and Learning, 2.* Retrieved October 9, 2008 from http://academics.georgiasouthern.edu/ijsotl/v2n2.html.

Darling, A. L., & Civikly, J. M. (1987). The effect of teacher humor on student perceptions of classroom communicative climate. *Journal of Classroom Interaction, 22,* 24–30.

Davis, J.H. (1968). Verbalization, experimenter presence, and problem solving, *Journal of Personality and Social Psychology, 8,* 299–302.

Delpit, L. (1988). The silenced dialogue: Power and pedagogy in educating other people's children. *Harvard Educational Review, 58*(3), 280–299.

Devitt, A. J. (2004). *Writing genres.* Carbondale: Southern Illinois University Press.

Di Vesta, F.J., & Rickards, J.P. (1971). Effects of labeling and articulation on the attainment of concrete, abstract, and number concepts. *Jouirnal of Experimental Psychology, 88,* 41–49.

Dillon, J.T. (1983). *Teaching and the art of questioning.* Bloomington, IN: Phi Delta Kappa Educational Foundation.

Do, S. L., & Schallert, D. L. (2004). Emotions and classroom talk: Toward a model of the role of affect in students' experiences of classroom discussions. *Journal of Educational Psychology, 96,* 619–634.

Doran, G. T. (1981). There's a SMART way to write management's goals and objectives. *Management Review, 70*(11), 35–36.

Dwyer, K. K. (2000). The multidimensional model: Teaching students to self-manage high communication apprehension by self-selecting treatments. *Communication Education, 49*(1), 72–81.

Eagly, A. H. (1987). *Sex Differences in Social Behavior: A Social-Role Interpretation.* Hillsdale, NJ: Lawrence Erlbaum.

Elgort, I., Smith, A. G., & Toland, J. (2008). Is wiki an effective platform for group course work? *Australasian Journal of Educational Technology, 24*(2), 195–210.

Emig, J. (1977). Writing as a mode of learning. *College Composition and Communication, 28,* 122–128.

Engstrom, Y. (199). *Learning, working and imagining: Twelve studies in activity theory.* Helsinki: Orienta-Konsultit Oy.

Ericson, P. M., & Gardner, J. W. (1992). Two longitudinal studies of communication apprehension and its effects on college students' success. *Communication Quarterly, 40*(2), 127–137.

Esser, J. K., & Lindoerfer, J. S. (1989). Groupthink and the space shuttle Challenger accident: Toward a quantitative case analysis. *Journal of Behavioral Decision Making,2*(3), 167–177. doi:10.1002/bdm.3960020304

Fassinger, P. A. (2000). How classes influence students' participation in college classrooms. *The Journal of Classroom Interaction, 35,* 38–47.

Forgas, J. P. (1998). On feeling good and getting your way: Mood effects on negotiator cognition and bargaining strategies. *Journal of Personality and Social Psychology, 74*(3), 565–577.

Fox, H. (2009). *When race breaks out: Conversations about race and racism in college classrooms* (Revised ed.). New York, NY: Peter Lang.

Fritschner, L. M. (2000). Inside the undergraduate college classroom: Faculty and students differ on the meaning of student participation. *The Journal of Higher Education, 71,* 342–362.

Frymier, A. B. (1993). The relationships among communication apprehension, immediacy and motivation to study. *Communication Reports, 6,* 8–17.

Fugimoto, E. (2002). South Korean adoptees growing up in white America: Negotiating race and culture. In J. N. Martin, T. K. Nakayama, & L. A. Flores (Eds.), *Readings in intercultural communication: Experiences and contexts,* (2nd ed., pp. 265–275). Boston, MA: McGraw Hill.

Gagne, R. M., & Smith, E. C. (1962). A study of the effects of verbalization on problem solving. *Journal of Experimental Psychology, 63,* 12–18.

Geertz, C. (1973). *The interpretation of cultures: Selected essays* (Vol. 5019). New York, NY: Basic Books.

Gibb, J. R. (1961). Defensive communication. *Journal of Communication, 11,* 141–148.

Gilbert, D. T., & Malone, P. S. (1995). The correspondence bias. *Psychological Bulletin, 117*(1), 21–38.

Goffman, E. (1967). *Interaction ritual: Essays on face-to-face behavior.* New York, NY: Pantheon Books.

Goldstein, G. S., & Benassi, V. A. (1994). The relation between teacher self-disclosure and student classroom participation. *Teaching of Psychology, 21,* 212–217.

Goodboy, A. K., & Myers, S. A. (2008). The effect of teacher confirmation on student communication and learning outcomes. *Communication Education, 57*(2), 153–179.

Gouldner, A. W. (1960). The norm of reciprocity: A preliminary statement. *American Sociological Review, 25,* 161–178.

Guilford, J. P. (1967) *The nature of human intelligence.* New York, NY: McGraw-Hill.

Hake, R. R. (1998). Interactive-engagement versus traditional methods: A six-thousand-student survey of mechanics test data for introductory physics courses. *American Journal of Physics, 66,* 64–74.

Hall, E.T., & Hall, M.R. (2002). Key concepts: Underlying structure of culture. In J. N. Martin, , T. K. Nakayama, & L. A. Flores (Eds.), *Readings in intercultural communication: Experiences and contexts* (2nd ed., pp. 165–171). Boston, MA: McGraw Hill,

Harvard Business Press. (2010). *Leading virtual teams: Empower members, understand technology, build team identity.* Boston, MA: Harvard Business School Publishing.

Hatano, G. (1993). Time to merge Vygotskian and constructivist conceptions of knowledge acquisition. In E.A. Forman, N. Minick, & C.A. Stone (Eds.), *Contexts for learning: Sociocultural dynamics in children's development* (pp. 153–166). New York, NY: Oxford University Press.

Heinich, R., Molenda, M., & Russell, J. D. (1989). *Instructional media and the new technologies of instruction.* Macmillan.

Heller, J. F., Puff, C. R., & Mills, C. J. (1985). Assessment of the chilly climate for women. *Journal of Higher Education, 56,* 446–461.

Helman, S., & Horswill, M. S. (2002). Does the introduction of non-traditional teaching techniques improve psychology undergraduates' performance in statistics? *Psychology Learning and Teaching, 2*(1), 12–16.

Herrington, A. (1981). Writing to learn: Writing across the disciplines. *College English, 43,* 379–87.

Hinds, P. J., Carley, K. M., Krackhardt, D., & Wholey, D. (2000). Choosing work group members: Balancing similarity, competence, and familiarity. *Organizational behavior and human decision processes, 81*(2), 226–251.

Hirokawa, R. Y., Cathcart, R. S., Samovar, L. A., & Henman, L. D. (2003). *Small group communication: Theory & practice* (8th ed.). Oxford University Press.

Hirokawa, R.Y., & Poole, M.S. (Eds.). (1986), *Communication and group decision-making.* Beverly Hills, CA: Sage.

Hofstede, G. (2002). I, we, they. In J. N. Martin, T. K. Nakayama, & L. A. Flores (Eds.), *Readings in intercultural communication: Experiences and contexts* (2nd ed., pp. 289–301). Boston, MA: McGraw Hill.

Hogan, K., Nastasi, B. K., & Pressley, M. (2000). Discourse patterns and collaborative scientific reasoning in peer and teacher-guided discussions. *Cognition and Instruction, 17*, 379–432.

Holtgarves, T. (1992). The linguistic realization of face management: Implications for language production and comprehension, person perception, and cross-cultural communication. *Social Psychology Quarterly, 55*, 141–159.

Hopf, T., & Ayres, J. (1992). Coping with public speaking anxiety: An examination of various combinations of systematic desensitization, skills training, and visualization. *Journal of Applied Communication Research, 20*(2), 183–198.

Howard, J. R., & Henney, A. L. (1998). Student participation and instructor gender in the mixed age college classroom. *The Journal of Higher Education, 69*, 384–405.

Howard, J. R., Short, L. B., & Clark, S. M. (1996). Students' participation in the mixed-age college classroom. *Teaching Sociology, 23*, 8–24.

Hurt, H. T., & Preiss, R. (1978). Silence isn't necessarily golden: Communication apprehension, desired social change, and academic success among middle-school students. *Human Communication Research, 4*, 315–328.

Hyde, C. A., & Deal, K. H. (2003). Does gender matter? Male and female participation in social work classrooms. *AFFILIA, 18*, 192–209.

Institute of International Education Network.(n.d.). Open Doors Data Tables. Retrieved from http://opendoors.iienetwork.org/?p=150810.

Jameson, J. K. (2004). Negotiating autonomy and connection through politeness: A dialectical approach to organizational conflict management. *Western Journal of Communication, 68*, 257–277.

Janis, I. L. (1972). *Victims of groupthink: A psychological study of foreign-policy decisions and fiascoes.* Oxford, England: Houghton Mifflin.

Jehn, K. A. (1995). A multimethod examination of the benefits and detriments of intragroup conflict. *Administrative Science Quarterly, 40*, 256–282.

Johnson, D. W., & Johnson, R.T. (1974). Instructional goal structure: Cooperative competitive or individualistic. *Review of Educational Research, 44*, 213–249.

Johnson, D.W. & Johnson, R.T. (1998). Learning together and alone: Cooperative, competitive, and individualistic learning. Boston, MA: Allyn & Bacon.

Johnson, D. W., Johnson, R., & Smith, K. (2006). Active learning: Cooperation in the university classroom (3rd ed.). Edina, MN: Interaction Book Company.

Jones, E. E. & Harris, V. A. (1967). The attribution of attitudes. *Journal of Experimental Social Psychology, 3*, 1–24.

Jones, S. M., & Dindia, K. (2004). A meta-analytic perspective on sex equity in the classroom. *Review of Educational Research, 74*(4), 443–471.

Jones, S., Barnlund, D., & Haiman, F. (1980). *The dynamics of discussion.* New York, NY: Harper & Row

Jordan, C., Au, K. H. P., & Joesting, A.K. (1983). Patterns of classroom interaction with Pacific Islands children: The importance of cultural differences. In M. Clarke and J. Handscombe (Eds.), *Comparative Research in Bilingual Education: Asian-Pacific American Perspectives* (pp.216–242). New York, NY: Teachers College Press.

Jussim, L., Soffin, S., Brown, R., Ley, J., & Kohlhepp, K. (1992). Understanding reactions to feedback by integrating ideas from symbolic interactionism and cognitive evaluation theory. *Journal of Personality and Social Psychology, 62,* 402–421.

Kao, C., & Gansneder, B. (1995). An assessment of class participation by international graduate students. *Journal of College Student Development, 36,* 132–140.

Karp, D. A., & Yoels, W. C. (1976). The college classroom: Some observation on the meaning of student participation. *Sociology and Social Research, 60,* 421–439.

Kerssen-Griep, J., Hess, J. A., & Trees, A. R. (2003). Sustaining the desire to learn: Dimensions of perceived instructional facework related to student involvement and motivation to learn. *Western Journal of Communication, 67,* 357–381.

Kerssen-Griep, J., Trees, A. R., & Hess, J. A. (2008). Attentive facework during instructional feedback: Key to perceiving mentorship and an optimal learning environment. *Communication Education, 57,* 312–332.

Kluger, A. N., & DeNisi, A. (1996). The effects of feedback interventions on performance: A historical review, a meta-analysis, and a preliminary feedback intervention theory. *Psychological Bulletin, 119,* 254–284

Krathwohl, D. R., Bloom, B. S., & Masia, B. B. (1964). *Taxonomy of educational objectives: Book 2 affective domain.* White Plains, NY: Longman, Inc.

Lakoff, R. (1975). *Language and women's place.* New York, NY: Harper & Row.

Lee, G. (2009). Speaking up: Six Korean students' oral participation in class discussions in US graduate seminars. *English for Specific Purposes, 28,* 142–156. doi:10.1016/j.esp.2009.01.007

Levine, D. W., O'Neal, E. C., Garwood, S. G., & McDonald, P. J. (1980). Classroom ecology: The effects of seating position on grades and participation. *Personality and Social Psychology Bulletin, 6,* 409–412.

Lim, T., & Bowers, J. W. (1991). Facework: Solidarity, approbation, and tact. *Human Communication Research, 17,* 415–450.

Lyons, P. R. (1989). Assessing classroom participation. *College Teaching, 37*(1), 36–38.

Mali, T. (2015). Totally like whatever, you know? Retrieved from http://www.taylormali.com/poems-online/totally-like-whatever-you-know/

Marks, M.R. (1951). Problem solving as a function of the situation. *Journal of Experimental Psychology, 41,* 74–80.

Martinez. (2002). Learning to see what I was never supposed to see: Becoming Chicana in a white world. In J. N. Martin, T. K. Nakayama, & L. A. Flores (Eds.). *Readings in intercultural communication: Experiences and contexts* (2nd ed., pp. 67–73). Boston, MA: McGraw Hill.

Martins, L.L., Gilson, L.L., & Maynard, M.T. (2004). Virtual teams: What do we know and where do we go from here? *Journal of Management, 30*(6), 805–835. doi: 10.1016/j.jm.2004.05.002

Mazer, J. P., Murphy, R. E., & Simonds, C. J. (2007). I'll see you on "Facebook": The effects of computer-mediated teacher self-disclosure on student motivation, affective learning, and classroom climate. *Communication Education, 56*(1), 1–17.

McCroskey, J. C, Booth-Butterfield, S., & Payne, S. K. (1989). The impact of communication apprehension on college student retention and success. *Communication Quarterly, 37,* 100–107.

McCroskey, J. C., & Andersen, J. F. (1976). The relationship between communication apprehension and academic achievement among college students. *Human Communication Research, 3,* 73–81.

McCroskey, J. C. (1977). Oral communication apprehension: A summary of recent theory and research. *Human Communication Research, 4,* 78–96.

Mehren, E. (1999, February 22). Colleges, like focus on speech. *The Los Angeles Times,* p. A1.

Miller, C. R. (1984). Genre as social action. *Quarterly Journal of Speech, 70,* 151–167.

More, A. J. (1987). Native Indian learning styles: A review for researchers and teachers. *Journal of American Indian Education, 27*(1), 17–29.

Morreale, S. P., & Pearson, J.C. (2008). Why communication education is important: The centrality of the discipline in the 21st century. *Communication Education, 57,* 224–240. doi: 10.1080/03634520701861713

Morton, J., & O'Brien, D. (2005). Selling your design: oral communication pedagogy in design education. *Communication Education, 54,* 6–19.

Moskal, B. M. (2000). Scoring rubrics: what, when, and how? *Practical assessment, research, & evaluation, 7*(3). Retrieved from http://pareonline.net/getvn.asp?v=7&n=3

Murphy, P. K., Wilkinson, I. A. G., Soter, A. O., Hennessey, M. N., & Alexander, J. F. (2009). Examining the effects of classroom discussion on students' comprehension of text: A meta-analysis. *Journal of Educational Psychology, 101*(3), 740–764. doi:10.1037/a0015576

Myers, S. A. (1995). Student perceptions of teacher affinity-seeking and classroom climate. *Communication Research Reports, 12*(2), 192–199.

Myers, S. A. (2004). The relationship between perceived instructor credibility and college student in-class and out-of-class communication. *Communication Reports, 17*, 129–137.

Nance, T. A. & Foeman, A. K. (2002). On being biracial in the United States. In J. N. Martin, T. K. Nakayama, & L. A. Flores (Eds.), *Readings in intercultural communication: Experiences and contexts* (2nd ed., pp. 35–43). Boston, MA: McGraw Hill.

National Association of Colleges and Employers. (2014). *Job Outlook 2015*. Bethlehem, PA: National Association of Colleges and Employers.

Nicol, D., & Pilling, S. (2000). *Changing architectural education: Towards a new professionalism*. New York, NY: Taylor & Francis.

Nitko, A. J. (2001). Educational assessment of students (3rd ed.). Upper Saddle River, NJ: Merrill.

Nunn, C. E. (1996). Discussion in the college classroom: Triangulating observational and survey results. *The Journal of Higher Education, 67*, 243–266.

O'Donnell, A.M. (2006). The role of peers and group learning. In P. Alexander & P. Winne (Eds.), *Handbook of educational psychology* (2nd ed.). Mahwah, NJ: Lawrence Erlbaum, pp. 781–802.

O'Donnell, A. M., & O'Kelly, J. (1994). Learning from peers: Beyond the rhetoric of positive results. *Educational Psychology Review, 6*(4), 321–349.

Odell, L. (1980). The process of writing and the process of learning. *College Composition and Communication, 36,* 42–50.

Ong, W. J. (1982). *Orality and literacy: The technologizing of the word*. New York, NY: Methuen.

Palmerton, P. R., & Bushyhead, Y. (1994, April). *It's not getting at real': Exploring alternative approaches to critical thinking*. Presented at the Central States Communication Association Convention, Oklahoma City, OK. (ERIC: ED-374-483).

Parker, G. M. (2003). *Cross-functional teams: Working with allies, enemies, and other strangers*. San Francisco, CA: John Wiley & Sons.

Pearson, J. C., & Daniels, T. (1988). 'Oh, what tangled webs we weave': Concerns about current conceptions of communication competence. *Communication Reports, 1*, 95–100.

Petress, K. (2006). An operational definition of class participation. *College Student Journal, 40*, 821–823.

Philips, S. U. (1983). *The invisible culture: Communication in classroom and community on the Warm Springs Indian Reservation*. Prospect Heights, IL: Waveland.

Piorkowski, J. L., & Scheurer, E. (2000). "It's the way that they talk to you": Increasing agency in basic writers through a social context of care. *Journal of Basic Writing, 19*(2), 72–92.

Powers, W., & Smythe, M. J. (1980). Communication apprehension and achievement in a performance-oriented basic communication course. *Human Communication Research, 6*, 146–152.

Putnam, L.L. (1979). Preference for procedural order in task-oriented small groups. *Communication Monographs, 46*, 193–218.

Reeder, G. D. (1982). Let's give the fundamental attribution error another chance. *Journal of Personality and Social Psychology, 43*, 341–344.

Requejo, W.H., & Graham, J.L. (2008*). Global negotiation: The new rules*. New York, NY: Palgrave Macmillan.

Rhoads, M. (2010). Face-to-face and computer-mediated communication: What does theory tell us and what have we learned so far? *Journal of Planning Literature, 25*(2), 111–122. doi: 10-1177/0885412210382984

Rhodes, R. W. (1988). Holistic teaching/learning for Native American students. *Journal of American Indian Education, 27*(2), 21–29.

Rhodes, T. (Ed.). (2010). *Assessing outcomes and improving achievement: Tips and tools for using rubrics*. Washington, DC: Association of American Colleges and Universities.

Richmond, V. P. (1984). Implications of quietness: Some facts and speculations. In J. A. Daly & J. C. McCroskey (Eds.), *Avoiding communication* (pp. 145–156). Beverly Hills: Sage.

Richmond, V. P., & McCroskey, J. C. (1997). *Communication: Apprehension, avoidance, and effectiveness*. Pearson College Division.

Roberts, C. (1983). Speaking and listening education across the curriculum. In R. B. Rubin (Ed.), *Improving speaking and listening skills* (pp. 47–58). San Francisco: Jossey-Bass.

Rocca, K. A. (2010). Student participation in the college classroom: An extended multidisciplinary literature review. *Communication Education, 59*(2), 185–213.

Rosenfeld, L. B. (1983). Communication climate and coping mechanisms in the college classroom. *Communication Education, 32*(2), 167–174.

Rothwell, J.D. (2010). *In mixed company: Communicating in small groups and teams* (7th ed.). Boston, MA: Wadsworth Cengage Learning.

Rubin, D. L. (2002). Help! My professor (or doctor or boss) doesn't talk English. In J. N. Martin, T. K. Nakayama, & L. A. Flores (Eds.). *Readings in intercultural communication: Experiences and contexts* (2nd ed., pp. 127–137). Boston, MA: McGraw Hill.

Russell, D. R. (1997). Rethinking genre in school and society. *Written Communication, 14*, 504–555.

Sattel, J. W. (1983). Men, inexpressiveness, and power. In B. Thorne, C. Kramarae, & N. Henley (Eds.), *Language, gender and society* (pp. 119–124). Cambridge, MA: Newbury House Publishers.

Schmidt, H. G., De Volder, M. L., De Grave, W. S., Joust, J. H. C., and Patel, V. L. (1989). Explanatory models in the processing of science text: The role of prior activation through small-group discussion. *Journal of Educational Psychology, 81*, 610–619.

Schwartz, D. L. (1995). The emergence of abstract representations in dyad problem solving. *Journal of the Learning Sciences, 4*, 321–354.

Scott, M. D., & Wheeless, L. R. (1977). Communication apprehension, student attitudes, and levels of satisfaction. *Western Journal of Speech Communication, 41*, 188–198.

Shaw, M. E. (1981). *Group dynamics: The psychology of small group behavior* (3rd ed.). New York, NY: McGraw-Hill.

She, H. C. (2001). Different gender students' participation in the high-and low-achieving middle school questioning-oriented biology classrooms in Taiwan. *Research in Science and Technological Education, 19*, 147–158.

Silvan, A., Wong Leung, R., Woon, C., & Kember, D. (2000). An implementation of active learning and its effect on the quality of student learning. *Innovations in Education and Teaching International, 37*(4), 381–389.

Slaven, R. E. (1995). *Cooperative learning* (2nd ed.). Boston, MA: Allyn & Bacon.

Smith, C. D., & King, P. E. (2004). Student feedback sensitivity and the efficacy of feedback interventions in public speaking performance improvement. *Communication Education, 53*(3), 203–216.

Smith, K. A. (1996). Cooperative learning: Making "groupwork" work. *New directions for teaching and learning, 67*, 71–82.

Spender, D. (1984). *Man made language.* London: Routledge and Kegan Paul.

Spitzberg, B. H., & Cupach, W. R. (1984). *Interpersonal communication competence.* Beverly Hills, CA: Sage.

Spitzberg, B. H. (1988). Communication competence: Measures of perceived effectiveness. In C. H. Tardy (Ed.), *A handbook for the study of human communication.* (pp.67–105). Norwood, NJ: Ablex.

Sprague, J. (1993). Retrieving the research agenda for communication education: Asking the pedagogical questions that are "embarrassments to theory." *Communication Education, 42*(2), 106–122.

Springer, L., Stanne, M. E., & Donovan, S. S. (1999). Effects of small-group learning on undergraduates in science, mathematics, engineering, and technology: A meta-analysis. *Review of Educational Research, 69*(1), 21–51.

Sternglanz, S. H., & Lyberger-Ficek, S. (1977). Sex differences in student-teacher interactions in the college classroom. *Sex Roles, 3*, 345–352.

Stevens, B. (2005). What communication skills do employers want? Silicon Valley recruiters respond. *Journal of Employment Counseling, 42*, 2–9.

Stuart, W. D., & Rosenfeld, L. B. (1994). Student perceptions of teacher humor and classroom climate. *Communication Research Reports, 11*(1), 87–97.

Tannen, D. (1990). Gender differences in conversational coherence: Physical alignment and topical cohesion. In B. Dorval (Ed.), *Conversational organization and its development* (pp. 167–206). Norwood, NJ: Ablex.

Tatar, S. (2005). Why keep silent? The classroom participation experience of non-native-English-speaking students. *Language and Intercultural Communication, 5*, 284–293.

Tatum, B.D. (1992). Talking about race, learning about racism: The application of racial identity development theory in the classroom. *Harvard Educational Review, 62*, 1–24.

Tatum, B. D. (1994). Teaching white students about racism: The search for white allies and the restoration of hope. *Teachers College Record, 95*, 462–476.

The Chronicle. (1999). Colloquy: Responses. Retrieved June 27, 2008, from http://chronicle.com/colloquy/99/speech/re.htm

Ting-Toomey, S. & Oetzel, J. G. (2001). *Managing intercultural conflict effectively.* Thousand Oaks, CA: Sage.

Ting-Toomey, S. (1994). *The challenge of facework: Cross cultural and interpersonal issues.* Albany, NY: State University of New York Press.

Ting-Toomey, S., & Kurogi, A. (1998). Facework competence in intercultural conflict: An updated face negotiation theory. *International Journal of Intercultural Relations, 22*, 187–225.

Trees, A. R., Kerssen-Griep, J., & Hess, J. A. (2009). Earning influence by communicating respect: Facework's contributions to effective instructional feedback. *Communication Education, 58*(3), 397–416.

Trice, A. D. (2000). *A handbook of classroom assessment.* New York, NY: Longman.

Tucci, L. (2007, May 16). Tech skills not so important any more, say CIOs. *TechTarget.* Retrieved from http://searchcio.techtarget.com/news/1254916/Tech-skills-not-so-important-anymore-say-CIOs

Tulchin, B., & Muehlenkamp, K. (2007, March 12). *Survey results on education among California business leaders.* Washington, DC: Greenberg Quinlan Rosner Research. Retrieved from http://www.calchamber.com/cfce/documents/cfcesurveysummary.pdf

Vogt, L. A., Jordan, C., & Tharp, R. G. (1987). Explaining school failure, producing school success: Two cases. *Anthropology and Education Quarterly, 18,* 276–286.

Vygotsky, L. S. (1978). *Mind in society: The development of higher psychological processes,* (M. Cole, V. John-Steiner, S. Scribner, & E. Souberman, Eds. and Trans.). Cambridge, MA: Harvard University Press.

Wambach, C., & Brothen, T. (1997). Teacher self-disclosure and student classroom participation revisited. *Teaching of Psychology, 24*(4), 262–263.

Weaver, R. R., & Qi, J. (2005). Classroom organization and participation: College students' perceptions. *The Journal of Higher Education, 76,* 570–601.

Webb, N. M. (1982). Peer interaction and learning in cooperative small groups, *Journal of Educational Psychology, 74,* 642–655.

Webb, N. M. & Palinscar, A.S. (1996). Group processes in the classroom. In D. Berliner & R. Calfee (Eds.), *Handbook of educational psychology* (pp. 841–873). New York, NY: Macmillan.

Webb, N. M., Franke, M. L., De, T., Chan, A. G., Freund, D., Shein, P., & Kelkonian, D. K. (2009). 'Explain to your partner': Teachers' instructional practices and students' dialogue in small groups. *Cambridge Journal of Education, 39,* 49–70. doi: 10.1080/03057640802701986.

Webb, N. M. (2009). The teacher's role in promoting collaborative dialogue in the classroom. *British Journal of Educational Psychology, 70,* 1–29. doi:10.1348/000709908X380772

Weir, M. W., & Helgoe, R.S. (1968). Vocalization during discrimination: Effects of a mixture of two types of verbalization patterns. *Journal of Verbal Learning and Verbal Behavior, 7,* 842–844.

Wiggins, G. P. (1998). *Educative assessment: Designing assessments to inform and improve student performance* (Vol. 1). San Francisco, CA: Jossey-Bass.

Wijeyesinghe, C. L. & Jackson, B. W. (Eds.). (2001). New perspectives on racial identity development: A theoretical and practical anthology. New York, NY: New York University Press.

Wilmot, W., & Hocker, J. (2010). *Interpersonal conflict.* New York, NY: McGraw-Hill.

Wood, J. T., & Inman, C. C. (1993). In a different mode: Masculine styles of communicating closeness. *Journal of Applied Communication Research, 21*(3), 279–295.

Yankelovich, D (1999). *The magic of dialogue: Transforming conflict into coopera-*

tion. New York, NY: Touchstone.

Yoder, J. D., & Hochevar, C. M. (2005). Encouraging active learning can improve students' performance on examinations. *Teaching of Psychology, 32*(2), 91–95.

Zernike, K. (1999, January 31). Talk is, like, you know, cheapened. *The Boston Globe,* p. A1

INDEX

About the Authors

Deanna P. Dannels (PhD, Communication, University of Utah, 1999) is Associate Dean of Academic Affairs in the College of Humanities and Social Sciences and Professor in the Department of Communication at North Carolina State University. She is the author of the book *Eight Essential Questions Teachers Ask: A Guidebook for Communicating with Students* (Oxford University Press) and the recipient of several teaching awards: the College of Humanities and Social Sciences recipient of the Alumni Distinguished Graduate Professor Award (2015) and Board of Governor's Award for Excellence in Teaching (2014); the Southern States Communication Association recipient of the John I. Sisco Excellence in Teaching Award (2010), the Western States Communication Association Master Teacher Award (2010) and the National Council of Teachers of English Best Article on Pedagogy or Curriculum in Technical or Scientific Communication (2009). Dannels has published widely in communication instruction/communication across the curriculum arenas and is considered one of the leading scholars exploring oral communication teaching and learning in various disciplines.

Patricia R. Palmerton (PhD, Speech Communication, University of Minnesota, 1984) is Professor and Chair of the Department of Communication Studies at Hamline University, Saint Paul, Minnesota. She has worked extensively with faculty across disciplines on integrating oral communication activities into the classroom, having consulted nationwide on curriculum development and faculty development. She has published and presented work on oral communication pedagogy, including research on the role of race, ethnicity, and gender in education; on communication in conflict situations; and on the impact of therapeutic horsemanship on communicative processes. She is the recipient of several teaching awards, including the Burton and Ruth Grimes Teaching Award, the Sears Roebuck Foundation Teaching Excellence and Campus Leadership Award, and the Central States Communication Association Outstanding Young Teacher Award. She teaches courses in communication and rhetorical theory, gender and communication, small-group communication, interpersonal communication, communication and conflict, and communication research methods.

Amy L. Housley Gaffney (PhD, Communication, Rhetoric, and Digital Media, North Carolina State University, 2010) is director of the Oral Communication Center at Hamilton College. Her research deals with the role of communication in teaching and learning as well as approaches to integrating communication instruction into courses across the curriculum. Her work explores the teaching of both public speaking and writing at the general education level and extends those principles of communication within specific disciplines. She was previously assistant professor in Instructional Communication & Research at the University of Kentucky, where she was active in the university's general education implementation and multimodal communication across the curriculum Quality Enhancement Plan (QEP) for SACS reaccreditation. She teaches at both the undergraduate and graduate levels.

CPSIA information can be obtained
at www.ICGtesting.com
Printed in the USA
JSHW031403250520
5884JS00002B/8